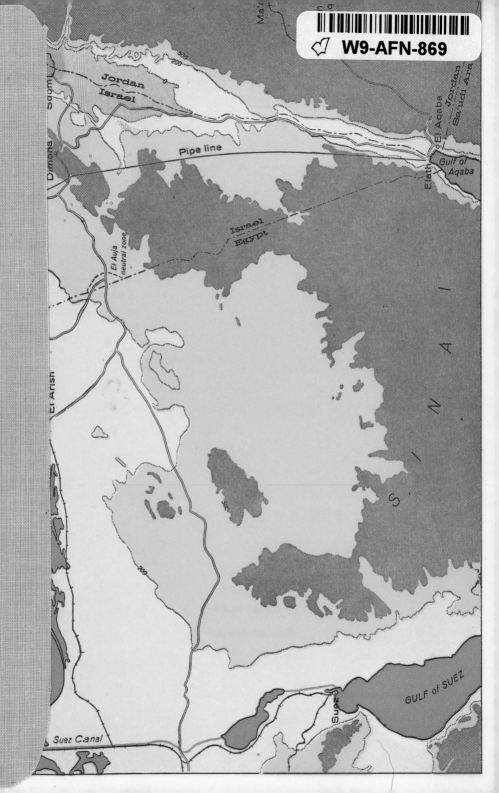

THE UNITED STATES
AND ISRAEL

THE AMERICAN FOREIGN POLICY LIBRARY

CRANE BRINTON, EDITOR

THE UNITED STATES
and Israel

BY NADAV SAFRAN

HARVARD UNIVERSITY PRESS
Cambridge, Massachusetts

1963

TO THE MEMORY OF MY FATHER

Contents

MAPS

Introduction

One of the first books published in the American Foreign Policy Library was Ephraim A. Speiser's useful volume, *The United States and the Near East* (1947), now for some time out of print. Is is a comment on changes that have taken place since then, both in the Near East itself and in the interests and commitments of the United States in that area, that a single volume of the size usual in this Library no longer seems at all adequate for the subject. We have therefore decided to treat Israel in this separate volume. Small though Israel is in area—it is not quite as large as Massachusetts—it has an importance in international politics, and therefore in our American politics, not in any sense to be measured by comparative statistics of area or population.

Few nations present a more testing challenge to an American anxious to make an objective approach to the study of a foreign country and to achieve a realistic understanding of the problems of our relations with that country than does Israel. Much in such a study will inevitably move him to profound and sometimes blinding sympathies. We still feel horror at the cruelties the Jews have suffered in our own times, and if we are conscientious must feel our own share of the guilt for historic anti-Semitism; we are by tradition committed to sympathy for the underdog, especially when he fights against great odds, as have the Israelis; nor are such sympathies diminished by admiration for the success with which the vastly outnumbered Israelis have hitherto faced their Arab enemies; we admire the Israelis as representatives of modernity in the midst of a Near East still barely emerging from an older culture and a primitive economy. All this and much more can make many Americans into unreasoning—and perhaps more important, unobserving —partisans of Israel.

Yet the emotional balance may quite easily swing other Americans into becoming unreasoning and equally unobserving enemies of Israel. There still are American anti-Semites, in spite of the very great diminution of their number and influence in the last thirty years; many Americans, not at all convinced of the moral validity of the title of, say, the Cherokees or the Seminoles, to their original lands, feel very strongly that, after all, the Arabs of Palestine did have moral and legal titles to their lands and that the Israelis are simply receivers of stolen goods; many American liberals, sure that nationalism is the root of all evil in international politics, sure that they themselves have risen above such nationalism, regard Zionism and its achievements in Israel as a regrettable backward step; many deeply religious individuals in the Judaeo-Christian tradition, both Jews and Christians, feel strongly that the whole concept of a Jewish homeland in the form of a territorial nation-state like all other nation-states on this wicked earth is a betrayal of the spiritual mission of Israel; feel that the Zion with which this book is concerned is a travesty on the Zion of Isaiah, cannot possibly be a "covenant of the people, for a light of the Gentiles." The accumulated weight of such feelings, too, is very strong.

The author of this book is clearly aware of all the judgments, opinions, prejudices, emotions, we have very briefly dwelled upon, and he would be less than human—would in fact be incapable of writing so good a book as this—did he not share some of them. But Mr. Safran does not let them corrupt his powers of observation nor his judgment. An editor must cherish, if not paternal, at least avuncular, feelings toward the product of his work; and uncles too are usually favorably prejudiced by their relationship. Yet this editor feels safe in asserting that Mr. Safran has here achieved a remarkable feat of fair-mindedness—not a cold-blooded, or dull, or peevishly superior work—there is here no trace of Mercutio's "a plague o' both your houses"—but a warm and sympathetic account of a great experiment in human relations. No book in our opinion does as succinctly, as justly, as effectively, what Mr. Safran has done in this book.

He has of course special qualifications for the task. He is familiar not only with Hebrew and with Jewish culture, but with the Arabic language and culture, a rare combination indeed among modern commentators. He has written an excellent scholarly study, *Egypt in Search of Political Community; an analysis of the intellectual and political evolution of modern Egypt, 1804–1952* (Cambridge, Massachusetts, 1961). He has traveled widely in the Near East, or rather, has lived there, and knows its peoples at firsthand and with the intuitive familiarity so hard for most Americans to acquire in that field. He has, finally, what is indispensable, the temperamental qualifications of both the scholar and the judge, a mating by no means as common as, for the good of us all, it ought to be.

The book is clearly outlined, so that the reader who will glance at the table of contents will know what to expect. It would be idle to point out here any special sections of the book. The interested reader will hardly be tempted to skip. For the editor, however, the very clear analysis in Chapter VI of the *aliyot* which built up the Israeli people of today, and the effects of the post-statehood *aliyot* on social stratification, was particularly enlightening; so too was the whole of Part IV, "The Struggle for Livelihood and Life." It is a real pleasure to welcome this volume to the American Foreign Policy Library.

CRANE BRINTON

Author's Preface

Readers who are not familiar with other books in Harvard's American Foreign Policy Library may be a little puzzled that a book entitled *The United States and Israel* should devote so much more space to various aspects of Israel's internal life than to the relations between the two countries that share the book's title. A conscientious diplomat would easily understand this procedure. He would know from his own experience how necessary it is to try to understand the temper and "inner workings" of a country before attempting to make an intelligent assessment of events and possibilities or to suggest effective moves relating to that country. It is true that this book is not written exclusively or even mainly for diplomats, but is addressed to a broader public. In a democracy such as the United States, however, and in an age of mass media, the public itself often exercises collectively a decisive influence on foreign policy and might therefore wish to learn certain things about Israel quite as much as the diplomat, whom it not infrequently overrules.

An author who attempts to understand the temper and inner workings of Israel while marshaling the data necessary for such an undertaking must necessarily be selective in his choice of subjects. It matters little that the nation we are concerned with here is new and small, for its people are ancient and its history and problems are as complex as those of any nation. I have used no definite criterion in my choice of subjects other than my own sense of what is necessary background and my own assessment of what are the most revealing and enduring forces at work in Israel; and I should not be surprised, therefore, if other observers should disagree with my choice. There is one subject, however, that I omitted not because I did not think it important and of lasting relevance but because of its intractability in the context of this book—and that is the problem of the Arab minority in Israel. I do speak of Israel's Arabs in various contexts but I do not give the question the special treatment it deserves. My excuse for this omission—and this might well be my own shortcoming—is that, try as I could, I was not able to do justice to the subject without becoming involved in the entire question of the rights and wrongs of the Palestine issue; and such involvement would have distracted me from my main subject and turned this book into something other than what it is intended to be. Of course, one cannot write about Israel, and accept her as an established fact—which is what I do—without thereby taking an implicit stand on the Palestine issue. If a reader wishes to interpret such a stand as placing the author morally on the side of Israel against the Arabs, he is of course free to do so. For my part, I believe that fundamentally both Arabs and Jews have an unassailable moral argument. A person who cannot see how this is possible does not understand the essence of tragedy; much less does he realize that his position serves only to assure that the Palestine tragedy should have another sequel, and yet another.

The object of this book has determined the style and mode of its presentation. I have tried to present the material simply, without referring to the sometimes massive, and often confusing, sources underlying the facts cited, and without always expounding in full the deliberations upon which the judgments are based. This method makes an author an easy target for criticism, but the risk had to be taken if the book was to attain the comprehensiveness of subject matter and easy accessibility to a broad public which are necessary to serve its purpose.

Through all the stages of my endeavor I received help from many officials of governmental and other institutions in the United States and Israel and from individuals in various walks of life in both countries. I cannot thank all of these people individually, especially since I may have shown some ingratitude toward some of them in the views I have expressed. A grant from the Rockefeller Fund awarded to me through the Department of Government, Harvard University, enabled me to spend the academic year 1961–1962 in Israel, refurbish my acquaintance with the country, and observe its progress and problems at first hand.

I am grateful to Professor Crane Brinton for smoothing out my path and for his expeditious handling of those aspects of the project connected with his editorship of the American Foreign Policy Library. I am indebted to Professor Frank E. Manuel for the very many hours he spent with me discussing and working over some of the subjects treated in this book. Professor John L. Rodman and Professor L. Carl Brown have brought their exacting minds to bear on the entire manuscript and have saved me from many a pitfall; and Professor H. A. R. Gibb and Professor Rupert Emerson have gone over the product in its penultimate stage and have given me needed reassurance by their silence as well as by their criticism. Needless to say, any merit this book may have is due largely to the assistance of these kindly colleagues, and all the defects of expression, analysis, and judgment are solely my own responsibility. I wish to thank Mrs. Elma Leavis for her patience while typing the manuscript and Miss Kathleen Ahern of the Harvard University Press for her unusual zeal in preparing the book for the Press.

Cambridge, Massachusetts   N.S.
December, 1962.

PART ONE: THE ORIGINS OF MODERN ISRAEL

Introductory

Israel is first and foremost the creation of Zionism. This movement is closely linked to the wave of nationalism that has swept the world in the last century and a half and gave rise to more than two score independent nations in the last decade and a half alone. Zionism cannot, indeed, be understood apart from its origin in the political, social, and intellectual currents that washed Europe in the nineteenth century and were the common source of many nationalist movements. Its success cannot be imagined apart from the two world wars of the twentieth century which broke up big empires, revolutionized international power relations, and made possible the triumph of many movements of national liberation. However, so different were the circumstances of the Jewish people from those of other peoples aspiring to sovereign national status, so different was the connection of the Jews to the territory they sought to make their national home from that of other peoples to their national territories, and so peculiar, therefore, were the tasks that confronted the Jewish nationalists and the conditions under which they had to work, that any attempt to understand Zionism by looking at it as just another nationalist movement is bound to obscure the subject rather than clarify it and is certain to become a handicap in any effort to grasp the forces that shape Israel.

Zionism endeavored to obtain national sovereignty for a people that had had no common national history for nearly two thousand years, in a land it had not effectively occupied for that long. The only link among the dispersed portions of the people had been religious, and between the people and the country the connection had been essentially spiritual. Yet Zionism, while capitalizing on these links, was not a religious movement in the commonly accepted sense of the term. It did not arise out of a religious impulse nor did it seek to meet some religious need. In fact, Zionism emerged when the hold of religion was weaker than in any previous period of Jewish history and when Jews themselves were endeavoring for the first time to blur any religious elements that stressed their separateness so as to be able to merge more easily among the Gentiles. The Zionist program did not seek to reverse this trend but sought rather to provide another way, in its view the only feasible one, to make the Jews in all respects like others.

The specific doctrine and ultimate program of Zionism were never accepted by more than a small minority of Jews in the world or in any country, and were in fact actively and vigorously opposed by many powerful Jewish groups in many communities. Nevertheless, the Zionist movement was able to mobilize the support of most Jews nearly everywhere for one aspect or another of its many endeavors in Palestine which the supporting groups viewed as ends in themselves but which the Zionists viewed as elements of their nation-building goal. At a critical moment in Jewish history, after the Nazi slaughter of most of Europe's Jews, the Zionists were able by this process to mobilize the backing of nearly all of world Jewry for the creation of a Jewish state as the only means to rescue the survivors and relieve the oppressed; but the Zionist doctrine remained even then the faith of a minority.

While Zionism provided the leadership and drive and mobilized the resources for the total Jewish endeavor in Palestine, the whole undertaking would have been impossible had not Britain sponsored the Zionist movement at the end of the first World War and given it the opportunity to establish a secure base in the country through the Balfour Declaration and the Mandate. A quarter of a century later, when Britain felt impelled to trade her support of Zionism for Arab good will, the embryonic Jewish national community that had emerged in the meantime in Palestine was already strong enough to defy its initial sponsor and, with aid from the Zionist movement and the benefit of favorable circumstances, to gain friends and supporters elsewhere who helped to bring about the termination of Britain's rule in Palestine and the establishment of Israel. One of these friends was the United States. American pressure on Britain immediately after the end of the second World War was crucial in compelling her to bring the whole Palestine question before the

United Nations in 1947, and American support was decisive in winning the decision of this organization in favor of partitioning Palestine between a Jewish and an Arab state.

Because of America's active support of the Zionist cause in those crucial years, some observers have claimed or simply assumed that she is "responsible" for the creation of Israel and have gone on to argue about the consequences of this act for her. Others go back three decades and condemn or praise the Balfour Declaration as the root from which Israel grew. Many, especially among the Zionists, tend to minimize the importance of either of the previous factors and to consider the Jewish state to have been historically "inevitable" from the moment Jewish national consciousness became crystallized in the Zionist movement three quarters of a century ago. Finally, not a few among Jews as well as Gentiles go back several thousand years and view the source of Israel in God's covenant with Abraham granting the Land of Canaan to his descendants for all time. The view taken in this book, which is evident perhaps from the preceding introductory remarks, is that all these conceptions express some truth but not the whole of it. Each of the factors mentioned made a larger or smaller contribution to the creation of Israel, but each of them alone would have been either inconceivable or ineffective without the others. This view will become clearer, it is hoped, as we consider more closely the origins of modern Israel, starting with the earliest in point of time.

I

The Jewish Connection with Palestine

1. THE ANCIENT HEBREW CIVILIZATION

The origins of the Jewish connection with Palestine go back to the remote realms in which history is merged with legend, myths, and religious traditions. The Bible tells the story of God's command to Abraham to go forth from his native land of Ur, in present-day Iraq, to what came to be known as Palestine, which country He promised to grant to his descendants forever though not before they had passed a period of four hundred years as persecuted strangers in an alien land. In accordance with the divine forecast, Abraham's grandson Jacob, or Israel, was compelled by famine to go to Egypt with his entire family in the circumstances described in the moving story of Joseph and his brothers and settle there in the land of Goshen. From seventy souls in all, the children of Israel multiplied so rapidly in the course of time that they aroused the anxiety of Egypt's rulers who took drastic measures to check their growth and keep them under control. At the proper time, God appointed Moses as His prophet and mouthpiece and entrusted him with the task of leading the Children of Israel out of Egypt and back to the land He had promised to Abraham. After many trials, during which God continually supported Moses with signs and miracles, and after forty years of wandering in the desert during which the multitude of the Children of Israel was forged into a "nation" vowed to the exclusive worship of God and endowed with His Own laws, Moses finally brought his people to the gates of the Promised Land. God called His servant when his mission was fulfilled and Joshua led the Israelites into their homeland.

In regard to most points of this story, history is able to tell us little that is certain. We know generally that during the second millennium B.C. there were periodical incursions of Semitic tribes from the Syrian desert into the lands lying on the seacoast of the Mediterranean; that one tribe or group of tribes who claimed descent from Abraham of Ur and were known as Hebrews, or Israelites, had migrated into the territory of Palestine; and that by 1100 B.C. the Israelites were in firm occupation of most of the hill country and were already distinguished by their religion from the Phoenicians and Philistines of the coast and from the nomads who dwelt on the eastern side of the Jordan.

For the next twelve hundred years the Children of Israel were settled in Palestine. They were never the sole occupants of the land, nor were they always its "sovereign" masters. But they were definitely rooted in it, and it was there that they developed the great spiritual heritage which they contributed to mankind.

During the twelfth and eleventh centuries B.C., the Israelites lived under a system of separate tribes which were often in conflict with each other and with their neighbors. This phase of their life is fairly amply described in the Book of Judges. But under the pressure of foreign enemies, particularly the Philistines, the tribes were driven to establish a monarchy which, following its halting beginnings under Saul, became consolidated and reached the height of its power under King David (1010–970 B.C.) and King Solomon (970–930 B.C.). David decisively defeated the Philistines and other enemies, and Solomon extended the influence of the realm he had inherited from his father over nearly the entire area lying between the two rival powers of Assyria and Egypt. The glory of Solomon's reign was crowned by the construction of the Temple in Jerusalem, which gradually became the focal point of the religious and national life of the Israelites.

On King Solomon's death, ten tribes inhabiting the northern half of the country seceded and formed their own kingdom which became known as Israel. The Philistines reasserted their independence in their coastal city-states as did other subject nations. What remained of Solomon's realm became known as the kingdom of Judah and continued to have its center in Jerusalem and its Temple.

The two small kingdoms, as well as the city-states of the coast, managed to preserve their independence for nearly two hundred years, despite their size and relative weakness, until 721–715 B.C. when the Assyrian giant conquered the kingdom of Israel, destroyed its capital, and deported the able and wealthy among the population to distant lands. Judah escaped a similar fate by submitting to Assyrian suzerainty. But several generations later, in 585 B.C., Nebuchadnezzar of the new Babylonian empire, which had dispossessed Assyria, conquered and drove out the Judeans as well. Jerusalem was sacked, and many were deported to Babylon. Thus ended the episode known in Jewish tradition as the period of the First Temple. Politically, the record of that period was rather unimpressive after the reigns of David and Solomon. Spiritually and culturally, however, it witnessed in its latter half the high soaring of the human spirit, the deepening of the moral conscience, and the flowering of the great rhythmic prose evident in the legacy of the prophets Amos, Hosea, Isaiah, and Jeremiah.

The captivity of Judah in Babylon did not last long. In 539 B.C., Cyrus the Great, the founder of the Persian empire, occupied Babylon and in the next year gave permission to the Judean exiles to return to their country. Nearly 40,000 of them, a small part of the total Jewry of Babylon, availed themselves of the opportunity and returned to their homeland to reconstitute their national life as a small vassal state and to rebuild the Temple. Little was known until quite recently about the life of the "men of Judah," or Jews, for the next three or four hundred years apart from the fact that they were under Persian suzerainty and afterwards came under the Ptolemaic Greeks. But recent research, much of it done in Jerusalem, indicates that it was in this period that the cultural identity of the Jews was fixed and secured. It was then that the Torah (the Pentateuch) took its final form and became the focus of Jewish life, and it was then that the books of Job, Ruth, the Song of Songs, Ecclesiastes, Proverbs, and some of the finest Psalms were written.

A new phase began with the conquest of Palestine by the Seleucid rulers of Syria. Hellenism had made deep inroads among the Jews, but when the Seleucids tried to hasten the historical process by banning adherence to rules of the Torah, a revolt broke out which succeeded in recovering the independence of Judea. The revolt had been led by the Hasmonean priestly family who set up a dynasty of priest-kings. Under some of its more able members, Judea expanded in all directions so that by 150 B.C. it had reached something like the limits of the kingdom of David and Solomon. Less than one hundred years later, however, Judea succumbed once more to the might of another great empire when, in 63 B.C., Pompey captured Jerusalem. For the next two thousand years Palestine was never to become an independent realm again, until Israel was established in A.D. 1948.

During the next century after their conquest the Romans ruled Judea indirectly and did not, on the whole, disturb the community life of the Jews. At times they allowed native rulers like Herod to assume the title and many of the prerogatives of a king. But the heavy burden of taxation, internal feuds, and above all the growth of a fierce national spirit which fed on a fanatic attachment to religion, led to continual strife and tension culminating in a general revolt in A.D. 64. It took Rome seven years of bitter fighting before she was able to subdue the Jews. The Temple, which was the seat of the last resistance, was burned to the ground by Titus and his soldiers. But the Jews were not yet completely crushed. They revolted again in 115 and in 132. This last revolt, which was led by Shimon Bar Kochba, was so successful that Rome determined to make its repetition impossible. In 135 Jerusalem was destroyed and its site was plowed up. Countless Jews were slaughtered and countless others were carried off to slavery. For two more centuries the pacified Jews of Palestine were able to maintain a communal life under the leadership of a patriarchate sanctioned by Rome, during which the great work of elaborating the Torah into the legal-moral compendia known as the Mishna was completed. But subsequent centuries saw the dwindling of Jewish life in Palestine until only a few thousand impoverished Jews remained in their ancient homeland. Long before this point had been reached, Jewish history had ceased to be the history of Palestine and began to be what it still is in large measure today: the history of Jewish communities dispersed over much of the world.

2. THE DIASPORA AND THE IDEA OF RETURN

The long, fascinating, and often tragic history of the Jewish communities outside of Palestine is beyond the scope of this work. However, a few paragraphs giving its bare outline might provide a useful background for many topics touched upon in this book, and are particularly important for setting the Jewish connection with Palestine in its historical context.

The history of the Jewish Diaspora, or dispersion, began long before the disastrous end of the Bar Kochba uprising in A.D. 135. Many, if not most, of the Jews who had been exiled to Babylon in 585 B.C. did not return in 538 B.C. or thereafter; and their descendants, swollen by waves of immigration, grew in the course of time into a very large community which kept in close touch with Palestine and developed a creative cultural-religious life centered on the Torah. When Palestine declined as the center of Jewish culture, around the third century of our era, that function passed to the Babylonian Jewish community and remained with it through the Arab conquest in the seventh century and the golden age of Arab-Islamic civilization in the next three centuries. In the course of this long span, the academies established by Babylonian Jewry collected and produced the immense corpus of commentaries and elaboration upon the Mishna known as the Talmud, worked out the principles of Jewish jurisprudence, assembled the homilies and legends known as the Midrash, and elaborated the first Siddur, or prayerbook. This body of material has served ever since as the core of traditional Jewish learning everywhere and has provided Jews in the Diaspora with a common heritage of doctrine, law, and lore which contributed enormously to preserving the unity of the Jewish people until the dawn of modern times. Even today, nearly one hundred Yeshivot —religious colleges—in Israel, and many others all over the world devote themselves mainly to the preservation and enrichment of the heritage bequeathed by Babylonian Jewry.

A Jewish community was established in Alexandria, Egypt, almost since the foundation of the city by Alexander the Great. In the course of time, the community grew to such an extent that it dared, in A.D. 115, to revolt against Roman power and was able to secure the relaxation of an old Roman law against mutilation of the body, which had been used in the years before the uprising to ban circumcision. But jealous as it was for its faith, that community nevertheless participated fully in the Hellenistic culture and shared in the glory of Alexandria when it was the center of Hellenistic civilization. The Septuagint—the Greek translation of the Old Testament —and the work of the great Jewish philosopher Philo testify to the effort made by that community to reach an accommodation with Greek culture and thought which, incidentally, influenced in turn the philosophy of the Church Fathers. In later Roman times, the Jewish community in Alexandria declined in importance and numbers, just as did Palestine's Jewry with which it had kept in close contact, but the Jews of Alexandria flourished again under the generally tolerant Arab-Muslim rule. Once more the Jews of Egypt adopted the language, way of living, and culture of the surrounding society while retaining their separateness in matters pertaining to their faith. Many of them attained positions of power and honor in the government, in finance, in science and in learning.

From the Near East, from Egypt, and from North Africa Jews migrated to Spain in the wake of the Arab conquest and reinforced Jewish groups who had migrated to that country in earlier times. There they became full-fledged partners with the Arabs in the brilliant civilization that developed under a succession of magnificent princes. All walks of life, rural and urban, were open to the Jews and many of them attained the highest positions in the economic, social, cultural, and political life of the various Spanish states. And while the Spanish Jews, like the Egyptian, assimilated by adopting Arabic names, the Arabic language, and Arab ways, they managed at the same time to produce a bright revival of Hebrew culture including religious and secular poetry. The record of the period between the tenth and twelfth centuries, studded with names like Hasdai ibn Shaprut, Samuel the Naguid, Solomon ibn Gabirol, ibn Janah, Bahya ibn Pakuda, Isaac al-Fasi, Moses ibn Ezra, Judah Halevi, Abraham ibn Ezra, and Moses ibn Maimun, or Maimonides, constitutes a glorious chapter in Jewish history. Unfortunately this period came to a premature end with the Almohade persecution of the Jews of Spain and North Africa, exceptional in its fierceness in the record of Muslim treatment of Jews, which compelled Maimonides, among many of his co-religionists, to seek refuge on the more hospitable shores of Egypt.

In the Western world, the Jews fared nowhere nearly so well as in the lands that came under the dominion of Islam. In Europe, the Jews were compelled to live an isolated community life, assimilating little of the culture and ways of the peoples among whom they lived until the seventeenth and eighteenth centuries. From Rome and other cities of Italy, where large Jewish communities existed by the first century, Jews had penetrated into the European provinces of the Roman empire and, after its collapse, into Germany and England. When Christianity became dominant in these areas, the Jews were submitted to various restrictions and prohibitions which marked them off as distinct and inferior people because of their denial of the central belief of Christianity. In the course of time, the gulf established by ecclesiastical discriminatory decrees was widened by the effect of social factors. The Jew could not find a place on the land or in the artisan guilds. Consequently, he became a middle man, merchant, or peddler; and since usury was forbidden to Christians, he also became the moneylender. Concentrated in the towns where they were confined to special quarters known as ghettos, foreigners and foreign-looking, keeping to themselves, occupied in unpopular albeit useful professions, clinging stubbornly to their faith, and viewed as bearing collectively and for all time the guilt of the crucifixion, the Jews became intensely disliked by the populace. This dislike came to a head in the period of the Crusades, when it became as much an act of piety to kill the Jews in Europe as to kill the Saracens in the Holy Land. A wave of persecution, increasingly brutal, spread all over Western Europe. In England, France, and Germany, Jews were despoiled, tortured, some massacred and the rest finally expelled. For a time, there was less brutality in the parts of Spain reconquered by Christians. But in the second half of the fifteenth century the Inquisition took up its task of hunting and burning heretics, and in 1492 all Jews who refused to be converted were expelled.

The refugees from western Europe went to the eastern frontiers of the expanding continent to Lithuania, Poland, and Hungary. This migration continued through the ages until half the Jews in the world were congregated in that area. At first, the Polish kings protected them; but the respite was short-lived. In the middle of the seventeenth century came the Tartar invasion and later on Russian rule. A sort of territorial ghetto, "the pale of settlement," was set up from the Baltic, north of Warsaw, to the Black Sea, near Odessa, to keep the Jews from penetrating Holy Russia; throughout this area, the ghetto system was enforced.

The refugees from Spain went mostly to the Mediterranean provinces of the Ottoman empire, to North Africa, Egypt, the Balkans, Asia Minor, and even to Constantinople itself. A few of them trickled into Italy and southern France and were followed in subsequent generations by Marranos Jews—Jews who had remained in Spain by bowing to the Inquisition in outward form but not in conviction—who also infiltrated Holland, Germany, and England and paved the way for the return to all these countries of undisguised, professing Jews. The Spanish refugees who went to the Muslim lands merged with the Jewish communities already existing there and enjoyed relative freedom from the worst forms of persecution. But just as these Jews had shared in the glory of the Muslim countries in the previous centuries, so in the centuries that followed they shared in the decay and stagnation that engulfed them at the very time when the western Christian peoples were forging ahead toward a new world.

By the time of the American and French Revolutions, Jews had lived in dispersion for one and a half to two and a half millennia without losing their identity and their essential unity. Certain minor differences in ritualistic details and much larger sociological and even racial differences had crept in among various communities or groups of communities over the centuries, giving rise to three major divisions: 1) the Ashkenazim—literally, Germans, but actually those who had lived under Christianity before the expulsion of the Jews from Spain; 2) the Sefaradim—literally, Spaniards, but actually the Spanish outcasts and all the communities of the Mediterranean basin with which they intermingled; and 3) various communities which existed uninterruptedly in the East from before the destruction of the Second Temple, notably the Yemenites and the Iraqis. But the differences among these divisions were outweighed by the enormous body of religious law, ritual, customs, lore, and knowledge which they shared in common, and above all by the common conception of the history and destiny of the Jews centering upon the ideas of *Galuth* and *Geullah* which they all held.

Galuth, meaning exile, defined the condition of the Jews in their own eyes, and Geullah, delivery from the exile and return to the ancestral homeland, defined their expected destiny. Among various Jewish communities at various times these two concepts were overlaid with metaphysical meaning, but never until the nineteenth century was the idea of actual return to Palestine missing in any interpretation. Assertions of the conviction of Jews that their current status was that of an exiled people and expressions of their faith in delivery and return are to be found in countless rituals, from the daily prayers through the ceremonials attending birth, marriage, and death. But the belief in these concepts found its strength in the roots it has in the traditional Jewish view of the world. This view, which saturates much of the Old Testament, conceives of the universe as governed by a divine design operating continuously, the chief motif of which is God's relation with His Chosen People. Empires rise and fall, nature pursues or modifies its prescribed course, and the earth proffers or withholds its bounty in order to serve an identifiable purpose in the cosmic moral drama that had its historical beginning in God's covenant with Abraham. It followed that such events as the destruction of the Temple and the scattering of the Jews, the most momentous since the Exodus, could not be accidental or definitive, but served a certain purpose and had to have a sequel. That purpose was viewed as the chastising of the Jews in exile, and the sequel was viewed as redemption and return to the land God gave to Abraham. The fact that both the Christian and Moslem societies among which the Jews served their sentence of exile conceded the special relation of the Jewish people with God in the past and confirmed the cosmic moral significance of its dispersion, even as they differed in assessing its present status and the sequel to its dispersion, further confirmed the Jew in his conviction. For the belief in the Delivery and Return yet to come became one of the most important criteria continuously separating and demarcating him from the peoples among whom he lived.

II

Zionism: The Dynamics
of Its Internal Success

Zionism has been viewed by some as a nationalist movement representing the ripening of the religiously inspired yearning for Zion and by others as an essentially secular movement of national liberation triggered by the difficulties and problems encountered by Europe's Jews in the course of the nineteenth century. Both views have their adherents among Zionists themselves and can find support in the facts of Zionist history. Indeed it is possible to draw a continuous line between the traditional yearning for Return and a certain branch of Zionism, just as it is possible to point out that the actual initiators of the Zionist movement, Pinsker and Herzl, were prompted to issue their call for a Jewish state by purely practical assessments of the conditions of the Jews in Europe and did not even consider Palestine as the only conceivable site for that state. But a critical look at the evolution of the Zionist movement as a whole in the context of a broad historical perspective would show that it could not have succeeded if it really were only one or the other. Its strength lay precisely in the fact that it combined the traditional yearning for Return with considerations of the practical needs of the Jews into a new synthesis in which those needs activated the traditional yearning even as they sheared it of its strictly religious content; while the yearning for Return endowed the practically inspired suggestion of a Jewish state with emotional power even as it directed it toward Palestine specifically.

1. ZIONISM, THE YEARNING FOR RETURN, AND THE JEWISH PROBLEM

The Return to the ancestral homeland has been viewed throughout most of Jewish history as something to be accomplished through miraculous divine intervention in the context of a cosmic upheaval and as the prelude to an era of universal peace and justice. This conception did not, however, preclude certain "minority opinions" which envisaged the Return as coming about through the divine will operating in what would appear as normal historical processes, nor did it prevent self-appointed Messiahs from arising now and then to lead the people back to their homeland and gaining considerable numbers of followers on the basis of flimsy credentials. The traditional conception did not, in any case, rule against anybody going to live in the Holy Land without awaiting the Messiah; on the contrary, Jewish tradition extolled such an act as a good deed, almost a religious obligation, and cultivated a fervent unconditional affection for the ancestral home in and of itself. Throughout history there never lacked individuals and groups who uprooted themselves from their environment and went to live in Palestine out of piety and yearning for Zion.

In the early part of the nineteenth century, the stimulus of general European nationalism began to awaken the traditional yearning for Return and give it a nationalist turn. Religious leaders in various parts of Europe, such as rabbi Judah Bibas (d. 1852) of Corfu, the Sefaradic rabbi Judah Alcalay (1798–1878) of Semlin, Serbia, and the Ashkenazi rabbi Zvi Hirsh Kalisher (1794–1874) of Posen, in Prussian-occupied Poland, basing themselves on the "minority opinions," urged that their fellow Jews take action to effect their Return to their homeland in the same way that other nationalists strove to redeem themselves. In the tracts they wrote and the sermons they preached they presented arguments and advocated measures which foreshadowed those subsequently adopted by the Zionist movement. But these appeals went unnoticed and made no impact until they were rediscovered and used by some groups in the Zionist movement several decades later.

The idea of Return was a tenet of faith not only for the Jews, but also for some influential groups among the Christian, particularly Protestant, powers in modern times. And for them too the idea was not only eschatological. During the nineteenth century, sympathy for nationalist causes in general and unsettled conditions in the Near East and Palestine encouraged the notion among some enthusiasts of the Jewish Return that the time for the fulfillment of the Biblical prophecy had come. These enthusiasts, while they were personally moved by religious sentiment, advanced all sorts of political arguments to win the support of their governments for their schemes. Some argued, for instance, that a Jewish settlement in Palestine would prove a reliable support for the tottering Ottoman regime when support of that regime seemed to be in the national interest. Others argued that the Jews in Palestine would be the most trustworthy successors of the Ottomans and the guardians of the eastern approaches to Suez in alliance with the power that would sponsor their settlement. Schemes of the sort engaged at times the attention and imagination of very serious statesmen like Palmerston; but, again, nothing enduring came of them until the Zionist movement appeared and was able to capitalize on them and on the sentiment underlying them.

The Zionist movement did not, in fact, produce any new idea when it advocated the establishment of a National Home for the Jewish people in Palestine, nor did it invent any new argument in approaching the various powers for support for its scheme. If it nevertheless succeeded where its antecedents among both Jews and Gentiles had failed, it was because it wedded the idea of Return to the Jewish problem as it appeared in the nineteenth century and thus responded to an urgent practical need with an emotionally rich formula.

In its modern version, the Jewish problem is the product of the Enlightenment and the issue raised by the emancipation of the Jews in many European countries in the wake of the French Revolution. We have seen that until the latter event, the Jews of Europe, comprising the majority of world Jewry, had led their own life in the ghettos in almost complete seclusion from Gentile society except for business contacts. The ghetto had been imposed on them together with other restrictions as a mark of the curse lying on them for rejecting the true faith, but they had rationalized their status and the frequent outbursts of active persecution in the concept of Galuth as a penance to be followed by Geullah; in the meantime, they had developed a complete, poor and inbred but spiritually satisfying way of life. The French Revolution upset this doctrinal and social order which had stood for centuries by offering to the Jews freedom and equality with the non-Jewish citizens, provided they ceased to look upon themselves as a separate nationality and assimilated into the national culture while retaining only their separate cult and faith.

After an initial period of hesitation and fear, the French Jews welcomed their new freedom and endeavored to live up to the terms under which it had been proffered. France became a model for the other European countries, and the emancipation of the Jews went hand in hand with the spread of the Enlightenment and the advance of the liberal creeds of the French Revolution, so that by the 1860's most European states had liberated their Jews. For their part, the emancipated Jews reinterpreted the concepts of Galuth and Geullah so as to free them of any separatist nationalist connotation, and many among them supported reforms in their religion designed to suit it to modern thought as well as to discard anything which might impose excessive barriers between themselves and their fellow citizens. But the Jewish question was not to be solved so easily.

Although most European countries emancipated their Jews in the course of the nineteenth century, Tsarist Russia, containing most of Europe's Jews, and Rumania, containing the next largest number, did not do so. During the reign of Alexander II, it looked for a while as though Russia's Jewry, too, was on its way to liberation as curbs on Jews were eased and as many of them acquired modern education and mixed with Russian society. But the assassination of the Tsar in 1881 inaugurated a period of general reaction in the country and of repression and pogroms against the Jews such as had not been seen since the height of the Middle Ages. Many Jews reacted in the tradition of their ancestors by taking to the road and seeking more hospitable lands, thus starting the most massive wave of migration in Jewish history. But among the millions who remained, the masses were caught in a mixture of despair and Messianic anticipation while members of the enlightened minority urged various courses and solutions. Some still believed in emancipation as the desirable solution, but, convinced that it could not be achieved under the existing regime, advocated participation in the efforts of the many Russian revolutionary groups to overthrow it entirely. Others lost all hope of emancipation from above and doubted its efficacy even if it was attained. One of these was a physician from Odessa by the name of Leo Pinsker who wrote a pamphlet in 1881 entitled *Auto-emancipation* in which he argued that anti-semitism was an inescapable passion provoked by the very character of the Jewish people as an abnormal nation, a "ghost nation." The only solution to the problem was for the Jews to take their fate in their own hands and seek to establish a state of their own which would convert them into a "normal" nation and thus eliminate the root of the fear and hatred of them.

Pinsker's pamphlet marked the beginning of Russian Zionism. Immediately after its publication, a congress of prominent Russian Jews was assembled and founded a society to promote the idea expounded in it. However, while Pinsker had not mentioned Palestine specifically as the site of the envisaged state, the founding members of the society, who were in closer touch with the mood of the people than Pinsker, the assimilated physician, insisted on it as the only conceivable choice. As if to stress the point, they adopted for the society the name *Chovevei Zion*—Lovers of Zion.

The Jewish problem in the nineteenth century was not confined to Russia and Rumania. Even in Central and Western Europe, the emancipation which had been achieved formally did not proceed smoothly in practice. In the first place, emancipation had been much more an act prescribed by rational consistency in an age that valued reason than an expression of a spontaneous feeling of brotherhood, equality, and justice. The ideas of the Enlightenment were hostile to medieval corporatism; the status of the Jews was part of that system; therefore it had to go. Liberalism, with its conception of society as a conglomeration of free and equal individuals united by a compact, was particularly impelled by its own logic to eliminate the abnormal status of the Jews as an inferior group within but not of society. Now emancipation on the basis of rational philosophical considerations alone could lead to political equality and economic freedom, but it could not and did not in fact lead to social acceptance. In matters that were outside the province of the law, the Jews were still often treated as inferior. Secondly, in the course of the latter half of the nineteenth century the rational philosophical theories of the Enlightenment and liberalism themselves came under heavy attack from political and social philosophies resting on evolutionism, historicism, romanticism, and race theories which viewed society as an entity which had been formed by many centuries of common history, as a living organism or as a compact of blood rather than a deliberate artificial creation. Such schemes had no room in the national society for the Jews, who were a distinct group and had lived their own life in seclusion until recently, and some of them explicitly regarded the Jews as harmful to the nation or necessarily disloyal to it. Finally, because liberalism was closely associated with the emancipation of the Jews, its political opponents endeavored to arouse suspicion and dislike of the Jews on every conceivable ground with the purpose of using these feelings as a means of embarrassing or overthrowing its proponents.

The pressures generated by these hostile trends caused many Jews to discard more and more of their specific Jewish baggage in the belief that greater assimilation would eventually prove a remedy to Jew-hating. Not a few crossed over and became formally baptized. Most tried to convince themselves that the progress of civilization and evidence of their own loyalty and attachment to the nation would finally eliminate the remaining prejudices against them. But a few gave up hope in the effectiveness of assimilation and suspected that anti-Semitism was ineradicable. One of these few was Theodor Herzl, the founder of the World Zionist Organization. Herzl had been a strong advocate and practitioner of assimilation. He was born in Budapest in 1860 and had achieved some fame as a writer and playwright. In the winter of 1894–1895, he was stationed in Paris as a correspondent of a great Viennese newspaper where he observed at close quarters the Dreyfus drama. For a year or two before, he had been preoccupied with the problem of anti-Semitism and had begun to have doubts about his earlier views on the efficacy and desirability of assimilation. The Dreyfus Affair now led him to the conclusion that assimilation was not realizable and that the only solution to the Jewish problem was a mass exodus of the Jews to a state of their own. He put his ideas in a pamphlet called *The Jewish State,* published in 1896, without being aware of Pinsker's pamphlet dated fifteen years before containing similar conclusions, reached on the basis of an assessment of the condition of the Jews in Russia. In the following year, however, when Herzl assembled in Basle, Switzerland, a congress of Jews from all over the world to promote his idea, representatives of the Russian Lovers of Zion attended together with representatives of Jewish groups in Europe and America, and all took part in establishing the World Zionist Organization.

In his pamphlet, Herzl had expressed preference for Palestine as the site of the Jewish state because of its historical association with the Jews, but, like Pinsker, he was also willing to consider a suitable place anywhere else. The first Zionist Congress, however, unanimously opted for Palestine. A few years later, the choice of Palestine was put to the test when the British government offered Herzl a territory in East Africa for Jewish settlement. Herzl and many of the Western Zionists were inclined to accept, but among Zionists from Eastern Europe there was bitter opposition to any alternative to Zion which threatened to pull the movement apart. Eventually, the seventh Zionist Congress, which met in 1905 soon after Herzl's death, rejected the East Africa proposal and rededicated itself to Palestine. Those who still favored any territory seceded from the movement and formed the Jewish Territorial Organization (ITO). The history of that organization is perhaps an indication of what might have happened to the Zionist movement as a whole had it not tapped the deeply rooted popular attachment to Palestine to sustain its endeavor to find a practical solution to the immediate Jewish problem. Despite its sponsorship by many outstanding Jews and its very able leadership, the Jewish Territorial Organization became converted into a philanthropic group which did some useful work in several countries but sank into insignificance within a decade after its foundation.

2. ZIONISM, WORLD JEWRY, AND THE BUILDING OF THE NATIONAL HOME

Zionism, as a doctrine that rejected outright the possibility of the Jews' being able to live as citizens of various countries on equal terms with non-Jews and asserted that Jews everywhere constituted a single nation for which it sought to secure a National Home in Palestine, was never more than the faith of a relatively small minority of Jews. In 1899, two years after its founding, the World Zionist Organization had a registered membership of 114,000, even though membership in practical terms involved no more than payment of a small biennial poll tax. Fourteen years later, on the eve of the first

World War, the number had increased to 130,000 after periods of considerable decline from the original number. In 1921, after the Balfour Declaration had been issued and the Zionists had proved that they were not merely a group of dreamers but an internationally recognized force worthy of the sponsorship of mighty Britain and the other Great Powers, the membership of the Organization attained 778,000. Granting that all these figures understated the strength of the movement, since Zionism was formally outlawed both in Tsarist and Soviet Russia, the adherents of the movement still represented a minority of the world Jewish population which counted at that time 14 million.

Not only was Zionism the faith of a minority, but it was actively opposed nearly everywhere by powerful Jewish forces. In Russia and Eastern Europe it was opposed vehemently by the Bund—The General Jewish Workers' Organization in Russia and Poland —which was founded in the same year as the Zionist organization. The Bundists argued that the Zionists were diverting Jewish energies to a hopeless dream to the detriment of their own more realistic efforts to improve the lot of the Jews where they were. They sought instead to marshal Jewish effort on behalf of a Russian revolution while safeguarding what they conceived to be the interests of the Jewish working class. In Western Europe and the United States, the Zionist movement was opposed by most of the established Jewish communal organizations whose leaders were particularly indignant at the Zionist suggestion that Jews everywhere were unassimilable and constituted one nation—a claim which tended to cast doubt on their loyalty to their respective countries and strengthen the hands of the anti-Semites who asserted just that. Everywhere, the movement was opposed by small groups of ultraorthodox Jews who objected to its secularism and accused it of tampering with the Messianic idea. So conscious were the Zionists of the Jewish opposition and so hemmed in by it that, until the rise of Hitler, their *bête noire* was not any persecutor of the Jews, nor was it, as in the case of other nationalist movements, a foreign occupying power, but other Jews—the non-Zionists and the anti-Zionists. If Zionism succeeded nevertheless in representing itself to the world as the spokesman of the national aspirations of the Jewish people and achieving its goal of a Jewish state, it was because of two crucial considerations: the comprehensiveness of its program, and the tragic history of the Jewish people culminating in the disaster of Hitler's program of extermination.

As a nationalist movement, Zionism was confronted with the peculiar task of having not only to win sovereignty for a dependent nation, but also of having virtually to create that nation before winning sovereignty for it. For even according to the Zionists, the Jews constituted only a disembodied abnormal nation that had to be normalized and given more substance before it could be called a nation in the full sense of the term. Zionism, therefore, had to gather the people in Palestine from the various countries, settle them on the land, teach them new skills and induce them to change their occupations, give them jobs, create towns and villages, build factories, hospitals and schools, revive a defunct national language, start a new national culture, history, and mystique, and do a hundred other things which nationalist movements elsewhere could take for granted. Now, many of these tasks taken separately appealed to Jews everywhere on philanthropic, religious, cultural, scientific, and humanitarian grounds and they gave their unstinting support to achieve them. The Bund, for instance, though violently anti-Zionist, strove vigorously to preserve and promote Jewish culture; non-Zionist organizations of German Jews helped build a technological institute in Palestine; French Jews founded agricultural schools and farms; British Jews supported agricultural research stations; American Jews supported the Hebrew university. Ultraorthodox Jews set up religious schools, settlements, and urban quarters to combat Zionist secularism. All of these enterprises, while they were set up by their supporters without political *arrière pensées,* did in fact contribute greatly to the creation of that organic national strength in Palestine which in due course made the Zionist political claims all the more powerful.

An even more important factor in the success of the Zionist movement in becoming the most powerful and most widely recognized voice of the collective will of the Jewish people was the renewal of active and brutal persecution of Jews in many countries in the last quarter of the nineteenth and in the present century. Jews everywhere were unanimous in viewing as an inescapable imperative the lending of help to their persecuted brethren. Such help took many forms, including relief aid and intercession directly and through intermediaries with the offending authorities. But when the trouble was serious, there was no other recourse for the persecuted than flight, and flight became more and more difficult in this century. As one country after another passed exclusion acts or adopted restrictive measures which blocked the way to massive Jewish immigration, Palestine became one of the few place of refuge and the only country which Jews could enter, in Churchill's words, "by right, not on sufferance." Increasingly, therefore, Jewish opinion in the world, regardless of political inclination, supported the struggle of the Zionists to keep the gates of Palestine wide open. When, after the massacre of European Jewry, the issue of providing a place of refuge for the survivors became inextricably involved with the issue of ultimate sovereignty in Palestine, virtually the whole of world Jewry, with its center by then in the United States, threw its weight on the side of the Zionists and pressed for a Jewish state. Thus it came about that, in the matter of building the foundations of a nation in Palestine as well as in the matter of winning sovereignty for it in most of the Palestinian territory, the Zionists were able to enlist the sympathy and support of most of world Jewry, though for motives other than their own and not on the basis of their complete interpretation of the position and destiny of the Jews in the world. This difference of motive and approach is at the root of the confused ideological wrangles which today characterize the relations between and among the leaders of Israel, the Zionist movement, and spokesmen for Jewish organizations outside Israel.

III

The Balfour Declaration
and the Mandate

The triumph of Zionism as expressed in the establishment of Israel was not only the outcome of the convergence of the wills and forces of the Jewish people just described. The support of powerful individuals, groups, and governments for various aspects of the Zionist case was also crucial on several occasions, even as it is essential today for the survival and development of Israel. One of the most important of these occasions was the issuing of the Balfour Declaration by the British Government on November 2, 1917. It was this Declaration which laid the foundations for the development of the Jewish community in Palestine from 56,000 divided and squabbling people scattered in two dozen settlements and a few mixed towns at the end of World War I into the disciplined and prospering embryonic nation of 700,000 which was able to withstand the combined assault of all the surrounding Arab states in 1948.

1. THE BALFOUR DECLARATION

The Declaration consisted of a single, long sentence in the form of a letter addressed by Foreign Secretary Balfour to Lord Rothschild as representative of the Zionists. It read: "His Majesty's Government view with favor the establishment in Palestine of a national home for the Jewish people, and will use their best endeavours to facilitate the achievement of this object, it being clearly understood

that nothing shall be done which may prejudice the civil and religious rights of existing non-Jewish communities in Palestine, or
the rights and political status enjoyed by Jews in any other country."

The reasons which had prompted the British government to issue
the Balfour Declaration are of interest not only because they reflect
the grounds for the appeal of Zionism to a great Gentile power
like Britain but also because they foreshadow the grounds for the
subsequent trouble in British-Zionist relations. A recent definitive
study by Leonard Stein (see bibliography) indicates that, in the
immediate sense, the British Cabinet approved the issuing of the
Declaration in the hope that the Jews of Russia, which was then
in the throes of revolution, might be able to exert a steadying influence on their country and keep it in the war; in order to counter
the apathy toward the war of a considerable section of American
Jewry; in the expectation of reaping some propaganda benefits in
all the countries where Jews lived; and, finally, with a view to
forestalling an expected German declaration in favor of the Jews.

Beneath these immediate political considerations, however, there
was a large variety of longer-range sentiments and motives in favor
of the object of the Declaration which were reflected at one time
or another in the course of the long process of interviews, discussions, and negotiations that preceded its issuance. Among these,
there was an intuitive sympathy with Zionist aspirations on the part
of many British statesmen which expressed itself as soon as Turkey
entered the war and its partition became a major war object of
the Allies; there was the impression made on the British government by men like Chaim Weizmann and Sir Herbert Samuel that
Zionism was a powerful force among Jewry and that Jewish good
will was an intangible asset worth acquiring; there was the response
of some imaginative British minds to the suggestion that a large-
scale Jewish settlement in Palestine might have a stabilizing influence in an area where important British interests were at stake and
might contribute to the regeneration of the Middle East as a whole;
there was the hope that a chance given to Zionism might serve as
an antidote to the subversive movements in which Jews, in rebellion
against their lot, were finding an outlet for their frustrated energies;
there were the romantic dreams of men like Mark Sykes to help a
great but corrupted people regenerate itself through the renewal
of its life in the cradle of its civilization; there was the desire to

use the sponsorship of Zionist aspirations as a means to help nullify French claims to parts of Palestine and bring the whole country under British auspices; and, finally, there was the more comprehensive view expressed by Balfour a few weeks after the Declaration that "the Jews ought to have their rightful place in the world: a great nation without a home is not right." In short, the Declaration was issued out of broad humanitarian considerations, for immediate tactical political advantages, and for long-range strategic interests—an irresistible combination to any imaginative Anglo-Saxon statesman.

The Declaration was approved by the chief Allied Powers, including the United States, and its principles were incorporated in the terms of the Mandate approved by the League of Nations by which Britain was to govern Palestine. The instrument of the Mandate recognized "the historical connection of the Jewish people with Palestine and . . . the grounds for reconstituting their national home in that country." The Mandatory Power was directed to encourage immigration and close settlement of Jews on the land; and, as a sign of the Jewish cultural renaissance, Hebrew as well as Arabic and English was to be an official language. The instrument prescribed the establishment of a Jewish Agency representing the Jewish people to advise and cooperate with the British Administration in economic, social, and other matters which might affect the establishment of the Jewish National Home and assist and take part in the development of the country.

2. THE APPLICATION OF THE MANDATE: INTERNAL DEVELOPMENT

The story of the application of the Mandate as far as the Jews are concerned appears as the history of increasing frustration, despair, turmoil, and strife in the external political sphere, and of steady growth, prosperity, and achievement in the internal economic, social, cultural, and political fields. In retrospect, it seems, oddly enough, that the frustrations as well as the achievements operated in favor of the creation of the state of Israel. For had the external political situation been less intolerable to the Jews by the end of the second World War, they might not have risen against the prevailing order for a few more years, at least, and this might very well have made all the difference in terms of obtaining international support for partition and the establishment of a Jewish state. In any case, the over-all development of the Mandate was such that by the time its initial spirit and purpose had been completely whittled away, the Jewish settlement had grown in every respect to the point when it could take its fate in its own hands and forge ahead to create and sustain the state of Israel.

In terms of internal development, the history of the Yishuv (the Jewish community in Palestine) during the Mandatory period is marked by three phases. The first, which lasted from the confirmation of the Mandate in 1922 until the end of 1932, was characterized by a rather slow evolution. The basic institutions of Jewish Palestine were established or consolidated during that period—the institutions of communal self-government, the Jewish Agency, the labor movement, the main forms of settlement, the political parties, the Hebrew education system, the university, a national press, and so on; but the flow of immigration was disappointingly, almost fatally, slow. In his appearance before the Peace Conference in 1919, Chaim Weizmann had estimated the expected level of immigration to ʾhe envisaged National Home at between 70,000 and 80,000 a year. Louis D. Brandeis had had notions of transferring a million Eastern European Jews to Palestine in a few years. In contrast, the number of immigrants in the period under consideration averaged slightly more than 10,000 a year, and in 1927–1928 the number of Jews who emigrated from Palestine actually exceeded that of Jews who immigrated to it. It is true that the closing of the exit gates before Russia's Jews was partly responsible for the disparity between the expectations of the Zionist chiefs and reality; but there can be no doubt that these men had grossly overestimated the eagerness of the Jews to avail themselves of the opportunity offered to them to build a homeland without the constant prodding of persecution. Thus, despite the important qualitative development of the Yishuv during that decade, its slow quantitative growth carried with it the danger that the Jewish National Home in Palestine might shrivel of its own accord to something not unlike the interesting but ultimately unimportant Jewish agricultural settlement in Argentina sponsored by Baron de Hirsh. That this did not happen was largely due to Hitler's coming to power in Germany.

The persecution of the Jews by the Nazis induced or compelled tens of thousands to leave Germany, then Austria, then Czechoslovakia and all of Central Europe, with nowhere else to go but Palestine. Such were the skills and qualifications of these people, or such was the capital they were able to take out, that very large numbers of them passed the tests of the Mandatory government devised to restrict immigration in accordance with the economic absorptive capacity of the country. And as those who entered invested their money in various enterprises and built houses and facilities, they created further absorptive capacity for more Jews from everywhere. Thus it came about that in the course of the six years from 1934 to 1939 more than twice as many immigrants came to the country as had come to it in the previous twelve years. By the outbreak of World War II, the Yishuv had not only grown to a substantial community of more than half a million, but its over-all potentialities had expanded tremendously by the injection of new capital and vast numbers of excellently trained professionals, technicians, entrepreneurs, and highly educated people generally.

The third phase in the growth of the Yishuv dates from 1940 until the foundation of the state. Because of the war and political restrictions, the number of immigrants who came in during this period was relatively small, averaging about 15,000 a year; nevertheless this phase was of great importance for the formation of the Yishuv in all other respects. It was a period in which the economic and technical capacities of the Yishuv were fully realized as the dwindling of imports to the entire Middle East and the Allied war effort stimulated the growth of new Jewish industry, the reorganization of agriculture, and the expansion of the entire economy through vast new expenditures. It was a period in which the Yishuv was able to acquire valuable military experience through the 30,000 men it contributed to the British forces, and to accumulate a substantial arsenal of clandestine weapons from the enormous stocks that circulated in the area. Above all, it was a period when the Yishuv, screened against its own will from any vast inflow of new immigrants, totally engaged in the war and fired by the shame, pain, agony, and hatred caused by the savage destruction of millions of fellow Jews, was able to merge all the previous waves of immigration into a national community as cohesive and fanatically determined as any the world has seen. It was the insufficient appreciation of this moral-psychological factor, the outcome of the strains of the war and its aftermath, that completely confounded the estimates of the Yishuv's real strength made in Cairo and Damascus as well as in London and Washington.

3. THE APPLICATION OF THE MANDATE: EXTERNAL POLITICAL ASPECTS

In the political sphere, the story of the Mandate is the history of the continual narrowing of its original intent and purport as these came increasingly into conflict with the interests of the Mandatory Power in the Middle East as a whole. Already at the beginning of the Mandate, the immediate tactical political calculations that stood behind the issuing of the Balfour Declaration had become irrelevant. The broad humanitarian impulse which had moved statesmen in London to adopt a decision of principle in favor of the Jews was naturally less effective when it became a question of influencing the decisions and actions of officials in London and Jerusalem concerned with the routine application of the Mandate in the face of mounting practical difficulties. Finally, the long-range strategic considerations began to turn more and more decisively against the Zionist case as Arab opposition to the Jewish National Home deepened and broadened and as the world headed toward an international crisis in which the good will of the Arab mass of the Middle East seemed to weigh more and more heavily in the eyes of the British government.

Even before the Mandate had been confirmed, the Palestinian Arabs manifested their resistance to the policy it embodied in serious riots in 1920 and 1921. The following year, the British government issued an interpretation of the Mandate designed to assuage Arab fears and to check any extravagant expectations on the part of the Jews. The interpretation, known as the Churchill White Paper, explained that the development of the Jewish National Home did not mean the imposition of Jewish nationality upon all the inhabitants of Palestine, but the full development of the existing Jewish community to become a center in which the Jewish people could take pride. Having given the purport of the Mandate this cultural twist, the White Paper then went on to insist that the Jewish community in Palestine was there "as of right, not on sufferance."

For seven years comparative peace reigned in Palestine. Then, in 1929, Arab religious and national feeling, excited by a conflict involving the Wailing Wall (a remnant of the Second Temple), which stands in an area sacred to both Arabs and Jews, burst out in a series of murderous attacks on the Jewish population. A number of British commissions visited Palestine to inquire into the causes of the trouble and recommend remedies. Their reports suggested the imposition of qualifications and restrictions on Jewish immigration and, in general, stressed those provisions of the Mandate safeguarding the rights of the non-Jewish inhabitants to as great an extent as those designed to secure the establishment of a Jewish national home, if not more.

Once again there was a seven-year period of peace followed by another outburst of Arab violence and another spate of commissions of inquiry which submitted recommendations designed to appease the Arabs. This time, however, the issues were more significant, the commissions were of a higher caliber, the recommendations were more basic, and the stakes were consequently much higher.

The grounds for the Arab outburst had been the sudden increase in the rate of Jewish immigration following Hitler's rise to power. Although this immigration gave a fillip to the economic life of the country from which everybody benefited, the Arabs became fearful of the prospect, now real for the first time, that the Jews might soon become a majority in the country. As a sop to their apprehensions, the Palestine government suggested in 1936 the formation of a Legislative Council in which Arabs would outnumber Jews and official members. But the scheme was severely criticized in the British Parliament and withdrawn; whereupon the Arabs initiated acts of violence which soon assumed the character of an open, all-out revolt against British authority.

A Royal Commission, sent to inquire and make recommendations, did not content itself with suggesting new restrictions, but reached the drastic conclusion that the Mandate itself was altogether "unworkable." Instead of the Mandate, the Commission suggested the partitioning of Palestine into an Arab and a Jewish state and a British zone. The Arabs rejected the scheme outright, the Jews accepted the principle of partition, and the British government sent another commission to work out the details of its application. The Arab revolt was resumed and was supported this time by popular agitation in the neighboring Arab countries and by propaganda, money, and some arms from Fascist Italy and Nazi Germany. The commission appointed to work out the details of partition submitted a report which concluded that partition was impracticable. To break the deadlock, the British Prime Minister Neville Chamberlain, summoned a conference of Arabs and Jews in London. In recognition of the character which the Palestine question had begun to assume by that time and as an indication of the context in which the British government now viewed it, not only the Jewish Agency and the Palestine Arabs were invited to attend, but also the representatives of all the neighboring Arab countries.

The conference assembled in London at the beginning of 1939 in the shadow of a new climax in the international crisis. Hitler had just violated the Munich agreement by annexing the rest of Czechoslovakia and even Neville Chamberlain realized by then that war could no longer be avoided. In this context, the foremost concern of the British government was to win Arab good will or at least to check the spread of pro-Axis sympathies in order to secure Arabian oil and protect the Middle East link of its imperial communications. Consequently, when the conference, as had been expected, got nowhere, the British government issued a unilateral statement of policy—*the* White Paper henceforward—which proposed to give up the Mandate in favor of an independent, predominantly Arab Palestine that would be established in ten years if a constitution protecting Jewish rights could be secured. In the interim period, Jewish immigration was to be fixed at a maximum of 75,000 in the entire first five-year period, after which it would depend on Arab consent. The Jews would be allowed to acquire land from the Arabs only in a very small portion of the country. In short, the Jewish National Home was to be frozen at the level it had attained by then, and Palestine was to remain predominantly Arab.

Throughout the years of the Mandate, the majority in the Zionist movement, under the moderate leadership of Chaim Weizmann, had perforce reconciled itself to the successive British restrictions of its aims as long as the residual policy still allowed the growth of the National Home at a reasonable rate. The general feeling was that the political future of Palestine would ultimately be determined more by the established realities of relative strength and number than by any legal or political formula. The promulgation of the White Paper policy, by foreclosing further growth of the Jewish proportional strength, disrupted this approach and threw the whole movement into agitation. Dissident rightist groups resorted to systematic terror against the British as soon as the Nazi threat to the area receded. The majority of the movement formally adopted a program which, for the first time since the Balfour Declaration, spoke no longer of a Jewish National Home but redefined its aim as the establishment of a Jewish state. A substantial minority on the left opposed the new program as impractical or premature and urged the establishment of a bi-national Jewish-Arab state with freedom of immigration. With all the ringing proclamations and programs, however, it is almost certain that all sections of opinion would have been content with the abolition of the White Paper and the restoration of the *status quo ante* with large-scale immigration.

For a moment right after the war, the chances of achieving just that seemed propitious. The Yishuv had made an important contribution to the war effort, the world was under the shock of the fantastic extent of the Nazi horrors perpetrated against the Jews, and the Labor Party had come to power in Britain soon after its Conference had adopted far-reaching pro-Zionist resolutions. But it soon became apparent that, under the aegis of Foreign Secretary Ernest Bevin, Britain's Palestine policy was more than ever wedded to the aim of winning Arab support for a new Middle East order based on an Anglo-Arab alliance. Pressure from President Truman on the British government to admit to Palestine immediately 100,-000 survivors of the Nazi extermination camps brought about the appointment of an Anglo-American commission to inquire into the whole much-inquired-into Palestine question. The commission reported favorably on the admission of 100,000 people but also made some political recommendations which included the need to dismantle and disarm all illegal forces. President Truman and the Zionists hailed the conclusion concerning immigration and pressed for immediate application, while the British government made it contingent upon the disarming of illegal armies and upon American financial and military support in the enforcement of the entire scheme. There was another committee, another plan, another conference, and a long series of embittered exchanges between British, Jews, Arabs, and Americans, but it was obvious that the whole issue was getting nowhere. In the meantime, tension in Palestine built up rapidly to a climax. The dissident groups extended their acts of terror. The Haganah—the underground army under the authority of the Yishuv leadership—engaged in sabotage and brought in numerous unauthorized immigrant ships; and the British responded with hangings, martial law, curfew, arrest of Yishuv leaders, and deportation of illegal immigrants to camps in Cyprus and even back to Germany. When the last device—an Arab-Jewish-British conference—collapsed, the harassed British government finally decided on April 2, 1947, to place the whole Palestine issue squarely in the hands of a special Assembly of the United Nations.

IV

The United States and the Birth of Israel

The Palestine problem was brought before a special session of the General Assembly of the United Nations on April 28, 1947, and seven months later the regular session of the world body adopted the well-known resolution to partition Palestine into an Arab and a Jewish state. Although all the practical arrangements made by the United Nations for the application of its resolution were nullified by British obstruction and Arab resistance, and although the Jews of Palestine had to fight a costly war for their state, the resolution was nevertheless crucial for the emergence of Israel. It was crucial because it liquidated the Mandate and defined the legal framework within which the Yishuv could conduct its struggle and establish its state while placing its enemies in the position of aggressors. It was crucial because it made it possible for the Yishuv to obtain material help from abroad and diplomatic support from the United States and the United Nations at critical moments in the war. It was crucial, above all, because it provided the Yishuv with a definite goal and a program around which it could rally all its forces. Only five years before the United Nations' resolution, the adoption by the Zionist movement of a program redefining its immediate aim as the setting up of a Jewish state instead of simply assuring the further development of the National Home had encountered great difficulties and in the end left a substantial minority in opposition. Only the year before the U.N. resolution, the energies of the movement had been concentrated on getting accepted the recommendations of the Anglo-American Commission which explicitly ruled out a Jewish state. It was only after the majority of the United Nations' own inquiry commission (UNSCOP) recommended partition and a Jewish and an Arab state that the stragglers, not to be less "Zionist" than the commission, and the extremists, not to miss the opportunity of getting what could be obtained, rallied to the center, and that the entire Yishuv, from Communists to Irgunists, could fight for a common program.

The United States was intimately involved in the adoption of the partition resolution as well as in the chain of events that had brought the Palestine question before the United Nations. In the very intense struggle that developed between supporters and opponents of partition, the United States not only stood on the side of partition, but in the crucial moments before the decision threw her full weight into the effort to mobilize the votes that were still needed. Without this effort, it is very doubtful whether the partition resolution would have obtained the statutory two-thirds majority of the General Assembly.

In many quarters in the United States, including some departments of the government, the role played by America in the Palestine controversy under the aegis of President Truman has been severely criticized as unwise and unfair in terms of the Palestine issue itself and as practically damaging to the interests of the United States. Actually, as we shall see, the United States stand in favor of partition can be justified on any and all of these grounds at least as adequately as the implied alternatives of its critics. The real trouble was that that stand as well as all the positions advocated or adopted in connection with the Palestine question, had not been carefully thought through by anybody in any terms. Various groups exerted pressure on the President to favor or oppose specific measures, but nobody presented him with any suggestion for a comprehensive, consistent policy on Palestine. The result was vacillation and inconsistencies which did more harm to the issue and more damage to American prestige and interest than the substance of the final position taken.

1. AMERICA'S PALESTINE RELATIONS PRIOR TO THE UNITED NATIONS RESOLUTION

The absence of a definite, comprehensive American policy on Palestine when its fate was being decided stemmed partly from the fact that though the United States had had connections with Palestine and the Middle East going back at least one century, she had few interests there until just a few years before the problem came up in the United Nations. Until Wilson's brief sally into world politics during the first World War and after it, United States concern with the area had been almost purely a function of the academic, missionary, and philanthropic interests of some of her citizens in that part of the world. The activities of the American government in connection with these interests were uncontroversial and worked directly or indirectly for the benefit of Arabs and Jews equally. On the Arab side, the government afforded indispensable protection to the educational work of American missionaries which helped spark a cultural revival that marked the birth of Arab nationalism. On the Jewish side, American consuls provided protection to large numbers of Jerusalem Jews under the capitulations system, and American representatives in Constantinople wrestled with discriminatory laws against Jews because they affected the few hundred American Jews then residing in Palestine. In the course of the war, American naval vessels helped evacuate Palestinian Jews expelled by the Turks from Jaffa to Alexandria, and were commissioned to transport food, petrol, medicines, money, and other relief to the Jews of the Holy Land, cut off from their sources of aid in the rest of the world by the British blockade and abandoned to their fate by the Turks. These activities derived from the concern of the American government that American citizens should not be discriminated against or placed under unjust laws, or they were undertaken out of humanitarian considerations in response to appeals of American Jews on behalf of their distressed brethren.

For a brief period after the end of World War I, the nature of America's involvement in Palestine and the Middle East changed abruptly. Although she had not declared war against Turkey, the United States became concerned with the political future of the area as part of the general peace settlement. The United States government still had no special interest of its own to advance; but its influence was vigorously contested by opposing forces which then began to crystallize and were destined henceforth to become a permanent factor in the Palestine question in its American context. As early as October 1917, President Wilson, under the influence of his Zionist friend and adviser Louis D. Brandeis, had conveyed to the British government his support for one of the last drafts of the Balfour Declaration, unknowingly helping its advocates in Britain to overcome the last obstacles on their way. But the President had given that support in an offhand way and did not act in the Peace Conference as though he had already committed himself on the Palestine question. To the dismay of Brandeis and his associates, the President and some of his aides from the State Department entertained suggestions about the future of Palestine and Syria which took no account whatever of the Balfour Declaration or were opposed to it. Such suggestions had been made among others by groups of missionaries who feared that their work would be undone by the Jews and unfolded instead the vision of a united Arab world under American tutelage. They were reinforced by the opposition of anti-Zionist Jews to the Declaration out of fear of the charge of dual allegiance, and by the opposition of some American business interests—notably Standard Oil—which had acquired concessions from the Turks in the Negev and feared the Zionists. In the end, President Wilson reaffirmed his support of the Balfour Declaration in strong and unequivocal terms; but his initial casual involvement, his subjection to opposing pressures, his vacillation and final commitment, were a remarkable preview of what was to happen on a grand scale with President Truman thirty years later.

With the failure of Wilson's internationalism and the return to isolationism, the United States government lost any interest it may have had in the political fate of the Middle East and Palestine, and its concern with the area reverted once more to being subsidiary to the private interests of American citizens there. By then, however, these interests were no longer confined to the sphere of religion, humanitarianism, and philanthropy but had come to include economic and political interests of increasing importance.

As early as 1920 American oil concerns had appealed to their government to secure for them equal opportunity in the Middle Eastern countries under the control of the French and the British. The American government responded to this appeal and obtained for a group of American companies a 23.75 per cent share in the Iraq Petroleum Company. Thereafter, the United States government strove to obtain from the powers controlling the Middle

Eastern countries commitments to an open-door policy that would not discriminate against private American business. In this connection, the United States concluded the Anglo-American Treaty of 1924 which regulated relations between the two countries in connection with the Palestine Mandate and secured the protection of business and missionary interests of Americans in Palestine. Incidentally, the preamble to this treaty included a reference to the Balfour Declaration, inserted at the insistence of the British negotiators, which was to be interpreted later by various parties as giving the United States the right to have a say in any changes in the Mandate.

As for the political interest of American citizens in the Middle East, this had already manifested itself in the pressure on President Wilson by American Zionists, headed by men like Brandeis, Frankfurter (later Justices of the Supreme Court), Judge Mack, and Stephen Wise, to support the Balfour Declaration and the granting of the Palestine Mandate to Britain. Having attained its object, the political activity of the American Zionists subsided for most of the inter-war period. But in the 1930's, as persecution of Jews in Hitler's Reich mounted and as the British put increasing restrictions on Jewish immigration to Palestine, the American Zionists bestirred themselves once more in an effort to induce their government to press the British to alter their policy. At that particular juncture, the Zionists did not obtain much satisfaction from the President or the State Department; but Congress was another matter. The legislature of the United States, partly because it was not directly responsible for America's foreign policy and could therefore afford to look at the matter in abstract humanitarian terms, and partly because its members were more sensitive to the electoral implications of their position, had by then an already established tradition of sympathy with Zionist aspirations and wishes. In 1922, for example, Congress had adopted a joint resolution in support of the Balfour Declaration; and the sponsor of the resolution in the Senate was none other than Senator Henry Cabot Lodge, the spearhead of American isolationism in the post-war years. Now, in 1939, a majority of the House Foreign Affairs Committee and twenty-eight senators publicly protested against the restriction of immigration to Palestine at that critical moment for the Jews. They called the defense of Jewish interests in Palestine "a moral obligation of the

United States" and declared that the White Paper was a violation of the Anglo-American Treaty of 1924.

During the second World War the private interests of American citizens in the Middle East became much more intense and, in addition, the American government itself developed new interests of its own in the area. In 1933, American companies had obtained from the ruler of Saudi Arabia extensive oil concessions which reached the stage of large-scale production by 1940. Toward the end of the war, the excessive drain on America's own oil reserves caused the government itself to show interest in the Middle East Oil. In 1944, for instance, Secretary of the Interior Ickes sought to give the government a stake in Arabian oil by suggesting to the companies concerned that it should finance the building of a pipeline from the Arabian oil fields to the Mediterranean. The oil companies balked at the proposal, but official concern with insuring the flow of oil from the Middle East continued in government quarters, especially after the oil companies themselves undertook to build the pipeline and to expand their operations at a cost of hundreds of millions of dollars.

The outbreak of war and the initial disasters which were inflicted upon the Allies made it difficult for the Zionists to draw much attention to the problem of Palestine and the Jews. But as the tide of the war began to turn and victory loomed upon the horizon, and as news of the Nazi projects for exterminating the Jews reached the United States, the American Zionists, supported by the entire Jewish population and by large sections of the non-Jewish public, exerted a persistent and desperate pressure on the government to persuade the British to open the gates of Palestine and to commit themselves to the support of a Jewish commonwealth. Congress responded with a series of resolutions and declarations in the period 1943–1945 in favor of unrestricted immigration and a Jewish state in Palestine. President Roosevelt gave a number of clear pledges during the election campaign of 1944 to help bring about the realization of a Jewish commonwealth in Palestine which he counterbalanced with ambiguous pledges to King Ibn Saud that he would take no action which might prove hostile to the Arab people without full consultation with both Arabs and Jews. The War Department expressed concern lest the declarations made by Congress and the President should endanger the war effort of the Allies, while the State Department held to the line that Palestine was Britain's responsibility, except insofar as the American government was interested in the general problem of the tragedy of European Jewry and was eager to help. This last qualification was quite important; it was to prove the opening wedge of the American government's involvement in the Palestine question right after the war, which began with President Truman's appeal to Prime Minister Attlee to admit 100,000 survivors of the Nazi camps to Palestine.

While the private interests of its citizens were drawing it into greater involvement in Middle Eastern matters, the American government itself was acquiring its own interest in the area. During the war, the United States became directly interested in the Middle East as a theater of operations, as a strategic base, and as a supply route to Russia. At the end of the war, it looked for a time as though the United States might pull out of the whole area and leave it under the responsibility of Britain. But the civil war in Greece and Soviet pressure on Turkey and Iran compelled the American government to become more and more engaged, first politically and on the side of Britain, and then both politically and militarily as the chief actor. The turning point came in the spring of 1947 when, after Britain notified the United States of her intention to divest herself of responsibility for Greece and Turkey, the United States proclaimed what came to be known as the Truman Doctrine. The Doctrine committed the United States specifically to guarantee the security of Greece, Turkey, and Iran and declared the intention of the American government to contain Communist aggression everywhere. Thus, both by implication and as the hinterland of the American defense perimeter established along the three above-mentioned countries, the Middle East now came directly into the orbit of American global strategy.

2. THE UNITED STATES AND THE EMERGENCE OF ISRAEL

When the Palestine question came up for decision before the United Nations in the fall of 1947, the implications of the various involvements of the United States in the Middle East had not yet been fully worked out. There was a general sense that it was important to have the good will of the governments of the Arab land mass right behind the American defense perimeter. There was a belief that an effort should be made to insure the undisturbed development and flow of Arabian oil. And there was a generally accepted notion that something ought to be done to relieve the survivors of the Nazi slaughter and thus assuage the agitation of Palestine's Jews, alleviate the pressure of their American brethren, and meet a demand endorsed by public opinion generally. But all these considerations had not been assessed together in the context of the realities and possibilities of the Palestine situation in an effort to formulate an appropriate policy. What happened, instead, was that different individuals and sections in the government and among the public seized upon one aspect or another of the question in disregard of other facts and endeavored to press it upon President Truman while impeaching the arguments and even the motives of others. The President was left to steer his own course by hunch or impulse amidst conflicting views and opposing pressures; and his instinct guided him now one way, now another.

In the fall of 1947, the President decided, apparently without much difficulty, to support partition, against the judgment of people in the State Department. He, like everyone else, had been impressed by the fact that a majority of a United Nations commission, composed of representatives of countries with no direct interest in Palestine which had just investigated the problem had recommended this solution. (These countries were Australia, Canada, Czechoslovakia, Guatemala, India, Iran, the Netherlands, Peru, Sweden, Uruguay, Yugoslavia.) The solution also seemed to accord well with the humanitarian impulse which had induced him in the course of the two previous years to press for the admission to Palestine of a large number of survivors of Nazi concentration camps. Moreover, the proposed partition plan had been accepted with barely hidden enthusiasm by the Jewish masses of America whose votes seemed particularly important in that election year when Truman was the underdog in the contest against Governor Dewey of New York.

But the partition plan did not work out according to the schedule prepared for it by the United Nations. The British refused to collaborate with the world organization in easing the transition to the new order and even seemed to be doing their best to make it difficult. At the same time, the Arabs of Palestine rose up in arms in December 1947 with the encouragement and support of the neighboring Arab states, and the country was plunged into a vicious civil war in which the Jews seemed to be getting the worst of it. The United Nations considered organizing an international constabulary to enforce partition, but a force of the size thought to be needed was impossible to raise without Russian participation, to which the United States was opposed. The President was under mounting pressure to send American troops to do the job, but he was disinclined to commit the country further and, moreover, his military advisers informed him that the United States did not have the necessary forces available in any case. In these circumstances, the President accepted the advice of the State Department and authorized the American representative in the United Nations to declare the partition plan impracticable and to submit instead a proposal for a United Nations Trusteeship over Palestine.

This reversal of policy brought frantic protests and appeals from American Zionists and Jews, congressmen and other politicians, and prominent and plain American citizens. It also encouraged the Arabs to believe that whatever the political decisions were, it was the military facts that counted. But while the United Nations became entangled in fruitless discussions about Trusteeship and how *it* could be enforced, the Jews of Palestine, having received a shipment of Russian arms and enjoying greater freedom of action as the British forces kept withdrawing from the country, launched an offensive which reversed the course of the civil war and brought most of the territory allocated to them by the partition plan under their effective control. On May 14, 1948, notwithstanding State Department advice to the contrary, they proclaimed their state, calling it Israel. A few hours later, as army columns from the neighboring Arab states poured into Palestine in an attempt to establish a new set of military facts, the American chief delegate to the United Nations had to interrupt a speech in favor of Trusteeship to announce that the American government, that is, the President, had just awarded *de facto* recognition to the new state of Israel. The Trusteeship proposal was, of course, buried.

President Truman's recognition of Israel, undertaken without even notifying the men who were in charge of executing America's foreign policy, was not the last act in the undignified spectacle of United States inconsistency. Once again, the Secretary of State himself was to support a modification of the partition resolution, known as the Bernadotte plan, in the forum of the United Nations only to see the President repudiate it publicly at home; and more than once the President was to go over the heads of his State Department, as he did in choosing and instructing the first ambassador to Israel. All this seesawing and confusion, besides causing great damage to the prestige of the United States and encouraging the belligerents to believe and act as though military facts were the only important considerations, has left as residue the notion that the United States' support of Israel and the partition plan had been forced upon a well-meaning but weak President by sinister pressure groups regardless of the damaging effect on America's interest. To what extent is such a notion justified?

3. APPRAISAL OF AMERICA'S POSITION IN 1947–1948

That the President of the United States was submitted to unusually strong and sharp pressures in connection with the Palestine problem which helped to confuse his judgment is beyond doubt. As the published records of the period indicate, however, these pressures came from the opponents as well as from the supporters of partition. As to the question whether or not America's support of the partition plan was unwise, unjust, and contrary to the national interest, an appraisal of the situation in 1947, taking into account the background of the Palestine problem and the three basic aims of the United States at that time—to maintain peace and gain Arab good will, to protect the oil interests, and to help the escapees of Hitler's massacres—would seem to indicate that partition was, if not the best, at least the only available solution worthy of support.

It should be recalled that by the fall of 1947, two basic facts in regard to the Palestine problem were clear to all. One was that the Mandate could not go on and had to be terminated. This was a conclusion which had been reached by the British, the Arabs, and the Jews and was included among the unanimous recommendations of the United Nations' inquiry committee. The second fact was that Arabs and Jews were determined to fight: the former to prevent large-scale Jewish immigration, the latter to achieve just that. These two facts must be taken as premises in any attempt to assess the most desirable and practical policy for the United States at the time.

Before the United Nations and the world, three competing solutions to the Palestine problem were presented. Two of these were suggested by the United Nations inquiry committee which, given its composition, could not be said to have had any interest in the question other than providing a fair and viable solution under the circumstances. The majority of the committee recommended partition into two sovereign, independent Arab and Jewish states and an international zone linked by an economic union, and allotted to the proposed Jewish state nearly 55 per cent of the territory of Palestine in order to give it some living space for future immigration. The minority recommended a single federal government for all of Palestine with two constituent states, Arab and Jewish, endowed with a considerable degree of autonomy. Immigration, together with defense and foreign affairs, was to be entrusted to the federal government whose legislature was to be bicameral, with equal Arab and Jewish representation in one house and proportional representation in the other. All legislation was to require a majority of both houses. Deadlocks were to be resolved by an arbitral committee in which the decisive voice would belong to an outsider. The third solution was suggested by the Arabs themselves. It called for an independent, unitary, sovereign state in Palestine in which the Jews would enjoy guarantees of their status as a minority and would be awarded a large measure of municipal and cultural autonomy. Immigration, as all other matters, would depend on the decision of the legislature, which would, of course, be predominantly Arab.

Now, the Arab solution was the one which least endangered the oil interests, and support for it would have gained for the United States the good will of the Arabs at least in the immediate sense. But from the point of view of the United States it had at least three major disadvantages. First, it precluded in practice any substantial Jewish immigration for which the United States had been pressing Britain. After all, an important factor in exacerbating the Palestine crisis right after the war had been the plea made by President Truman to the British government to admit a large number of survivors of the Nazi massacres into that country in the belief that such tragic necessity could hardly be resisted. Even the Morrison-Grady plan of 1946, agreed upon by the State Department and the British but rejected by the President, had envisaged an immigration of 100,000 immediately and held out the promise of more thereafter. It is true that the embarrassment of appearing inconsistent did not prevent the United States government from changing its mind several times later on; but at least in these cases it could plead *force majeure* whereas, in this instance, supporting the Arab plan would have required it to accept and even urge something much less than what it had previously rejected as inadequate at a time when the United Nations commission was recommending more. Secondly, it was extremely doubtful that the Arab solution, even with American support, would have gained the required two-thirds majority vote of the General Assembly considering its extreme remoteness even from the minority report of the United Nations commission. Thirdly, the application of such a solution would have required measures to suppress the Jews of Palestine even more drastic than those which had been adopted by the British to no avail in the previous two years. It would have needed something like an international force or a great power sealing the country while the armed forces of the Arab states crushed the Jewish settlers. And this right after the Nazi massacre of Europe's Jews.

We have deliberately dwelt at some length on the Arab solution because it was the only one which seemed to offer the prospect of satisfying the "real," tangible, and immediate interests of the United States, and it is therefore important to stress how infeasible it was. The other two proposals, that of the majority and that of the minority of the United Nations commission, were labeled "absurd" by the Arabs and were vehemently rejected. Consequently, United States support for either seemed to entail a risk of alienating the needed Arab good will and endangering the oil interests. It is of course true that in the perspective of later events it became clear that the Arabs would have preferred the minority plan; but in this same perspective the Arabs have expressed their acceptance of partition too. As things stood in 1947, support for the minority plan would have entailed almost the same risks for United States interests without satisfying the Jewish aspirations and having the Jewish support which the majority plan enjoyed. Furthermore, supposing the minority plan were capable of mustering, with United States' active support, the needed vote—which is not at all certain —its realization and viability depended so much on continual Arab-Jewish cooperation that once the two partners of the envisaged state opposed it they in fact doomed it. The realization of the plan in the face of such opposition would have required the indefinite presence of a third power which almost surely was not to be found and which in any case would gain the hostility of both sides very quickly. The problem of Palestine would have remained to plague the United Nations and, in all likelihood, one of the federated states would have seceded sooner or later and reopened the entire issue.

In the light of the circumstances of 1947, there seems to be no doubt that the partition plan offered the best hope for a solution of the Palestine problem. It had the support of the Jews, which greatly simplified the problem of application. Violence and difficulties might have been expected from the Arab side, but if handled wisely and with determination, the extent of the violence might have been limited and, after a transition period, there would have been two independent states capable of taking care of themselves. From the point of view of the United States, there were undoubtedly some risks of losing her standing among the Arabs and endangering the oil interests of her citizens in which she too was interested; but these were in less danger from the quick surgical operation of partition than from the festering open wound of a federal state or some similar scheme. Finally, the partition plan did offer some prospect of closing the painful episode of Jewish martyrdom which weighed heavily on the conscience of the Western world. If subsequent circumstances disproved the calculations that might have been made in 1947, it was in great degree because the calculations were *not* made and therefore the support given to partition was uncertain, hesitant, and incomplete. Who knows whether the Arab armies would have intervened had the United States as well as the Soviet Union provided arms to the Jewish militia in March and April of 1948 instead of knuckling under to Arab violence and repudiating the partition plan? The Jewish state might have been erected then within the boundaries provided for it by the United Nations, and a Palestinian Arab state might have emerged at its side. Further, the bulk of the refugee problem would not have existed, much bloodshed and misery would have been spared, the entire heritage of the tragedy of Palestine might have been less bitter, and a salutary precedent might have been set for Arabs and Jews, as well as for other nations, in those crucial formative years of the international body, that the United Nations' will cannot be flouted with impunity.

PART TWO: THE PHYSICAL, HUMAN,
AND CONSTITUTIONAL ENVIRONMENT

V

The Country

1. POLITICAL GEOGRAPHY

The State of Israel was carved out of former Palestine in the War of 1948 and includes almost four fifths of its territory; the rest was annexed by Transjordan (which thus became the Hashemite Kingdom of Jordan) except for 135 square miles of territory known as the Gaza Strip which fell to Egypt. Although the name of Palestine goes back to Roman times, it did not designate a distinct political entity until recent times when Palestine was formed out of the dismembered Ottoman Empire in the wake of the first World War. It consisted then of the southern halves of the Ottoman provinces of Beirut and Syria and the entire district of Jerusalem. No sooner was that entity established than it underwent its first division. In 1920, Britain, then in the process of acquiring a Mandate from the League of Nations over that territory, divided it into two administrative segments separated by the river Jordan. The eastern segment was ruled by an Arab prince advised by British officers, while the western portion was directly administered by the British. Though both segments formally constituted the Mandate of Palestine, the eastern territory grew into the independent Kingdom of Transjordan (later Jordan) and only the western part retained the name of Palestine. The fact that Palestine had been for many centuries almost indistinguishable from the Syrian provinces was a factor in the involvement of Arabs outside Palestine in the country's destiny; while the fact that the original Mandate of Palestine included the territory that became Jordan is a factor underlying irredentist claims among some Israelis.

Israel is situated on the eastern shore of the Mediterranean at a meeting point of three continents. The successive invasion of that part of the world by Assyrians, Babylonians, Persians, Greeks, Egyptians, Syrians, Romans, Arabs, Mongols, Turks, and British testify to its importance as a bridge or a buffer between the Nile and the Euphrates, between Africa and Eurasia. That area also connects the Mediterranean and the Atlantic to the West with the Red Sea at the Gulf of Aqaba and the Indian Ocean to the East. Present-day Israel, occupying the only land route between Egypt and the countries of the Fertile Crescent, serves as a buffer rather than as a bridge between the Arab countries to her south and southwest, and those to her north, east, and northeast. Though this fact is outwardly lamented by all the Arab states and has been a crucial factor in their unrelenting hostility to Israel, it has actually been of benefit to several Arab regimes by standing as an obstacle to Cairo's drive for hegemony over the Arab nations. Israel's position linking the Mediterranean and the Red Sea is only beginning to be exploited for oil passage and transit trade and may become a factor of vital national and international importance in the future.

Israel's shape is awkward and vulnerable. On the map it looks like an irregular triangle standing on its apex, connected by a long, narrow, and very irregular rectangle to a small, very irregular square. The clumsy frontiers, the result of the freezing of the battle lines of the War of 1948, look as though they had been drawn to achieve the maximum length and unmanageability. Thus for a territory of 8000 square miles, Israel has 600 miles of land frontier in addition to 150 miles of sea front. At the tip of the triangle, the country is only 8 miles wide; at the triangle's base, where it achieves the maximum width, it spreads only 69 miles from border to border; through the long rectangle, the width varies between 9.5 miles to 16 miles; and in the north, the square is never wider than 41 miles. A traveler is thus never far from the frontiers, wherever he goes; and in a place like Jerusalem he meets them while walking down the street since the city itself is divided between Israel and Jordan. The oddity of the boundaries, and the fact that they connect Israel with four Arab countries—Lebanon, Syria, Jordan, Egypt—has had much to do with the frequent border inci-

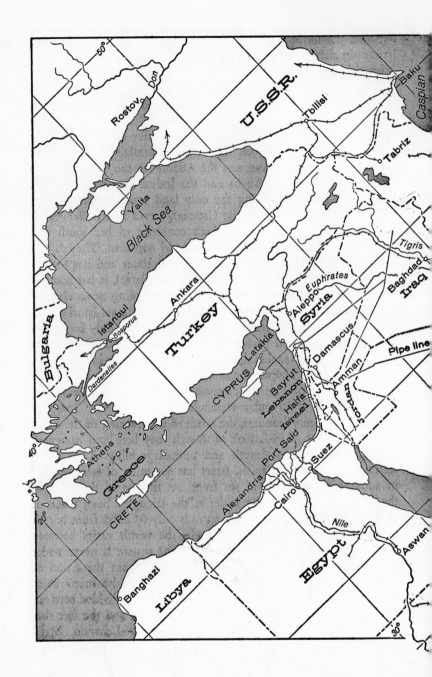

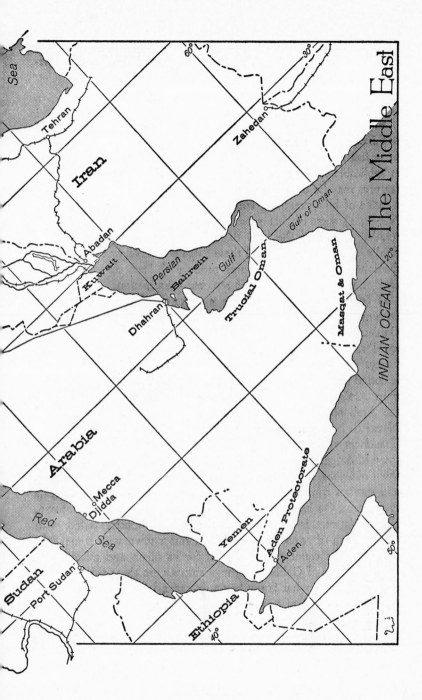

dents that have characterized Israel's history and with the obsessive preoccupation of Israel's leaders with the problem of national security.

2. PHYSICAL AND ECONOMIC GEOGRAPHY

Although Israel is only the size of Massachusetts, she encompasses within her borders a great deal of geographical variety, including some features to which the superlative, in world-geographical terms, is applicable. Taking Palestine as a whole, four basic geographical features may be discerned: 1) at the center of the country there is a range of hills stretching from Lebanon down to the heart of the Negev; 2) west of that range there is a coastal plain of varying width; 3) east of the hills there is the Jordan depression; and, finally, 4) to the south of all these there is the Negev desert. Modifications in these basic features produce at least six geographical regions which are worth brief separate examination.

1) In the extreme north, the mountains of Lebanon continue without a break though at lower altitudes to form the hills of Galilee, whose highest peak is just under 4000 feet. Abundant seasonal rainfall has eroded the hillsides and formed small fertile valleys which may be farmed without irrigation. The countryside is dotted with a considerable number of Jewish settlements but with more Arab villages and townlets, this being the area where most of the Arab population of Israel is concentrated. Here the town of Nazareth is located and many other places mentioned in the New Testament as associated with the life of Jesus; and here too is the town of Safed, the old seat of Jewish mystics. Today Nazareth is a town of 25,000, mostly Arabs, engaged in commerce, light industry, and services connected with the numerous religious establishments in the area. On hills overlooking Nazareth, a new all-Jewish town, Kiryat Natseret, is being built on the basis of industry. Safed, with a population of 10,000, is essentially a resort town with some light industry. The country is renowned for its olives and tobacco.

2) The hills of Galilee fall away abruptly on three sides. On the east they end at what is the beginning of a long, narrow rift with a maximum width of 14 miles in which the river Jordan flows. The Jordan rises partly inside Israel, partly just inside the frontiers of Syria and Lebanon, thus constituting a source of contention between the three countries. Moreover, after flowing for 60 miles in

Israel, it continues for another 97 miles in Jordanian territory, adding another interested party, before ending in the Dead Sea. A few miles from its source, the river used to flow into Lake Huleh, a shallow, marshy expanse of water that was a breeding ground for malaria. This has now been drained by Israel and converted into 10,000 acres of extremely fertile land. Further down its course, the Jordan flows into Lake Tiberias—the Biblical Sea of Galilee—which covers an area of 122 square miles, all included in Israel, and constitutes the most important water reservoir of the country. Up to a point south of Lake Tiberias, the Jordan rift is blessed with conditions which favor a very rich and variegated agriculture, including rice, cotton, groundnuts, corn, and tropical fruits in the area around Lake Tiberias which is more than 600 feet below sea level. From there on, the river flows in Jordanian territory through barren country very little of which is cultivable until it reaches the Dead Sea. This is a salt-water lake 40 miles long and 10 miles wide which is under Israeli sovereignty at its southwestern corner. The shore of the Dead Sea lies 1300 feet below sea level and is the lowest spot on earth. Its waters are fabulously rich in salts and minerals which are exploited on a large scale by Israel.

3) To the west, the hills of Galilee fall away to a coastal plain which stretches from a point south of the Lebanese border all the way down to the Gaza strip. From its starting-point to Haifa, the plain assumes the shape of a crescent curving around the Acre-Haifa bay with the mountain reaching down to the sea at the crescent's tips. Not far from the Lebanese border is the town of Nahariya with 20,000 inhabitants, having grown twelvefold since the establishment of Israel. Further south is the ancient town of Acre, the Hellenistic Ptolemais of St. Paul, the principal harbor and stronghold of the Crusaders, today a mixed Arab-Jewish town of 25,000 people. Still further south is the city of Haifa, climbing on the slopes of Mount Carmel, including a modern harbor which constitutes Israel's main gate to the world. At the end of the Mandate, Haifa had a population of 120,000, two thirds of whom were Jews and the rest Arabs. During the fighting that preceded the War of 1948, the Arab population fled and has since been replaced by twice as many Jews, bringing the total population to about 160,000. The area from Nahariya to Haifa is a major industrial center going back to Mandate days. Clustered together are found-

ries, flour mills, spinning mills, shipyards, power stations, big oil refineries, cement works, railway repair shops, automotive plants, and an entire steel complex recently finished, the "steel town." At the northern outskirts of Haifa runs the small perennial river of Kishon, once marshy but now cleared and its mouth enlarged to take in large ships.

Going south from Haifa, the coastal strip opens into the fertile plain of Sharon which broadens into a wide but increasingly sandy expanse some twenty miles south of Tel Aviv until it eventually becomes loose sand dunes and merges into the Sinai Desert. The coastal plain is the heart of Israel. It is the center of Israel's citriculture which provides the country with its most important export. It is the site of most of the country's industry. There two thirds of Israel's population are concentrated and most of her cities and towns. About halfway between Haifa and the Gaza Strip border rises the city of Tel Aviv, the economic center of Israel and her largest urban concentration. Started in 1909 as a garden suburb of neighboring Arab Jaffa, Tel Aviv has since grown into a city of more than 400,000 which has swallowed its mother town. Together with the townships of Bat Yam, Holon, Ramat Gan, Petach Tikva, and Herzliya, which merge with it physically, the Tel Aviv area forms an urban conglomeration of nearly three quarters of a million, all but a few thousand of them Jews, the Arabs having fled or been expelled during the fighting that preceded the establishment of Israel. A twelve-mile-long perennial river, the Yarkon, cuts across "greater Tel Aviv"; half of this stream's waters are carried away by pipeline to the south for some seventy miles. Midway between Tel Aviv and the Gaza Strip lies Ashdod Yam, the ancient Philistine city of Ashdod, where an economically and strategically vital second deep-water harbor is now under construction. To the east of it is the Lachish region, one of Israel's show pieces of land reclamation and planned settlement.

4) To the south, the hills of Galilee look down upon Emek Yizreel—the Vale of Esdraelon—or, as the Israelis call it, *The* Emek. This is a valley descending southeastward from the Mediterranean to reach the Jordan Valley. At its western end by the Haifa-Acre bay, the vale is 15 to 20 miles wide, but it narrows inland to only a mile or two before opening up once again where it joins the Jordan valley. For millennia the Emek has been a corridor of major

importance linking the Mediterranean coast and Egypt with the interior of Southwest Asia and has served as a passageway for ethnic, cultural, and military invasions. In the centuries prior to World War I, this lowland of very fertile soil, adequate rainfall, and abundant water springs had become converted by a chain reaction of nomad raids, desertion of the settled population, and neglect into a largely uncultivated malarial area. In the 1920's, the Jews bought up most of the valley, drained the swamps by relatively primitive methods which cost the lives and health of many, and transformed it in the course of time into a vast granary and garden. Looking down from one of the many hills around the Emek with its dozens of neat settlements tucked in the midst of woods, the geometric designs of its meticulously cultivated multicolored fields and its resplendent fish ponds, one beholds the spirit of the Jewish endeavor in Palestine at its inspiring best.

5) South of the Emek, the central chain resumes its course in the form of an upland plateau 3000 feet in height extending for nearly one hundred miles to a point south of Hebron, where the hills come down to meet the Negev. In the north, where there is adequate rainfall, the plateau has been eroded into valleys some of which are fertile. This region, the site of the ancient country of Samaria, centers around the two towns of Jenin and Nablus. Further south, rainfall is reduced, streams are less frequent, and the hills are more bare. This is the land of ancient Judea, with Jerusalem, Bethlehem, and Hebron its principal towns. The entire central plateau had been almost exclusively Arab during the years of British rule, Arab resistance having successfully prevented large-scale Jewish settlement. Consequently, in the War of 1948, this entire country fell to the Transjordanian army without much struggle, and only a small strip became part of the state of Israel. This is a corridor running east and west, fifteen miles long and ten to fifteen miles wide, which pierces the plateau through the Judean hills to connect the coastal plain with Jerusalem. The western entry of the corridor is through the Shefelah, a lowland of fertile soil and moist climate containing the towns of Ramleh, the center of Arab administration after the Islamic conquest, and Lydda, or Lod, the home of ancient rabbinical schools and of Saint George. Both towns were exclusively Arab during the Mandate and are at present exclusively Jewish, their population having been displaced during

the war. Adjoining the town of Lod is Israel's chief international airport bearing the town's name. Jerusalem itself is perched on the heights of the Mount of Olives, Zion, and Moriah. The city and its surroundings are replete with holy places and historical sites of great meaning for Jews, Christians, and Moslems. The absurd legacy of the War of 1948 has left the city divided into two rigidly isolated parts. The old walled city together with the northeastern suburbs is in the Arab state of Jordan. The new city, with a population of 165,000, is the capital of Israel. Like Washington, D. C., Jerusalem is of little economic importance and is primarily the center of government. In addition, the capital of Israel is the seat of many of the country's most important cultural and religious institutions. It houses the headquarters of the Chief Rabbinate and contains scores of religious schools of varying size and caliber; it is the site of the Hebrew University, the National Museum, the International Center for the Study of Man, now under construction, and the renowned Hadassah Medical Center.

6) At the southern end of the central plateau lies the Negev. This is an area comprising more than half the territory of Israel which is shaped and acts like a wedge driven into the surrounding Arab expanses. Geographically, it is divided in two by a vertical range of hills which is a continuation of the central plateau, and horizontally it is crossed by an imaginary line running somewhat south of Beersheba which delineates the progress of the Israeli settlement frontier. The northern part of the Negev was populous until late Byzantine times; but in the centuries that followed it turned into a desert after the nomads had driven off the cultivators. Since the establishment of Israel, water has been brought to the area from the Yarkon and from springs and wells in the coastal plain, and this together with science, hard work, and a lot of money, has managed to bring the countryside to life once again. The center and symbol of this area is Beersheba, a sleepy market townlet of 2000 people in 1948, now grown into a bustling, booming town of 45,000 well endowed with industry, hospitals, an Institute for the Study of the Wilderness, and all the urban amenities. The southern part of the Negev is mostly an extension of the Sinai Desert, though here too irrigation schemes for the potentially productive areas are being developed and a few urban centers are rising based on mining and industry. One of the latter is Dimona, a lively and fast-growing

town 20 miles southeast of Beersheba which serves as residence for the workers and employees of the multimillion dollar potash and chemical works at Sodom, on the Dead Sea, and also has its own textile industry. A less successful center is Mitzpeh Ramon, halfway between Beersheba and Eilat, planned to be based on the exploitation of nearby stone and ceramic clay quarries. The Timna copper mines, reputedly exploited in the days of Solomon three thousand years ago, are a few miles before Eilat itself, lying at the southernmost tip of the Negev touching the Gulf of Aqaba. The function of this growing town of 7000 as a gate to the East makes it a vital spot in the country. Today Eilat has a small operating harbor which is already the base of a regular freight line to Africa and the Far East and is the starting point of a 16-inch oil pipeline leading to the refineries in Haifa.

The Road and Rail Network

Israel inherited from mandatory days a good network of roads which was then and still constitutes today the most important means for the transportation of passengers and freight. In the fourteen years of its independent existence, the new state expanded that network very considerably to meet the requirements of defense, the immense growth of the population and its very substantial redistribution, the needs of economic development and of bringing new areas into use. In terms of coverage, Israel's road system is better than good today, comprising nearly 2000 miles of metaled road which reaches almost every corner of the land actually inhabited or planned for development in the next few years. In terms of quality, however, it leaves much to be desired, especially in the heavily inhabited coastal plain. In addition to the roads, practically all of the railway system of mandatory days remains in the area belonging to Israel; but that system was not very extensive and its chief importance as an international link in the Paris-Cairo system is nullified by the hostility between Israel and her neighbors. The principal railway line, laid by the British army in 1918, runs from Sinai northward to Haifa and the Lebanese frontier along "the way of the sea." An important extension links this line to Beersheba. Work is now in progress to carry this branch to Dimona, 20 miles south and east, and from there the line might be extended to Eilat. Another line, built by the French in Ottoman days, goes from Jaffa

to Jerusalem through Lod. The tracks of this line constitute the
boundary line between Israel and Jordan at several points in the
Tel Aviv–Jerusalem corridor. Finally, a third line—a branch of the
Hidjaz railway—runs through the Vale of Jezreel to Damascus.
Under Israel, the railway has been relaid in several places and re-
equipped with modern rolling stock and diesel engine to allow
faster traffic. The total length of track currently in operation is
about 400 miles.

Climate

Israel has a typical Mediterranean climate modified considerably
by varying altitude. There is a cycle of hot, dry summers when the
temperature reaches 90 to 100 degrees Fahrenheit, and short, mild,
rainy winters. But while Jerusalem and Judea may have several
inches of snow in winter and Galilee several feet, the lowlands
rarely see any, and Tiberias, by the lake of that name, and the
Negev never do. The valleys, especially the Emek and adjacent
parts of the upper Jordan, which lie below sea level, can become
extremely hot (over 100 degrees) and humid. Rainfall, too, fluctu-
ates a great deal from one part of Israel to another. Galilee receives
an average of 42 inches annually and parts of it even more; Jerusalem gets about 26 inches, the Gaza plain rarely gets more than 10
inches, while Eilat gets less than one.

Natural Resources

Israel is relatively poor in natural resources, but the little there
is has been or is being intensively exploited. Of her known mineral
resources, the most important are potash, bromine, magnesium,
salt, and other minerals which can be drawn from the unlimited
reserves of the Dead Sea. Actual production was about 135,000 tons
of potash and 2000 tons of bromine in the year 1960–1961 and there
are plans under way to treble potash production in the next few
years with the help of a loan received from the International Bank.
Mining of phosphates began at Oron, in the Negev, ten years ago
and important new deposits have been discovered since. Today's
production amounts to close to 300,000 tons of ore annually with
31 per cent content. At Timna, near Eilat, geological surveys have
found proven deposits of 50 million tons of low-grade copper ore

(1.43 per cent content). A mill was completed in 1958 to process these ores and has produced more than 6000 tons of copper in the year 1960–1961. Current plans call for the expansion of the smelting facilities to bring production up to 15,000 tons of purer copper than that actually produced. Oil was discovered in the south in small quantities in 1955 and is being produced now at the rate of 130,000 tons of crude a year, meeting about 8 per cent of the country's oil consumption in 1961. An additional field was struck in 1962 and is being presently assessed. In 1959, 1961, and 1962, gas fields were discovered in the Dead Sea area, two of which have an estimated annual capacity of 20 million cubic feet of gas equivalent to 200,000 tons of crude oil. Other mineral deposits currently exploited on a significant scale include gypsum, ball clay, marble, and glass sand. Israel has no known deposits of iron or coal and has no important source of hydroelectric power. She relies for her energy on electricity generated from steam produced mostly by imported fuel.

Agricultural Land

Land for agriculture is the most important natural resource of Israel, and the use made of it is still the greatest feat of her people despite growing diversification of the economy and industrialization. Men and women of diverse nationalities and backgrounds have disagreed violently about the ultimate rights and wrongs of the Jewish-Arab conflict over Palestine; but there are few who fail to be impressed by the great work of reconstruction and conservation that the Jews have accomplished in the land. For the country which they "invaded" or to which they "returned" had long ago ceased to flow with milk and honey. It was a country whose valleys were largely malarial swamps, whose pastures had been grazed down to the ground and turned into dustbowls, whose hills had been denuded of forests and washed off to bedrocks, whose terraces were mostly in ruin, and whose hundreds of ancient prosperous villages had become mounds of dirt or heaps of weather-beaten stones. To this land the Jews brought organization, skill, capital, science and, above all, infinite devotion—the early settlers had developed literally a cult of the soil, nature, and work. They drained its swamps, checked spreading sand dunes, planted tens of millions of trees, improved seeds and farming methods, and made the land yield a farm produce which supplies nowadays all but the meat and grain needs of the population on a Western European level and leaves large quantities for export.

Potentially usable agricultural land is plentiful in Israel; but water resources are relatively scarce. According to surveys of land-use potential carried out by the Israeli government, it is estimated that of the total area of the state of 20.7 million dunams (a dunam equals approximately a quarter of an acre), more than 4 million dunams are potentially available for dry farming, and more than 5.5 million dunams are potentially available for farming under irrigation. Of the potential dry farming area, nearly 70 per cent is actually cultivated; while of the area available for farming under irrigation only 22 per cent is actually worked. To realize even that degree of irrigated agriculture, Israel has had to use nearly 80 per cent of her total potential usable water supply, thus leaving little room for expansion.

The crucial need to tap new sources of water to allow for future development explains Israel's unflagging determination to carry through her Master Water Plan at all costs and the frequently voiced Arab threats to resist it by force. The purpose of the $200 million plan is to divert a substantial part of surplus water from the Jordan and from other sources in the north to the Negev, to store excess supplies from winter to summer and from periods of heavy rainfall to periods of drought, and to regulate the various regional water-supply systems. Its central feature is a great 108-inch prestressed concrete pipeline to carry Israel's share of surplus Jordan waters from Lake Tiberias for a distance of 90 miles to Plugot in the northern Negev, from where water will be distributed further south. The diversion operation is expected to take place in 1963–1964 though the Master Water Plan is not expected to be completed in its entirety before 1970. The quantity of water to be diverted is in the order of 200 to 350 million cubic meters a year, or nearly 20 per cent of present total resources. When the plan is completed, all the available water resources within Israel will have been brought into use; further expansion of agriculture would depend then on desalinization of brakish water, a field in which Israel is today one of the pioneering countries of the world.

3. LAND TENURE SYSTEM

Israel's mineral resources are the property of the state and the most important known ones are exploited by companies owned wholly or partly by the state. This is fairly common practice in many parts of the world. But what is unusual is that the land itself, especially agricultural land, is overwhelmingly the property of the state and not merely in the nominal sense in which land in many Latin American countries, for instance, is said to belong to the state, but in a very real sense which effectively determines its use.

Of the total area of Israel, 94.5 per cent belongs to the National Land Company, which was set up in 1959 to administer all the lands formerly under the authority of the Jewish National Fund and the state; only the remaining 5.5 per cent is privately owned, half by Jews and half by Arabs. If account is taken only of the farmed area, then the proportion of privately owned land increases to 20 per cent; but this means that virtually all the land reserves of the country are in the hands of the National Land Company.

The idea of public ownership of the national land goes back more than fifty years ago to the establishment of the Jewish National Fund by the World Zionist Congress to purchase Palestine land for settlement piecemeal. The principle prescribed for the disposal of lands acquired by the Fund was the Biblical injunction that "the land shall not be sold in perpetuity. . . ." This principle was not adopted, however, for the reason given in the rest of the injunction, namely, because the land and its fullness belongs to God, but because it was thought to be suitable for the practical purposes of the Zionist Organization. These purposes were essentially two: to insure that colonists settled on land acquired through public funds used the land for making a living, not for speculation, and to prevent as far as possible the reversal of land acquired by Jews to non-Jewish hands. Consequently, the Fund gave out land in 49-year leases, which would be invalidated if the lessee did not work his land for no sufficient reason or if he worked it with the help of hired labor. With the establishment of the state of Israel and its assumption of control over most of the land of the country as the custodian of refugee property and heir to the Mandatory government, the practical purposes which had moved the National Fund either became irrelevant or could be achieved by other means; but by that time social considerations reinforced the already established tradition and led to the retention of the Fund's basic principles.

There are other conditions for leasing national land which also had their origins in practical grounds but were later reinforced by considerations of social policy. In the days when the Jews constituted a minority of the population in Palestine, living in the midst of a hostile environment, it was largely impractical to lease out Fund lands to individual private farmsteads if only for security reasons. The practice therefore developed of awarding land leases mainly to small groups, organized in some form of cooperative or collective association. Since the establishment of the state, security conditions changed considerably, at least in regard to many parts of the country; nevertheless, the practice of leasing land only to groups has continued with few exceptions because cooperation and association have come to be viewed as desirable for social, economic, and ideological reasons. Thus, though there is no rule prohibiting it, a potential private farmer cannot in practice set himself up on leased national land; he has to join with other aspiring farmers and form a cooperative settlement which must undertake to employ no hired hands. The alternative for him is to lease or buy the land he needs from the very limited private sector at costs that are likely to affect severely the competitiveness of his products.

Within the frame of the formal and informal conditions of land rental mentioned before, publicly owned agricultural land is almost free for Jews. The rents charged for such lands average about one half of one per cent of the gross value of the agricultural product, and even this trivial rent is not exacted regularly. In contrast, a private Arab farmer, for instance, usually has to pay his landlord about one third of his crop or its equivalent in money as rent.

The reasons for this extraordinary policy go back, once again, to the nature of the Zionist endeavor in Palestine. The Zionist movement wanted to create a class of Jewish land settlers out of people who had had almost no agricultural tradition for centuries. It would have been difficult enough for inexperienced, often frail, urbanized young Jews to transform themselves into farmers even in the best of circumstances. In the period before the establishment of the state this difficulty was compounded by the fact that the new farmers had to settle on land which had been neglected for ages, in areas often infested with malaria and almost always surrounded by hostile neighbors. The elimination of rent made the task somewhat easier economically and constituted a sort of subsidy given to the products of Jewish farmers to enable them to compete with those of the Arab, accustomed to a very low standard of living. By the time the state came into being, the material conditions had eased a great deal; but the people who came to the country in the massive waves of immigration were far less ready than earlier settlers to accept any hardships. The rent-free land system was therefore retained as an inducement to attract people to agriculture.

In addition to these reasons, the free rent system served another purpose. The leaders of the Yishuv and the state of Israel wanted not only to create a class of agricultural settlers, but also wanted the settlements to be located sometimes in areas which were important from a political or strategic point of view though they may not have been the best in agricultural terms. The elimination of rent made it easier for the authorities to direct aspiring settlers to the desired areas. Of course, other factors have a bearing on the settlers' choice, such as access to water and proximity to markets; but here too the authorities have set up various equalizing schemes and are considering more. Right now, for instance, a scheme is under discussion which is designed to equalize the cost of water all over the country, where it now averages seven times more in the south than in the north.

Economists and free-enterprise-minded Americans may find many features of this system objectionable. For Israel, however, deficiencies in the details notwithstanding, the system as a whole has so far proved of enormous benefit. Thanks to it, Israel is, for instance, free from the agrarian problems that beset many developing societies and have been at the root of many social upheavals everywhere. She has no masses of land-hungry peasants confronting a few big landowners; no oligarchy deriving its power from its ownership of land; no vast ecclesiastical estates; no class of absentee landowners interested only in collecting rents and leaving the work entirely to tenant farmers who have neither the means nor the incentive to care for the soil; and she has experienced a soaring of land values as a result of speculation only in some urban areas where private ownership has prevailed. How viable the system will prove to be cannot, of course, be foretold; but the increasing resort to hired labor, which the authorities pretend to ignore, should serve as an illustration of how it might gradually become subverted altogether over the years.

VI

The People

The physiognomic and cultural diversity of Israel's population is a commonplace observation. It was, after all, very recently formed by immigrants from all parts of the world whose sense of common Jewish identity and destiny, besides varying greatly in degree and meaning, often lay buried under thousands of years of acculturation in different host societies. Also commonplace is the observation that the Israeli people is undergoing rapid change both in the demographic sense and in the more elusive sense of national character. For nearly half of Israel's present population consists of immigrants who came after the establishment of the state fourteen years ago, and no one knows how many more will come in the next five or ten years. The cultures brought by these immigrants affect substantially the character of Israel's people even as they themselves and their children undergo important change under the impact of the environment into which they come. Beyond these generalities, and because of them, it is extremely difficult to convey a meaningful idea of the people of that young state, of the extent to which it is becoming a nation in more than the political sense, and of what will be its likely character or even its size ten or twenty years hence. We shall approach this task by looking first at the process by which Israel's people was formed through successive layers of immigration and will then follow this historical description with an analysis of some of the main features of that people at present. Finally, an attempt will be made to assess the prospects of growth of Israel's population in the next ten years since the size of that country's population has many crucial implications.

1. THE FORMATION OF ISRAEL'S PEOPLE

Israel's people was formed by a succession of immigration waves over a period of eighty years. The waves are known in Zionist historiography as Aliyot, plural of the Hebrew term *aliyah,* denoting ascent or immigration to the Holy Land. Each Aliyah had its own characteristics, made a particular impact on the existing population, and brought its special contribution to the development of Israel's people as a whole. A broad distinction may, however, be drawn between the aliyot that preceded and those that followed statehood which is useful for many purposes.

The Pre-Statehood Aliyot

The First Aliyah began in 1882 and continued until 1903. It brought to Palestine 25,000 Jews, mainly from Tsarist Russia, whose arrival doubled the Jewish population of the country. Most of the previous inhabitants were Sefaradi and Oriental Jews who were thoroughly Turkified or Arabicized except for religion, and the rest were Ashkenazi Jews, mainly old people who had trickled into the country over the years for pious reasons. The initial inhabitants were concentrated in the holy cities of Jerusalem, Hebron, Safed, and Tiberias where they led a thoroughly apolitical, traditional existence and were primarily concerned with religious observance and study. They eked out a living from crafts and petty trade or subsisted on donations made by Jewish communities all over the world. In the 1870's, the first winds of change came to ruffle the settled life of the community. Eliezer Ben Yehuda, a young man obsessed with the idea of reviving the Hebrew language and putting it to daily use, appeared in Jerusalem and began to preach and practice his gospel. In 1878, a group of Hungarian Jews set out from Jerusalem to found an agricultural colony eight miles from Jaffa which they called Petach Tikva—The Gate of Hope. A few years before, the Alliance Israelite Universelle, a French Jewish philanthropic-cultural organization, founded an agricultural school near Jaffa—Mikve Yisrael, The Refuge of Israel. But when the new immigrants arrived, Ben Yehuda was encountering fanatic resistance from the older inhabitants who held that the use of Hebrew for secular purposes was sacrilegious. The Petach Tikva settlement had failed, and the graduates of Mikve Yisrael had nowhere to practice their skills outside the school's farm.

The newcomers radically differed from the older inhabitants in almost every respect. They were young and had been exposed to modern education and ideas. They had come to Palestine in the wake of the Russian pogroms of 1881 with the express intent of paving the way for a restoration of Jewish national existence in Palestine. Their slogan was the verse from Isaiah (2:5): "O house of Jacob, come ye and let us go," from the initials of which in Hebrew they derived their name as the Biluim; but they were not themselves religious. They meant to pursue their aims by leaving behind them in Europe the customary Jewish occupations and engaging in manual work and in tilling the soil. Some of them refounded Petach Tikva while others set out to establish the new colonies of Rishon le-Zion, Nes Zionah, Rosh Pinna, Zichron Yaacov—all in areas which were by the standards of those days far removed from the relative security and the "amenities" of the existing towns. The Biluim were thus the initiators of Jewish colonization in Palestine fifteen years before the World Zionist Organization had been conceived.

The first Biluim did not have an easy time in the country of their adoption. Their own inexperience, malaria, and a long untended soil, the suspicious Turkish officials, the predatory Arab neighbors and the sullen hostility of Jews of the old settlement conspired to make their life miserable. The whole experiment would probably have collapsed were it not that Baron Edmond de Rothschild of Paris came to their assistance after Chovevei Zion had interceded with him. The Baron bought land and built houses for the settlers, advanced money, tools and stock, subsidized or bought their products and sent instructors from France to organize them and teach them farm management. But the settlers had to pay for all that by giving up many of their brave ideals and settling down to a comfortable life as docile farmers relying primarily on cheap Arab labor and depending on the munificence of the Baron and the good will of the bureaucratically minded supervisors he sent. For the Baron's motives at that stage were purely philanthropic and he was opposed to any nationalist, not to speak of radical social, aspirations on the part of the settlers which might create difficulties with the Turkish authorities and nullify the prospect of Palestine's serving as a place of refuge for persecuted Jews. Had Jewish colonization continued along the same pattern, the history of Palestine and the fate of hundreds of thousands of Jews might have been quite different. Instead of a nation, or at least the makings of one, there would have grown in Palestine a class of Jewish *colons* which might have led a comfortable existence for a shorter or longer period only to be swept away eventually by the tide of awakening indigenous nationalism. That this did not happen was largely owing to the character and drive of the men of the Second Aliyah.

The Second Aliyah, too, came overwhelmingly from Russia and brought to the country nearly 40,000 Jewish immigrants in the decade between 1904 and 1914. This wave of immigration was prompted by the renewal of large-scale pogroms in Russia in 1903, but the newcomers were moved by much more than the desire and need to escape terror and oppression. The pogroms, renewed Tsarist repression, and the dislocation of Jewish life caused by the beginning of the industrial revolution in Russia had set in motion the most massive Jewish migration in history which carried westward over two and a half million Jews in the years between 1882 and 1914. But the majority of these Jews went to the United States and most of the remainder went to other non-European countries. Only three per cent went to Palestine, and more than half of these arrived after 1904 and constituted the men of the Second Aliyah. These were people who chose Palestine because, like the Biluim, they aspired to build a national home there, but they were much more conscious of themselves as part of a nationalist and socialist movement on the rise. They were affiliated with the World Zionist Organization and were also members of labor and socialist movements, founded almost simultaneously with the Zionist movement, which aspired to transform the Jews as individuals and as a people by revolutionizing their thought, their life, and their occupation and above all by rooting them in the soil of their ancient homeland. They were for the most part sons and daughters of middle-class families who sought deliberately to become farmers and workers in order to establish the base for a new, "normal," healthier occupational pyramid for the Jewish people while striving to ensure that the new society should be free of injustice and exploitation.

The men and women of the Second Aliyah and those of the next set their stamp indelibly on the development of Jewish Palestine. They endowed the country with its most typical institutions and spirit and decisively shaped its orientation for two generations. If there is any "aristocracy" in present-day Israel, it is definitely composed of the survivors of the Second and Third Aliyot. They are to be found in all the leading positions in the country and include the President of Israel, her Prime Minister, and the Speaker of her parliament, the Knesset.

The immigrants of the Second Aliyah immediately launched a struggle against the comfortably settled men of the First for the replacement of Arab by Jewish labor on their farms. The struggle was long and bitter because Arab labor was cheaper and better than that of the inexperienced newly arrived youth and because the latter considered that on its issue hinged not only their immediate livelihood but the future of their dreams of turning the country into a self-supporting Jewish homeland resting on a Jewish society built from the bottom up. Their victory in this struggle was crucial for the entire Jewish endeavor in Palestine.

Men of the Second Aliyah developed unions of rural and urban workers, cooperative enterprises, and mutual aid societies which became the foundation of the Histadrut—the impressive General Federation of Jewish Workers—of which more later. They gave a powerful impetus to the Return to the Soil movement and endowed it with an ideology that made a cult of manual labor much of which still persists today. They founded the kibbutz—collective settlement—movement which gave Palestine-Israel a unique institution and an instrument that rendered inestimable service to the Zionist endeavor and to the survival of Israel. They gave a decisive stimulus to the revival of the Hebrew language and ensured its triumph as the national tongue over several rivals.

The Third Aliyah began in 1918 and brought 25,000 Jews, mainly from Russia, in the course of the next five years, after which the exit of Jews from that country was barred. Essentially, this was in most respects a continuation of the Second Aliyah which had come to an abrupt end with the outbreak of the first World War, except that the new immigrants now came into a country ruled by a new master, Britain, which had committed itself to promoting the Zionist endeavor. The people of the Third Aliyah were predominantly pioneers belonging to the Zionist-Socialist movements and shared the ideologies and aspirations of the men of the Second. They confirmed the patterns already set by their predecessors and brought some of the enterprises begun by them to full fruition. Thus the kibbutz was transformed from an uncertain experiment to a growing movement and the Histadrut from a project to a reality. In addition, the two aliyot established an autonomous Jewish school system from kindergarten to university where Hebrew was the language of instruction, and laid the foundations for self-governing institutions encompassing all the Jews of Palestine. Also, the Third Aliyah set up the moshav—a smallholders' cooperative village—which became the other main form of settlement in Palestine alongside the kibbutz.

The *Fourth Aliyah,* lasting from 1923 to 1926, brought in 60,000 people, mostly from Poland. This wave was already substantially different from the Second and the Third. It was composed for the most part of middle-class people who intended to continue their occupation in their new country. They tended to cluster in Tel Aviv, founded fifteen years previously, in Haifa and in Jerusalem. The Aliyah in which they came had in fact been triggered by a series of measures taken by the Polish government which had hurt Jewish business in particular, and it came to an abrupt stop when an economic crisis in Poland and the devaluation of the zloty caused an economic crisis in Palestine itself. The relatively large size of that Aliyah was attributed at the time to the tightening of the immigration law in the United States, which deflected remnants of the great Jewish Eastern European migration to Palestine.

As the depression in Palestine gradually faded, immigration resumed at a slowly increasing pace. In 1932 it suddenly spurted to 12,000 and heralded the beginning of the *Fifth Aliyah,* the biggest wave of immigration in all the period preceding the establishment of Israel. From 1932 until 1939, nearly 225,000 Jews came into Palestine. About one third came from Eastern Europe and constituted in fact a continuation of the previous flow which had been interrupted between 1927 and 1930. But another third came from Germany and Central Europe as a result of the Nazis' rise to power and brought a new element into the Yishuv. There were very many doctors, lawyers, engineers, journalists, technicians, men with experience in administration, finance, and business organization, scholars and scientists, some with an international reputation, in addition to a large number of people with substantial capital. The Fifth Aliyah thus gave a powerful impetus to the development of industry, commerce, science, culture, and many other aspects of the Yishuv's life. It also gave the Yishuv a decidedly European character and composition. The old Sefaradi-Oriental core, though reinforced continually by a thin stream of immigration and by a high rate of reproduction, was reduced by 1939 to a mere fifth of the total Jewish population.

Although the Fourth and Fifth Aliyot were impelled by necessity, the immigrants, once in Palestine, became quickly integrated into the Yishuv and strengthened its national drive. For one thing, these aliyot, though predominantly middle-class, still contained many *chalutzim*—pioneers—who had been brought up in their countries of origin on the ideals of the men of the Second and Third Aliyot and came to Palestine ready to join them in doing the most difficult work. Moreover, many others among the new immigrants, though not ready to become workers, live in a kibbutz, and drain marshes, were convinced Zionists and fitted quickly into the ethos of the Yishuv. Even those who had not been Zionists abroad, were at least familiar with the Jewish national movement and, once in Palestine, considered themselves part of it. Thus, by the time World War II broke out, the very young Yishuv was no formless conglomeration of immigrants and refugees but a well-organized, politically conscious national community which was able, through voluntary discipline alone, to raise an army of 30,000 people to serve with the British forces. The tragedy of Europe's Jewry, news of which became known early in the war, only tightened the community more and permitted it to absorb another 120,000 immigrants by 1948 without any strain.

The Post-statehood Aliyot

The establishment of the state brought about a revolution in the size and composition of the aliyot. Since 1948, there have been two big spurts of immigration. In the first four years after its establishment, the Jewish state received 700,000 immigrants, or as many as its initial Jewish population. From the beginning of 1952 until the first half of 1954, there was a lull due to economic difficulties, the adoption by the state of a temporary policy of selective immigration, and the imposition of restrictions on Jewish emigration in some Eastern European countries. Fewer than 40,000 immigrants came in during that period. Beginning with 1955, a large flow started pouring in again and continues to the present, bringing to the country between 30,000 and 80,000 immigrants each year. Thus, sometime in 1961, the millionth immigrant since the establishment of the state set foot on Israel's soil.

The immigrants came from more than fifty countries; but over 90 per cent of them came from the eighteen countries specified in the following table, giving approximate figures for the period between 1948 and 1960.

Sources of Immigration May 1948 to May 1960
(approximate figures)

Europe		Asia	
Rumania	145,000	Iraq	120,000
Poland	130,000	Yemen	50,000
Bulgaria	39,000	Turkey	36,000
Hungary	27,000	Iran	33,000
Czechoslovakia	18,000	India	5,500
Yugoslavia	7,500	Total Asia	244,500
U.S.S.R.	5,000		
Other European countries	45,000	Africa	
Total European	416,500	Algeria, Tunisia and Morocco	150,000
America		Libya	32,000
U.S.A.	5,000	Egypt	25,000
Other American countries	10,000	Total Africa	207,000
Total America	15,000		
Undetermined	22,000		
GRAND TOTAL:	905,000		

The most notable feature about these waves of immigration, aside from their extraordinary size in relation to the original population, is their composition in terms of continent of origin. While 88 per cent of the pre-statehood immigrants had come from Europe and only 10 per cent from Africa and Asia, the last two continents accounted for half of those who arrived after 1948. This not only diluted the European character of Israel's people, but brought into the country masses of Jews whose historical background, typical occupations, culture, mentality, and physiognomy differed radically from those of the European Jews, both the newcomers and those already established in the country. Thus serious social and cultural problems arose in addition to the enormous practical difficulties involved in the attempt of a community to absorb a mass of newcomers more than one and a half times its size. What these problems are, how Israel is managing to meet them and the image her people as a whole present today, are the next questions to be examined.

2. ISRAEL'S PEOPLE TODAY

The flood of a million immigrants with bewilderingly varied backgrounds into the country which held an initial population of 717,000 Jews could not fail to have very far-reaching effects on Israel's people. With three out of every four adult Israelis born elsewhere, of whom three fifths came to the country after 1948, it is appropriate to begin an assessment of Israel's people today by asking whether one can speak at all of the Israelis as "a people" in anything but a purely formal sense.

One Israeli Nation or Two?

That one can speak of an Israeli people in several substantive senses is a conclusion any casual visitor to the country today is sure to reach very quickly. Like the visitor to any new country, one of the first things that will draw his attention will be its language. He will notice Hebrew on all signs and papers and hear everyone speaking it, and may not even realize that three out of every four adults he sees had had a different mother tongue and that most of them had had to learn and adopt Hebrew within the last thirteen years. This will be only one manifestation of a national will and a sense of national unity, more of which are likely to strike him again and again. He will probably notice that Israelis seem to have a passionate stake in the country and exhibit the liveliest interest in the minutest details of its life. In most affairs, he will find out, Israelis argue vehemently and are given to splitting hairs several times; but on certain basic points—the rights and wrongs of the Palestine issue, the ins and outs of Israel's dispute with her neighbors, the universal unity of the Jewish people and a notion of mutual obligation between it and Israel, the primacy of national defense and the justification of most measures taken by the government in that connection, the desirability of immigration and the sanctity of the open-gate principle, to mention the most important ones—the visitor will encounter an almost complete and most assertive unanimity of views. In addition, he will meet even among the most disgruntled Israelis a sense of pride in the national achievement as a whole and a readiness to fight for it that would arouse a nostalgic envy among leaders of older, well-established nations.

The visitor's sense of national oneness is apt to be strengthened by the uniformities he will observe in many surface aspects of the people and its life. The Arab minority of 237,000 people, most of whom still wear the typical headdress and live in towns, quarters, and villages that definitely recall the East, certainly strike the observer as a different group with a distant culture standing apart from the rest of Israel's people. By contrast, the Jews present on the whole an outward look that is quite uniform even though 28 per cent of them came from Eastern countries and cultures, most of them less than twelve years ago. Western dress is universal except among a few older women from Yemen, Kurdistan, or Persia, who are seldom to be seen in public anyway. The architecture is "Mediterranean" in style throughout, mixed here and there with nostalgic outcroppings of Lodz, Minsk, or German rural style. The theater, concerts, painting, places of entertainment, including cafés, nightclubs, bars, movies and so on are overwhelmingly Western in form and substance. Food and popular music show an impact of the East, but the end product is generally regarded as "Israeli" and is in fact quite different from the "purely" Oriental.

Although the existence of a strong sense of patriotism and of a consensus in regard to certain broad points of policy and principle undoubtedly makes the Israelis a "nation" in the operative sense that it can act as one vis à vis others, and although the surface uniformities do convey a certain flavor of very general cultural unity, it would nevertheless be rash to conclude that the Israeli people is anywhere near being an integrated nation, or, for that matter, that it is even on the way to becoming one in the foreseeable future. For beneath these unifying aspects there is a profound cultural, economic, and social cleavage among the Jews themselves—between the "Europeans" on the one hand and the "Africans and Asians" on the other—which divides the people into "Two Israels" that have so far defied all the efforts of the authorities to integrate them.

Israel's population in 1961 consisted of three broad groups in terms of country of birth: immigrants born in Europe constituted 35 per cent; immigrants born in African and Asian countries accounted for 28 per cent; and native-born Israelis amounted to 37 per cent. The significance of the native-born is, however, much less important than their proportion might indicate. For one thing, nearly 70 per cent of them were in that year children of fifteen or less, which means that, both because of their age and because they are mainly the offspring of recently arrived immigrants, their impact as "natives" on Israeli society at large is less important than their numbers. But, more important, the great majority of the children are of Oriental (that is, African or Asian) descent and follow in most essential respects the pattern of their parents rather than that of the native-born children of European parents. The much-romanticized image of the *Sabra,* the indigenous Israeli, allegedly a New Jew, a species of noble savage, blond, tough, direct, uncomplicated, free of all the "Jewish complexes," yet good and generous at heart—to the extent that it corresponded to anything in reality—does not in any case apply to the native Oriental children. For the Sabra of European descent, when he in fact differed in character and culture from his parents, was nevertheless reacting against their particular cultural-historical background and was therefore still motivated by the European experience of his parents. The native-born Oriental, if he reacted at all against his parents, was actuated by their quite different experience. Finally, and this is perhaps the central point, in terms of formal education and later earning patterns, the native-born Orientals actually fall into the patterns of their parents and perpetuate their underprivileged status.

Although the Africans and Asians as well as the Europeans differ considerably among themselves according to country of origin, the two groups of communities constitute two recognizable sectors differing from one another in several ways. The fundamental differences between these sectors go back to their different historical background to which we have alluded in previous chapters. One major distinction is fairly obvious and has to do with the general conditions of the society of origin. The Europeans came from societies which varied greatly from one another but were all relatively advanced by comparison with almost any of the Oriental societies, which included at best some that were in the process of emerging from their traditional patterns and at worst some that were still sunk in the obscurity of the dark ages. A less obvious but equally important disparity is related to the different experience of "the Jewish problem" that the two groups of communities had had, which determined to a very large extent their fundamental outlook on Israel. The Europeans had experienced the Jewish problem in several immediate and practical ways. They had sensed it as an intellectual conflict between modern thought and norms and the traditional Jewish faith and practice, or as an internal conflict between the desire to become equal partners in the surrounding society and culture and the fear of losing their Jewish identity, or as an external contradiction between their will to assimilate and their rejection by non-Jewish society, before finally experiencing it as active persecution culminating in extermination camps. The Orientals, on the other hand, had faced the Jewish problem mainly as a religious-metaphysical question for which the ideas of Galuth and Geullah provided a satisfactory answer. They had suffered none of the crises of their European brethren and lived within the surrounding society which was organized for the most part on a regional and communal basis. Even where the host society's traditional structure had begun to break up under the impact of nationalism and modernism, the bulk of the Jews had not yet been called upon to make any drastic adjustments to that society, and only a few of them had been tempted or impelled to make them voluntarily.

The different historical experience of the Jewish problem is reflected in the very different conceptions that Orientals and Europeans have of Israel. The Orientals revere the country as the Holy Land; they understand immigration as the promised "gathering of the exiles" and they are good patriots; but they do not see the Jewish state as a means to solving any individual or national problems of identity or religious-intellectual conflicts. To most of them, the atheist or agnostic European Jew who is a Zionist and lives in Israel is there simply because he had been expelled from his original country; any other explanation is incomprehensible. It follows that for them the act of coming to Israel is the realization of their yearning for Zion and the completion of their aspiration as members of the Jewish collectivity. From the moment of their arrival, their primary commitment is to their families and themselves except for the obligation of national defense. The dreams of the founders of Zionism and the builders of the Yishuv envisaging the Jewish state as a means or an opportunity for creating a model socialist society or a perfect liberal democracy, for allowing the "Jewish ethical genius" to flourish and be a light to humanity, or for raising a New Jew free from all the horrible and mean characteristics he allegedly acquired in the ghetto—these and many other ideas which had their roots in the conditions and predicaments of the Jews in various countries of Europe and had become moving forces in Palestine-Israel, are beyond the ken of most Eastern Jews. They are moved by no historical compulsion to change themselves, others, or anything, or to prove any point; they mainly take things as they are, try to continue their traditional way of life and make adjustments only on a pragmatic basis of necessity, utility, or convenience. They are inclined to take an "objective" view of the government, the law, institutions and policies of the country, seeing them as "given" things which might affect them for better or for worse but about which they cannot as a rule do much.

The difference in the conditions of the societies from which they originated is reflected in very substantial social and demographic differences between Europeans and Easterners. The average income of a European family is at least 50 per cent more than that of an Oriental family while the Oriental family is on the average three times larger than the European, thus making an enormous difference in standard of living. Nearly one out of every six Oriental families has eight or more members, whereas only one in a hundred European families is of that size. More than one in three Oriental families includes six or more members, while among the Europeans one in twenty-five families is of that size.

The large size of the Oriental family is the outcome of the traditional outlook of the parents and the sanitary conditions of Israel. Inquiries have shown that Oriental parents who had completed their families in the country of origin had had more children than parents who had most of theirs in Israel; however, nearly all Israeli children survive whereas a very high proportion of children born in the original country died young. The traditional outlook of the

Oriental parents is also reflected in the rate of literacy, which shows that only 44 per cent of the immigrant Oriental females over fourteen are literate. For the Oriental males the rate is much higher, reaching 74 per cent; but this is still well below the 95–99 per cent rate for Europeans, both males and females.

Poor education of the parents, large families, and low income mean inadequate education for the children and the perpetuation of the cycle. For though kindergartens and primary schools are free and compulsory in Israel, secondary education, which is the critical dividing line in the correlation between education and income, social outlook, and family size, is neither and is, moreover, rather expensive. Oriental children have constituted for several years 60 per cent of the entrants to the kindergartens but only 5 per cent of the graduates of secondary schools and 2 per cent of recipients of university degrees. Moreover, many if not most, of those who spend the statutory number of years in primary school come out only slightly improved in learning and barely touched in outlook, due to lack of suitable conditions for study and development at home and the pressure to go to work before or after the few hours spent at school in order to help the family make ends meet.

The gap between Orientals and Europeans is revealed further in every index one may pick up: among the Orientals, in substantially higher rates of overcrowded housing, slum dwelling, juvenile delinquency, criminality, and so on, and in their very low representation in the government, the senior civil service, the officers' corps, the professional and managerial positions. Perhaps the gravest aspect of the problem, however, is that the gap is not merely objective; it is consciously felt and expressed, often in a distorted light, by people in both camps. Some Orientals complain continually that they are deliberately kept down and discriminated against by the Europeans, while not a few among the latter convey the impression that the Oriental is intrinsically inferior to the European. Even when there is agreement among people on both sides on the causes of the disparity, there is violent disagreement on the nature of the remedial action to be taken and on the adequacy of the measures actually applied. Europeans tend to stress progress achieved and the improvement that has actually taken place in the conditions of the Orientals, while the latter look mainly at the remaining gap.

The truth is that in many, perhaps most, instances the standard of living of the Orientals has improved substantially in Israel over what it was in their countries of origin, but in nearly all cases the Oriental households have suffered a drastic decline in status. In their original societies these households, however low their standard of living, were still far better off in most respects than the vast majority of the indigenous families; whereas in Israel, however improved their standard of living, they are at the lowest end of the social scale. Perhaps the most telling single fact about the whole communal problem in Israel is the low rate of intermarriage, not only between Europeans and Orientals but even between members of the various communities within these two major groups. Assuming an index of 1 to mean absolute endogamy, or marrying strictly within one's community in the narrowest sense, the actual index for Israel in 1959 was 0.79.

Fortunately for Israel, the problem of communal divergence has not so far assumed the proportions of a racial or tribal conflict. Local acts of violence have occurred, but no sustained major outbreaks guided by united organization and national leadership. This is largely to the credit of the topmost leadership of the country which is committed to a policy of integration and does much, though not enough, to apply it. It is also to a substantial extent a result of the fact that there is a great deal of leeway for the capable and the ambitious among the Orientals to make their way to the top. Above all, however, it is due to the underlying feeling that Israelis cannot afford to indulge in communal conflicts while the enemy is poised at the gates.

The Over-all Stratification of Israel's People

When Israel started her career as a sovereign state, hers was probably the most egalitarian community in the world, the nearest approximation to a "classless society." Since then, mass immigration, especially its Oriental component, together with rapid economic development has loosened up the egalitarian social structure just as it has diluted the ideological compactness and relative homogeneity of the initial settlers. When Israel was established, her economy was young and small and had not given the opportunity for any significant number of people to accumulate large amounts of capital; since then, very rapid economic development and in-

flation have given rise to a substantial class of successful entrepreneurs and *nouveaux riches*. At the beginning of the state, Israel
had had for a decade and a half an excessive supply of highly
educated and professional people so that the difference between the
salaries of these people, and the wages of the manual workers was
very small; since then, the needs of the economy and the low
proportion of highly educated people among the massive Oriental
immigration have reversed the situation and have brought about
greater differentiation of salaries and wages. When Israel began,
the traditional difference in standard of living, social characteristics,
and outlook which exists everywhere between town and country
people was practically nonexistent because farm incomes were high
and the farmers were themselves city people who had taken to
tilling the soil out of "idealism"; since then farm incomes have
declined in relation to urban incomes, and masses of unprepared,
uneducated Orientals burdened with large families have been diverted to agriculture, creating a new class of farmers with limited
income and limited horizons. In the early days, the pioneering,
cooperative, and socialist-egalitarian tradition of the Second and
Third Aliyot still reigned supreme; since independence, reliance
on the sovereign state, economic development, and a massive immigration of people devoid of pioneering and Zionist background
have washed away much of that tradition.

Today the distribution of income in Israel shows a very considerable measure of inequality. A recent study indicates that in 1957–
1958 the lowest tenth of the urban income units received only 1.6
per cent of the total income while the highest tenth received as
much as 24.2 per cent. The poorer half of the units received only
one quarter of the total income while the richer half received three
quarters. One half of the urban families, in other words, had an
average income three times higher than that of the other half,
while the top 10 per cent families received more than 16 times the
income of the lowest 10 per cent. Between these two extremes, income rises or falls gradually. Reliable comparable figures for the
period around 1948 are not available, but all existing indications
point to a very substantial increase in inequality. A remarkable
thing is that this spreading of the income structure took place even
though the natural resources of the country, including most of the
land, are publicly owned and despite the fact that the government and

the Histadrut own and operate almost half of the country's industry and control very large portions of every other aspect of its economy.

Having stated the facts, it is now necessary to dwell briefly on what they mean. First of all, one must mention that the new distribution of income still leaves Israel among the most egalitarian countries in the free world; that distribution is at least as egalitarian as Sweden's in the same year, and is somewhat more so than the distribution of income in Britain in 1952, after six years of rule by the Labour Party. Secondly, as in Britain and Sweden, the inequality is considerably modified by a progressive taxation which falls heavily on the rich, and by extensive state welfare services which benefit the poor. Thirdly, and most important, several factors, such as the newness of the wealthy class and the importance of past contributions to the country and present service to it, especially in the security field, limit the extent to which wealth bestows status. Being a man of the Second or the Third Aliyah or having a bright military record to one's credit continues to some degree to overshadow wealth, which is still viewed as tainted with devious dealings. On the other hand, it should be noted that Israel's movement away from egalitarianism is contrary to the general trend among developed countries and that wealth is beginning to be associated with status. This will probably become increasingly true as the country gets older and the origins of that wealth are forgotten. Above all, one must never lose sight of the communal problem which has relegated whole sections of the population to an inferior status and tends to perpetuate their position there.

Occupationally, nearly 17 per cent of Israel's working population is engaged in agriculture, 32 per cent in industry and construction, 7 per cent in transport and communications, and 42 per cent in commerce, banking, personal and government services. This structure is still heavily weighted on the side of traditional Jewish occupations, but there can be no doubt that the founders of the Yishuv and the leaders of Israel have accomplished the Zionist dream of creating a "normal" structure for Jewish society in its homeland resting on a broad new base of farmers and workers. That this real revolution has been achieved without compulsion or violence and largely through self-sacrifice makes the accomplishment all the more impressive.

Israel's population is heavily urban. In 1961, 77 per cent of the total population lived in about 60 cities and towns and 25 per cent lived in about 800 rural settlements. Among Jews, the urbanization is even heavier, reaching about 84 per cent, in contrast with the Arabs, only 13 per cent of whom live in urban settlements. Today, as in 1948, most of the Jewish population is concentrated in the three districts, out of the country's six, which are composed of Tel Aviv, Haifa, Jerusalem, and their respective surroundings. But thanks to a deliberate and very expensive effort on the part of the government, a substantial redistribution has taken place in the last thirteen years. Thus the Tel Aviv district, which accounted for 43 per cent of the Jewish population in 1948, now accounts for only 35 per cent; while the South district, including the Negev, which comprised only 1 per cent of the Jewish population in 1948, now accounts for 8 per cent of an almost trebled population. The Haifa and Jerusalem districts, too, have had their share reduced, while that of the Central district, including the hilly corridor between Tel Aviv and Jerusalem, had correspondingly increased from 15 to 20 per cent. The North district, including Galilee, retained its share at 11 per cent, though of course it gained in absolute numbers.

3. PROSPECTS OF GROWTH

According to the provisional results of the census taken in May 1961, Israel's total population at that date amounted, in rounded numbers, to 2,170,000 people. Of these, 1,933,000, or 89 per cent, were Jews and 237,000, the remaining 11 per cent, were Arabs—three fourths Moslem and one fourth Christian. In the same area occupied by Israel, there were, in 1948, 717,000 Jews and 156,000 Arabs; thus the Jewish population has grown by 170 per cent in thirteen years and the Arab population by 52 per cent in the same period. Most of the Arab increase was due to natural growth, which took place at the phenomenal rate of over 40 per thousand in recent years, while only one fifth of the Jewish growth was due to natural increase (the rate in recent years has been 20 per thousand or less), the rest coming from immigration.

Clearly, the size and make-up of Israel's population in the future will depend very heavily on immigration as in the past; and the past history of immigration has included so many surprises that one can only conjecture about the future. Generally speaking, large-scale immigration has come from countries where political, social, and economic unrest stirred anti-Semitic feelings and endangered the status of the Jews, provided that the authorities in those countries allowed them to leave. In the past only a few outbreaks of unrest occurred abruptly, as in Hungary and Poland in 1956, and could not have been predicted; but the permission of the authorities has in most instances been quite capricious. Egypt and Iraq, for instance, very surprisingly let their Jews go, while Tunisia and Morocco have wavered back and forth. Bulgaria allowed a complete exodus, Poland and Rumania changed their policies many times, while Hungary and Czechoslovakia have maintained a strict ban since about 1950–1951. Soviet Russia has not allowed her Jews to leave since the early twenties, though a tantalizing few hundred a year on the average have trickled in since 1948. Looking at the immigration prospects for the next ten or fifteen years with these two very unsatisfactory guides in mind we get the following picture:

As of 1959, there were about 10.3 million Jews in the world outside of Israel. Of these, about 5.7 million lived in the United States and Canada, one million lived in Western Europe, 2.3 million in Soviet Russia, 400,000 in the rest of the Soviet bloc countries, 700,000 in Latin America (more than half of them in Argentina), 110,000 in South Africa and about 450,000 in the Moslem countries, chiefly Tunisia (50,000), Algeria (130,000), and Morocco (200,000). If the past is any indication of the future, then the 6.7 million Jews of North America and Western Europe must be excluded as important sources of immigration. The few thousands contributed annually by these areas in past years were more than offset by emigrants from Israel going there. At the other end of the spectrum, the 450,000 Jews of the Moslem countries may be expected to contribute about half their number despite the vacillations of the governments concerned. The same may be said, though with somewhat less assurance, of the 400,000 Jews of the Soviet satellites. Latin America as a whole has contributed a thousand or so people a year, but has taken in more as immigrants from Israel. This situation may change in the future, however, in view of the increasing restlessness of the area. Argentina, in particular, with its 400,000 Jews may prove an important source of emigration if the present political and economic instability with accompanying outbreaks of anti-Semitism continues, though Israel's share of it would depend largely on whether the Argentine Jews would be able to go else-where in Latin America or to the United States. South Africa has been losing an increasing trickle to Israel in the last few years which may reflect a mounting uneasiness of its Jews and their fear of getting caught in the midst of that country's racial trouble. The biggest and most decisive unknown is Russia's Jews. Israeli authorities claim that vast numbers, perhaps most of them, would emigrate to Israel at once if their government would let them go. How valid this claim is, this writer does not pretend to know, any more than he can assess the repeatedly expressed faith of Ben Gurion that the Soviet government *will* eventually let its Jews go.

Assuming there is no serious economic trouble in Israel, we might make three guesses about the size of the immigration to that country by 1971. The most likely minimum would lie between 300,000 and 400,000 over the entire period, which if added to natural increase would bring Israel's Jewish population to about 2,750,000 by the terminal year. Leaving the Soviet Union aside, the maximum immigration that might reasonably be expected would be in the order of 600,000 to 700,000, which would bring the total Jewish population close to the three and a quarter million mark. Finally, were we to take the Israelis' assertions in regard to Soviet Jewry on faith, we would add another million to either of the previous two estimates of immigration and more to the estimates of population. In all cases, about 70,000 to 100,000 Arabs should be added to the total population. The disparity between the lowest and the highest guesses—2,750,000 or 4,400,000 Jews—might make this game appear quite absurd. But, as we shall see further on, so important is the size of Israel's population for her future survival that we may be excused for indulging in it briefly.

VII

The Constitutional Order

1. THE FOUNDATIONS OF THE DEMOCRATIC SYSTEM

Israel is a parliamentary democratic republic; that is the character of her regime in fact, not by virtue of any self-definition in a constitution. For one of the unique features of that young state is that it does not have a constitution at all in the proper sense of the term. Certain laws enacted by the Knesset (Israel's parliament) are tagged "Basic Laws" and are intended in due course to form the basis of an integral written constitution; but for the time being most of these laws have no extraordinary legal standing. They do not require any special majority for their passage or amendment, as articles of a constitution normally do, and therefore do not constitute any particular limitation on the usual powers of the legislature. Thus, in theory at least, the legislature can alter the nature of the regime altogether and change completely the structure of government by the same process it follows in enacting the simplest of laws.

The existence of a working democracy in Israel despite the absence of a constitution may provide a refreshing contrast to the habit of so many states, new and not so new, of adopting high-sounding democratic constitutions which have little relation to actual practice. Nevertheless, the American observer, accustomed to a fairly rigid constitution and a delicate system of checks and balances which he regards as necessary for the protection of democracy and liberty, is apt to find the Israeli arrangement somewhat dangerous. It seems to grant too much power to a simple majority of the legislature which, in the circumstances of modern politics, often means the few leaders of the party or parties commanding that majority, and exposes the entire regime to the passions of a fleeting popular will. True, Britain does not have a constitution or any limitations on the power of Parliament, and her democracy does not seem to be the worse for it. But then, could a young nation-state such as Israel be expected to have the equivalents of the long parliamentary tradition, the political experience, and the kind of public opinion which have acted as informal restraints on the power of the majority and as buttresses of liberty in Britain?

Israel does have some unwritten checks and balances which have enabled her to do without a constitution so far. These consist of a balance of political forces in the country and a tradition of voluntary cooperation and egalitarianism going back to Yishuv days. With respect to the first of these factors, we shall see in our discussion of political parties that such is their character and their relative numerical strength that not one of them could achieve exclusive control of the legislature, and no combination of them could agree on any comprehensive program that might subvert the existing order. As a matter of fact, the absence of a constitution is largely due to the failure of any combination of parties to produce an appropriate majority in favor of any integral constitution to replace the existing *ad hoc* arrangements. But this balance of forces may not endure for any length of time in view of the rapid changes in the country's economy, the composition of its population, its leadership and its culture.

As for the democratic tradition of the Yishuv, this rested primarily on two basic facts. One was that Jewish society in Palestine had been newly founded by idealistic pioneers imbued with a utopian socialist spirit and rested overwhelmingly on self-supporting labor. No important social barriers or vested interests arose, therefore, which needed to be overthrown or suppressed. The large labor movement that developed did not grow in antithesis to capital but had the conditions for its existence within itself: it created the work that made the workers. All this has altered a great deal in the last fourteen years. Israeli society may still be driven to some extent by the momentum of the Yishuv tradition, but that momentum has been slowed down considerably under the impact of rapid economic expansion and massive immigration, especially of Oriental Jews. The other fact at the root of the democratic tradition of the Yishuv was that the community as a whole had no means of compulsion at its command and needed the cooperation of all its members for its immediate nation-building endeavor and its ultimate struggle to win sovereign statehood. Consent and cooperation were therefore its only means not only on the all-communal level of organization, but also on the level of each undertaking connected with nation-building, such as a village, a town, a school system, or self-defense. This situation naturally altered with the establishment of the sovereign state of Israel with its power to compel. True, the tasks of national defense, the reclamation of the wilderness, and the absorption of massive immigration call for a spirit of dedication and participation beyond anything that can be achieved by laws, and have in fact acted to mitigate the spirit of extreme partisanship in Israel. But there can be no doubt that the urge to obtain the consent of the minority and to elicit popular cooperation has diminished greatly and the temptation to rely on mechanical majorities and compulsion has increased accordingly. Altogether, then, it seems that if Israel's leaders had some good grounds for not being overly concerned with the adoption of a constitution immediately after the establishment of the state, they may be guilty of shortsightedness if they allow too long a time to pass without adopting one.

2. THE BASIC FRAMEWORK OF GOVERNMENT

The institutional framework of Israel's government was largely established by the Provisional Government which ruled the country in the first nine months of its independent existence. That government consisted of a Provisional Council of 38 members which acted as a legislature and a cabinet of 13 members which acted as an executive. Oddly enough, the Provisional Government exercised a tremendous influence on the form of government in Israel though it had no legal authority, strictly speaking; it was a self-appointed body composed of leaders of the Zionist movement residing in Israel and active in the Jewish Agency for Palestine, leaders of the communal institutions of the Yishuv, and delegates of parties and groups not represented in the previous two organizations. The respect and support it commanded, which have not been surpassed by any elected assembly or cabinet since, were due to its success in organizing the urgent services of the state out of the chaos left over by the Mandate and leading the nation to victory in the war that accompanied its birth.

The Provisional Government set the pattern for the present form of Israel's government by organizing itself on a parliamentary basis, whereby the cabinet derived its power from the Council, exercised it with its approval and under its scrutiny, and remained in power for as long as it retained the Council's confidence. By its Elections Ordinance of November 1948, the Council established the method of representation in the legislature of Israel, fixed that body's size, and determined the mode of its election. Finally, the Provisional Government provided for the continuation of the laws of the Mandate with some exceptions (notably the restriction of immigration and land purchase by Jews) and of the judicial system of the British administration, adding to it a Supreme Court.

All these crucial acts and many others of slightly lesser importance were adopted by the Provisional Government with a minimum of discussion and hardly any dissent. This was due partly to the enthusiastic mood and the sense of national emergency that gripped all Israelis in those fateful days, and to the fact that the acts made no radical innovation in the spirit and forms familiar to Israelis from the institutions of the Yishuv, the Jewish Agency, and the Zionist Organization. Above all, however, this was due to the realization that these were after all only temporary measures, subject to confirmation or revision by a constituent assembly which would draft a constitution. But what actually happened afterward was that the various combinations of parties were unable either to agree on any constitution that would modify the status quo established by the Provisional Government or to make that status quo itself final by embodying it in a constitution. The result was a compromise decision to leave things as they were but to work out the elements of a future constitution on a piecemeal basis over a period of years, which is what the Knesset has done since 1950.

The Knesset

As things stand today, the Knesset is the supreme authority of the land. This is a single chamber of 120 members elected by universal suffrage of adults eighteen years of age and older on the basis of proportional representation of party lists. A cabinet, now formally called "government," is considered legally constituted only after it faces the Knesset and obtains its confidence. A vote of no confidence at any time must entail the immediate resignation of the government. The Knesset also elects the President of the republic and can impeach and dismiss him.

The Knesset is the sole legislative authority; although the Prime Minister, the competent minister, and the President must sign bills before they become law, none of them has veto power, and the signatures of all three denote merely a compulsory formality. The Knesset fixes the budget of the government by a new law each year and checks on its application through a State Comptroller appointed by it. It exercises continual control over the executive and the administration by means of a question period at the beginning of its meetings, the right to ask for a plenary discussion of any subject whatsoever (the "motion for the agenda"), the right of the Knesset committees to inquire into the subjects under their jurisdiction and call for witnesses and records, and, again, through the State Comptroller who reports not only on accounts but also on the efficiency of government offices and government-supported enterprises in the country.

Unlike the practice in Britain, which has served as a model for Israel in many respects, no authority in the land—neither the Prime Minister nor the President—can dissolve the Knesset and call for new elections. Even the resignation of the government does not necessarily mean the termination of the Knesset. Only the Knesset can dissolve itself and fix the date of the new elections. Moreover, until 1958, when a Basic Law was passed fixing the term of all Knessets at four years unless any decides to dissolve itself, each Knesset fixed its own duration and could, presumably, prolong it indefinitely. That law also fixed the time of the convening of the Knesset, which was previously left up to its chair, and established for the first time different majority requirements for certain functions. Thus an absolute majority of Knesset membership (61 votes) was set for the election of a President on the first and second ballots, a three-fourths majority for dismissing him, and a minimum vote of 80 was made necessary to amend the Basic Law of the Knesset by means of emergency regulations. No quorum is needed for the Knesset to transact its business.

Formally, then, the Knesset has even more powers than the

British Parliament, of which it was said that it could do everything except turn a man into a woman and vice versa. But, as in the case of the British Parliament and unlike that of the American Congress, the exercise of the tremendous powers of the Knesset is, in practice, overwhelmingly under the control of the government, which commands a Knesset majority through strict party discipline and which has by law a decisive say in fixing the Knesset's agenda.

The Government

Israel, like Britain, has a much less definite separation of powers among its three branches, especially between the legislative and the executive, than the United States. The executive (the government), as has been said, is under the authority of the Knesset. After elections, the President charges the head of one of the parties with the task of forming a government from Knesset members as well as from outsiders; but the government is not considered legally installed until it confronts the Knesset and receives an explicit vote of confidence. There is no fixed number of ministries or ministers, and these have generally varied to suit the needs of the country as well as the political considerations attending the formation of a government.

The government has very broad capacities in law and even broader ones in fact. In practice, the government leads the Knesset in most essential functions more than it is led by it, and has charge, in addition, of the executive functions which are all its own. It not only determines internal and foreign policies and executes the laws, but possesses the initiative in legislation almost exclusively. Unlike the practice in Congress, it is virtually impossible for a Knesset member to initiate a law, though he is legally entitled to do so, unless the government is willing to surrender the priority it has for its own business and to allow its supporters in the Knesset to back the private member's bill. The government collectively, and each minister in his own sphere singly, are empowered to issue the regulations necessary for the execution of legislation, and these regulations have the force of law subject to the tacit consent of the Knesset and the interpretation of the courts. In foreign affairs, the government can enter into international agreements which commit the country itself without reference to the Knesset, though the latter can discuss all acts of the government and vote it out of office any time. By usage though not by law, treaties are submitted to the ratification of the Knesset.

Powerful as the government is in Israel, it is less powerful than the British cabinet in theory as well as in practice. It lacks the right of dissolving the Knesset, and its freedom of action has been limited by the fact that the division of political forces in the country has made possible only coalition governments, which lack internal cohesiveness and unity. The Israeli Prime Minister does not have the power of his British equivalent to nominate or ask for the resignation of any or all of his ministers. The parties forming the coalition appoint their own ministers whom the Prime Minister cannot dismiss unless he resigns himself and thus brings down the entire government. All in all, the pattern of legislative-executive relations that has emerged in Israel seems to strike a compromise between the continental European tradition favoring an omnipotent assembly and the British system of an extremely powerful cabinet.

The President

The President of Israel presides but does not rule. He has only formal and ceremonial functions except for two prerogatives: that of granting pardon and that of designating a person to form a government. The latter right is usually circumscribed since the President has to choose a candidate who can muster the support of the majority of the Knesset and this, in the circumstances of Israel so far, has meant the leader of the largest Knesset faction. It is conceivable, however, that under certain circumstances this right may become of practical importance. Should the leadership of the largest party not be settled on one person, for instance, or should two factions emerge which would both be capable of marshaling a coalition, the President would have a real choice in appointing the Prime Minister.

The President is elected by the Knesset for a term of five years. On the first and second ballots he needs to obtain a majority of the total Knesset vote, or 61; thereafter a majority of the votes cast is sufficient. He can be impeached by a vote of three quarters of all the members of the Knesset Committee, and can be dismissed by three quarters of the entire Knesset itself on the grounds of behaving in a manner not in keeping with his position. The Knesset can also depose him on the grounds of incapacitating ill health. The extremely weak position of the President provides an assurance against conflicts between him and the other branches of the government. On the other hand, it has also deprived the Israeli political system of a potential stabilizing influence which could have been very useful in view of the extremely fragmented nature of political opinion in the country.

The Judiciary and the Legal System

Israel has an eclectic judicial and legal system in which British influence is nevertheless predominant. There are two networks of courts in the country, one general and one special. Not all the courts operate on the basis of legislated laws. The Ecclesiastical Courts and the Arbitration Courts, though sanctioned by the state, operate on the respective bases of the religious law of the state's residents and of equity and tradition. The special courts deal with matters that fall under municipal, military, and administrative laws and regulations; the general courts supervise the special courts and deal with all the matters not covered by them. They are organized in a three-tier hierarchy culminating in a Supreme Court of nine members which acts as the highest court of appeal and as High Court of Justice to hear charges of arbitrary and illegal action by public authorities. In 1948 and 1949, when a constitution was being considered, it was suggested that the Supreme Court should have the power of judicial review, but the proposal found no favor. The Supreme Court has therefore no such power with respect to the conformity of any legislation with the "Basic Laws" of the country, but it has, together with other courts, the power to void regulations as unauthorized by the law on which they rest or as unnecessary for its proper execution.

All judges are nominated by an Appointment Committee which consists of the Minister of Justice, two members of the Knesset elected by secret ballot, three justices of the Supreme Court, two ministers, and two elected representatives of the Israel Bar Association. The nominations are forwarded to the President who makes the appointments subject to Knesset confirmation. This procedure is perhaps the only important innovation in the emerging constitution of Israel. Together with other, more conventional, measures, it is intended to secure the independence of the judiciary, which has in fact availed itself fully of its position. Judges hold office during good behavior and are required to retire with pension at the age of seventy. Their salaries are fixed by the Finance Committee of the Knesset and are at present set on a level which gives the Chief Justice of the Supreme Court a salary equivalent to that of the Prime Minister.

The laws applied in Israel derive from several sources. Upon the establishment of the state, the Provisional Government adopted the entire body of law which ruled in Mandatory Palestine with the exception of a few laws which restricted Jewish immigration and land purchase and laws which were contradicted by ordinances issued by it. The establishment of the Knesset brought an addition of new laws and modifications of old ones, but did not change the situation with any large-scale new codification. The laws inherited from the Mandate themselves derived from three sources. One was the Ottoman laws which prevailed in Palestine on November 1, 1914, the day Turkey joined in the war against the Allies, to the extent that they were not subsequently changed or cancelled by the Mandatory. These laws were themselves a composite body which included survivals of Muslim religious law, important elements of French law, laws enacted by the Ottoman legislator, and the religious law of the non-Muslim communities. A second source of Palestinian law consisted of laws and ordinances issued by the Mandatory government and the Palestinian local authorities. Finally, a third source consisted of the common law and laws of equity of Britain, which were used to fill the gaps in the previous two sources to the extent that they were deemed suitable to the local conditions. Among the legal elements from the British tradition inherited by Israel were the prerogative writs of *habeas corpus, mandamus* and *certiorari,* and the order *nisi* which, in the hands of the Supreme Court sitting as a High Court of Justice, have been used very effectively to protect citizens against arbitrary or illegal behavior by public authorities and to instill respect for the rule of law.

These, then, are in brief the basic institutions and procedures of the government of Israel. They fall far short of a constitution not only in the sense, already mentioned, that they rest on acts which have the standing of simple laws and which can be abrogated or modified by a relatively easy process, but also in the sense that they leave many gaps which need to be filled. There is, for example, no period fixed by law or usage within which elections must take place after a Knesset dissolves itself, but each Knesset fixes anew the date of the election of its successor. Similarly, there is no fixed period within which a new government must be formed after the demise of the old, and governments that had resigned have sometimes continued to serve "temporarily" for up to ten months—a dangerously long transition period, especially since in the course of it the various partners of a coalition are usually at odds and only routine business can be transacted. The legal qualifications of a presidential candidate are not fully established, and it seems, whether by design or not, that the President of Israel can be technically a foreign citizen. The relations between the state and the various religions are still technically governed by Mandatory and Ottoman laws whose foundations were completely altered by the establishment of the state of Israel. No law exists to regulate the status of the Holy Places. There is no Bill of Rights, and the protection of the citizens' liberties rests mostly on the assumption that everything is permissible which is not specifically prohibited by the regular law or by the emergency regulations which have been kept from Mandatory and wartime days. As may be gathered from all these examples, some of the gaps have remained because the need to fill them has not yet been practically felt. But others exist because the circumstances of party politics have conspired to leave them unfilled, and still others because they relate to highly divisive subjects such as religion, or such delicate issues as the balance between civil liberties and the needs of national security.

As the state of Israel enters into the fifteenth year of its existence, the absence of a constitution symbolizes both its basic internal strength and weakness. There is evidence of basic strength in the fact that the democratic regime of the country has rested for fourteen years not on formal constitutional definitions and arrangements but on a practical *modus vivendi* worked out by the political forces active in it. But insofar as these forces have been unable to extend that *modus vivendi* to fill remaining gaps and to transform it into a normative pattern enshrined in a constitution, there is evidence of a combination of rigidity and tension in the system which may undermine it without allowing it to make the necessary adjustments. These deficiencies will be encountered again and again in the specific topics discussed in the next chapters. To overcome them is a serious internal challenge confronting Israel.

THE GOVERNMENT OF ISRAEL
November 1961

MAPAI

David Ben Gurion	Prime Minister and Minister of Defense
Levi Eshkol	Minister of Finance
Golda Meir	Minister of Foreign Affairs
Abba Eban	Minister of Education
Moshe Dayan	Minister of Agriculture
Guiora Yosephtal	Minister of Development
Pinchas Sapir	Minister of Commerce and Industry
Bechor Shitrit	Minister of Police
Dov Yoseph	Minister of Justice
Yoseph Almogui	Minister without Portfolio

NATIONAL RELIGIOUS PARTY

Moshe Shapiro	Minister of Interior and Health
Yoseph Burg	Minister of Social Welfare
Zerach Warhaftig	Minister of Religions

ACHDUT HAAVODA

Yitzhak Ben Aharon	Minister of Transport
Yigal Allon	Minister of Labor

INDEPENDENT
(Mapai-supported)

Eliahu Sasson	Minister of Posts

PART THREE: POLITICAL DYNAMICS:
CHARACTERISTICS, ACHIEVEMENTS,
PROBLEMS

VIII

The Pattern of Party Politics

Israeli political parties bear many external resemblances to analogous organizations in America and in Britain, but it is their unique character rather than their similitude which holds the key to an understanding of a form of political behavior which is frequently bewildering to an outsider. We shall try to analyze their character in terms of four distinguishing qualities. In the course of the discussion, we shall attempt to explain the origins of these distinctive traits and to illustrate the manner in which they affect the operation of the political system and we shall venture a prognosis about the future evolution of Israel's parties and politics. For the political physiognomy of that country is undergoing significant changes as it moves into the fifteenth year of its independent existence.

1. First off, an observer accustomed to the two-party system, with an occasional intrusion of a short-lived third element, is struck by the sheer multiplicity of the Israeli parties. In the elections to the Knesset in 1961 two dozen political groupings presented their separate lists to an eligible electorate of about a million and a quarter voters, and eleven of the parties returned one or more Knesset members.

2. If a stranger tries to capture the temper of political life in Israel he is immediately impressed with its extraordinary emotional intensity. Political commitment is not a temporary intermittent passion which flares up chiefly during the period of national electoral contests and then remains relatively quiescent. Membership in a

party is all-absorbing, and the ardor it generates colors the whole of existence for a substantial number of citizens.

3. The political party is not a loose organization whose functions are centered exclusively on the winning of elections and the formulation of party programs. Virtually all major Israeli parties have ramified their activities into spheres which would in Anglo-American society be considered the province of the public authorities, of the church, of autonomous nonpartisan social service agencies, or of trade unions. Cultural programs which in the West would ordinarily be sponsored by apolitical private associations have become integrated into the party functions.

4. Finally, party leadership is highly centralized in a small group at the main seat of authority; local leaders, whose continuing pressure on the party executive every American politician of national prominence must reckon with, are of minor significance in Israel.

1. THE MULTIPLICITY OF PARTIES

The political parties of Israel had their origins in the complex and feverish life of the World Zionist Organization and in the self-governing organization of the Yishuv of the Mandatory period. For decades before the establishment of the state, groupings which called themselves parties or movements competed vigorously with each other for control and influence in the ruling institutions of these two organizations. By the time Israel declared her independence, these parties had been so completely formed that they simply changed the target of their operations and otherwise continued to operate without the least disturbance. All the characteristics previously enumerated, including the multiplicity of the parties, were already fixed. To escape the detrimental effects of some of these characteristics has become one of the major problems of contemporary Israel.

In the elections to the First Knesset of Israel which took place in January, 1949, twenty-four parties and organizations competed with lists of their own and sixteen managed to elect one or more candidates. In the elections to the Fifth Knesset which took place in 1961 after thirteen years of statehood, during which an active process of fission and fusion took place among the parties, twenty-three parties and organizations competed and eleven succeeded in returning one or more candidates. Of the successful lists, nine represented "major" parties and two represented more ephemeral Arab parties. In the accompanying table is the list of the major parties as of 1961 together with the percentage of the total vote that each of them polled in the elections which took place in that year. In order to give an idea of the range of strength of each party the percentages they drew in the elections to the First (1949) and the Third Knesset (1955) are also included.

	Percentage of total votes		
	1961	1955	1949
Mapai (Party of Israel's Workers)	34.7	32.2	35.7
Herut (Liberty)	13.7	12.6	11.5
General Zionists ⎤		10.2	5.2
Progressives ⎦	13.6	4.4	4.1
(now Liberal Party)			
Mapam (United Workers Party)	7.6	7.3 ⎤	
Achdut Haavoda (Unity of Labor)	6.5	8.1 ⎦ 14.7	
Hapoel Hammizrachi (Mizrachi Workers) ⎤		7.5	4.9
Mizrachi (Spiritual Center Party) ⎦	9.8	1.6	3.1
(now National Religious Front)			
Agudat Yisrael (Community of Israel)	3.7	2.4	1.8
Poalei Agudat Yisrael (Workers of Agudat Yisrael)	1.9	2.3	1.6
Communists	4.1	4.5	3.5

Students of political parties have pointed out two basic features which characterize all multiparty systems, wherever they may be: 1) the multiaxial division of opinion, or the crystallization of organized opinion around a number of issues which cut across each other; and 2) proportional representation. Both features are present in Israel and seem indeed to have most to do with the profusion of parties there.

In Israel today opinion is divided in terms of at least five major issues which cut across each other. The first and most important is the issue of basic socio-economic doctrine. It divides Israeli opinion into a group of six leftist parties consisting of the Communists, Mapam, Achdut Haavoda, Mapai, the Poel Hammizrachi, and Poalei Agudat Yisrael; and five rightist parties consisting of the Progressive Party, the General Zionists' Party (these two recently united to form the Liberal Party), the Herut Movement, and the two religious parties, the Mizrachi and the Agudat Yisrael. In general, left and right in this context signify, as they do in Europe, a division between those committed to social equality, collective ownership, and planning in greater or lesser degree, and those still attached to the basic economic, social, and political tenets of capitalist free enterprise. This does not, however, preclude certain paradoxical deviations from the European pattern on some specific issues arising from the particular circumstances of Israel. Thus, for example, because the Histadrut—the Israeli federation of trade unions, dominated by the secular leftist parties—has developed a health insurance system which encompasses the majority of the population and gives the federation a powerful means of influence, it is the right-wing parties which demand a national health service for Israel while the left-wing parties argue for the adavntage of voluntary association over a compulsory national system. Similarly, we find the right-wing parties demanding the nationalization of the cooperative monopoly of urban and interurban bus services while the left-wing parties defend it.

Within each group of parties there are significant doctrinal and practical differences in socio-economic matters. But among some of them, at least, these are not greater than the differences which obtain among various segments of the Labour and Conservative parties in Britain, or even the Democratic and Republican parties in the United States. In Israel such parties would have had little theoretical justification for separate existence were it not that other issues cut across their similar socio-economic views and differentiated them on other grounds. One of these is the religious question, which constitutes the second of the main axes of opinion.

The issue of the place of religion in the state separates the Poel Hammizrachi and Poalei Agudat Yisrael from the other left-wing parties, and the Mizrachi and Agudat Yisrael from others of the right. All of these four parties seek to establish in Israel a state founded on the Jewish religious law. But the Mizrachi and its labor offspring, the Poel Hammizrachi, have adopted for many decades a more flexible religious posture which had allowed them, for example, to take part fully in the Zionist enterprise, while Agudat Yisrael and its workers' offspring, the Poalei Agudat Yisrael, had opposed root and branch the Zionist endeavor as an encroachment upon the idea of redemption through miraculous divine intervention and have reconciled themselves to the Jewish state only reluctantly since it has become a fact. This historical difference is reflected today in the fact that the Mizrachi parties tend to be dominated by lay leaders active in all walks of life, while the Agudat parties tend to be dominated by a Council of the Learned composed of professional clerics. On socio-economic matters, as well as on other questions, the Poel Hammizrachi and Poalei Agudat Yisrael stand near to Mapai, while the Mizrachi and Agudat Yisrael stand near to the Liberals (the recently united Progressives and General Zionists). But the primary importance that all four of them attach to the religious issue has led the pairs of parties to prefer close cooperation with their religious counterparts across the socio-economic divide than with their neighboring nonreligious parties. The Poel Hammizrachi has actually merged with the Mizrachi to form the National Religious Party. Previously all four parties had formed a United Religious Front.

The religious parties confront in the other parties varying attitudes in regard to the religious question. All the other parties are opposed to a theocratic state, and all but the Communists are willing to recognize the national cultural value of the Bible and certain elements of Jewish tradition. On other matters specifically relating to religion their attitude ranges all the way from the general indifference of Herut and the Liberals, through the sporadic and moderate anticlericalism of Mapai, to the militant secularism of Achdut Haavoda, Mapam, and the Communists.

Another basic issue which has served to justify the division within both the right- and left-wing sectors is connected with the definition of the territorial claims of Zionism. This issue has weakened considerably since the establishment of the state of Israel in its present form and boundaries, but the divisions it had caused have not been repaired and they are still reflected in secondary issues. Until the Soviet Union announced its support of partition and the establishment of a Jewish state, the Communist Party of Palestine had opposed altogether the Zionist endeavor and aspiration to statehood. This opposition defined that party's main difference from Mapam's antecedent, the Shomer Hatzair, which was Zionist but otherwise shared with the Communists their orthodox Marxist doctrine and attachment to the Soviet Union. The Shomer

Hatzair, in its turn, differentiated itself from the other left-wing parties by advocating a bi-national Jewish-Arab state instead of an exclusively Jewish state in Palestine. On the other side of the socio-economic divide, the antecedents of Herut—that is, the Revisionist Party and the underground military movement, the Irgun— differentiated themselves from the General Zionists, with whom they shared the same basic socio-economic tenets, and from the other parties in general by their claim to the whole of Palestine west and east of the Jordan in its most extensive Biblical boundaries, and by their readiness to "go it alone" and fight for their goal outside the framework of the Zionist Organization and its institutions. The past attitude of Communists, Mapam, and Herut is seen in a modified form in today's Israel. The Communists, for example, while accepting the fact of Israel's existence as long as Moscow does, echo with relish every Soviet charge against Israel. Mapam, while giving up the idea of a bi-national state, considers itself the guardian of the rights of the Arab minority in Israel and would do away with all the restrictions imposed on it on grounds of security. Herut, while repressing open talk about Israel *irredenta,* is always pressing for greater militancy and greater show of force in the country's various conflicts with its neighbors. The attitude of the other parties toward the entire issue of the territorial claims of Zionism has been strongly pragmatic. Today, they are willing to operate in good faith within the terms of the international armistice agreements of 1949. But should these agreements be repudiated by military action on the part of one or more of the Arab states, they would probably endeavor to gain the best realizable boundaries within the very loose limits of the historical frontiers of the ancient Jewish state. Such at least was the impression conveyed during the Sinai War of 1956.

Another issue underlying the multiplicity of parties has to do with foreign-policy orientation. Like the question of the definition of the territorial claims of Zionism, to which it is in fact closely related, this issue is of reduced importance today, though it too contributed a great deal to the crystallization of party divisions in the past and is reflected today in secondary manifestations. The complete subservience of the Communist Party to Moscow has kept it apart from the other leftist parties even after it accepted the fact of Israel's existence. The advocacy of a clear pro-Soviet orientation had also kept Mapam away from Mapai after the establishment of Israel had rendered academic the difference between the two parties in regard to the question of a bi-national or Jewish national state. That same question split Mapam in 1954 into two parties when the former Shomer Hatzair leadership within the party continued to advocate a pro-Soviet orientation in the face of the evident hostility of Russia toward Israel. At the other end of the spectrum, the Liberals and Herut are profoundly anti-Soviet and favor a policy of open alignment with the West. Between the two groups stands Mapai whose nondoctrinaire socialism commits it to neither East nor West but which has found itself taking the lead in a pro-Western orientation on pragmatic grounds.

A fifth issue creating political division has to do with ethnic origins. Arabs have formed several small parties whose members feel that this is the only way to make their grievances heard. Similarly the Sefaradi, Yemenite, and Central European Jews at one time believed that they needed separate political agencies to protect their interests in the face of the ruling Ashkenazi and Eastern European Jews. As of today the separate ethnically based Jewish political organizations have collapsed or merged with other parties. But the ethnic factor is still a strong element in Israeli politics and may express itself again in the form of separate party organizations.

The proliferation of parties in Israel, and, before its establishment, in the Zionist Organization and the Yishuv, has been strongly encouraged by the system of proportional representation adopted by all three of them. In the election system current in the United States and Britain, the candidates for office, be it the presidency, a governorship, or a seat in Congress or Parliament, compete with each other in a given constituency and the candidate who receives a plurality is elected while his rivals get nothing. A defeated candidate for the presidency may obtain many votes in many states, or a defeated candidate for governor may obtain many votes in his state, but all these votes entitle him to nothing because he did not make up the required plurality. Similarly, a party may run scores of candidates for Congress or Parliament in scores of constituencies and thus obtain a very large vote over the country as a whole, but unless it can get pluralities in specific constituencies, all its votes are wasted. Since elections involve a lot of work and expenditure, a party under this system is not likely to run a candidate unless he has good chances of winning. Moreover, in elections to Congress or Parliament, unless a party is able to get a sufficient number of members elected so as to give it some leverage in these assemblies it will tend to drop out of the race altogether or to pool its forces with some large party. This system of single-member constituencies and plurality elections thus discourages political fragmentation and encourages concentration.

In the system of proportional representation, on the other hand, everything conspires to produce the opposite results, especially when the system is applied consistently and without any modification as it is in Israel. There, the entire country is considered a single constituency to which all the Knesset seats are assigned, and these are divided after the elections among the various parties in proportion to the number of votes each of them drew. Thus a party may draw only a few votes in each locality—in the American system they would be completely wasted—but these may add up over the country as a whole to give it a few mandates. This in itself is an incentive for many parties to enter the elections independently; but the effect of the system goes further. Because many parties enter the elections and manage to gain some seats, the final result is that no single party is able to gain a majority in the Knesset, and only coalition governments can be formed. This gives even a very small party a chance to place one or more of its members in the government and thus makes its whole effort worthwhile and worth continuing. There is no incentive for small parties to merge since this would not give them any significant advantage and there is, on the contrary, every inducement for a discontented minority within an existing party to split off and form a party of its own. Accordingly, the entire system discourages political concentration and encourages fragmentation. It encourages political groups to lay stress on the issues and features that divide them rather than on those interests which they may have in common.

Having seen how the multiaxial division of opinion and proportional representation conspire to produce a multiplicity of parties, the next question is why these two factors became established in Israel or in the political organizations which preceded the establishment of the state—the World Zionist Organization and the Yishuv self-government. But before answering this question some comment must be made on the relationship between these two factors, not just in Israel but everywhere.

In general, where a society is already divided into a number of fixed positions which cut across each other when it comes to set up a representative system, and where that society does not want, or is unable to repress by force, one or more of these positions, there is no escape from setting up a system of proportional representation which perpetuates and multiplies that initial division. Certain modifications of the system of proportional representation may reduce to some extent the number of divisions; but a basic remedy can be achieved only by mutual accommodations and voluntary mergers among the parties which may then be consolidated by a reform of the system of representation. On the other hand, where opinion is divided into only two crystallized positions or two sets of related positions at the time a representative system is to be set up, the community is free to choose any system of representation, and the system it chooses will have a decisive influence on the number of parties that may emerge in the course of time. If it adopts a system of single-member constituency and plurality election, the dual division is likely to become perpetuated. Many new issues may arise all the time, but the tendency will be for them to fall within the existing dual framework. They may upset the balance of forces between the two parties, change their character and their names, but they will not alter the dual pattern. Occasionally, a crucial issue may temporarily give rise to a third party, but the system of representation is likely in the long run to restore the dual division either by the existing parties' "plundering" the successful ideas of the new party or by the new party's pushing aside one of the existing parties and becoming itself the second major party. But if the society initially divided into two set positions adopts the system of proportional representation, the next issue that may arise or the next conflict within one of the existing parties is almost sure to produce another party, and yet another; and once this happens, it is difficult to change altogether the method of representation without recourse to repression. The critical questions, then, affecting the number of parties are: how was crystallized opinion divided at the time the system of representation was set up? And, if opinion was not yet crystallized, or if it was crystallized in a dual division, what sort of system of representation was adopted?

When Herzl set up the World Zionist Organization to speak and act on behalf of the national political aspirations of the Jews, its adherents embraced a vast diversity of views. Coming from all over the world, from all sorts of environments, and from all levels in the social structure, they brought with them a wide variety of ideal political-social images derived from their different environments. And although at the time the Organization was founded and for a few years thereafter, these attitudes and images had not yet assumed the form of organized parties, the nature of the Organization and the circumstances in which it operated precluded the setting up of a system of constituency and plurality elections and prescribed the establishment of a method which quickly developed into proportional representation with all its inevitable consequences.

The Zionist Organization was called by its founder "the Jewish State on the way," and its institutions were often thought of in terms analogous to state institutions. These descriptions and comparisons, though they proved to be prophetic in a general historical sense, are least useful when one seeks to understand the political nature and dynamics of the Organization and its institutions. Except for some formal analogies, these had nothing in common with the objects with which they were compared. In fact, the Zionist Organization even differed substantially from other nationalist movements —many of which, incidentally, may also be called "states on the way"—because the people on whose behalf the Organization claimed to speak were dispersed all over the world and constituted an insignificant minority in the territory which was the object of its aspirations. Because the Zionist Organization, unlike a government, was not involved in ruling a given territory, a territorial constituency representation was pointless. And even if constituency representation were desirable on some other ground, it was highly impractical because the Organization did not operate within defined territorial limits. In any case, a plurality vote was wholly undesirable because it involved an element of compulsion and, above all, because it was bound to leave unrepresented a substantial number, if not most, of the members—an absurd situation for an organization whose sole authority was the moral one of claiming to represent all sorts of

Jews and which therefore needed every additional member almost as much as he needed it. Nothing seemed more natural, therefore, than for the Organization to adopt the system it did, which simply allocated to every so many members the right to send a delegate to Congress, the supreme representative institution of the movement.

As the Zionist movement progressed in its endeavors and became a force of importance among the Jews and in the international political arena, the diverse background of its members combined with the method of representation adopted by its organized institutions to produce a large number of factions and parties. Some differentiated themselves on grounds of tactics to be followed by the movement, others on the grounds of personalities, others still on the grounds of the religious, social, and economic character of the state to be. Some drew their inspiration from the liberal democracy of Western Europe, others from Wilhelmian German authoritarian capitalism, and others still from Eastern European idealist utopianism or revolutionary socialism. The varied orientations, coming together for a brief meeting in a biennial World Zionist Congress, could not be stamped out by a single overriding direction without crippling the whole Organization, even if such direction had majority support. The Zionist movement, as a voluntary organization, was too weak to impose unqualified majority rule since the losers in an important showdown might depart and form separate Zionist bodies, fragmenting Zionism into feeble cliques. Thus, because of the vital need to preserve the formal unity of the World Zionist Organization, the rights of the minor parties were always respected; they were granted representation on the Executive and the Council which ran affairs between World Congresses, and their members were appointed to posts in the Zionist bureaucracy.

In time, the Zionist parties developed their own organizations and agencies in countries of heaviest Jewish concentration; and when their members immigrated into Palestine, they brought with them the party baggage and flag. In the 1920's the newly arrived Zionists set up a constitutional framework for the entire Jewish community in Palestine and sought recognition for it from the Mandatory administration together with the right to levy rates from the community's members. Both recognition and right were granted, but on condition of ensuring a proportional representation to ethnic groups in the community and of reserving to every individual the right to contract out of the community altogether. Thus the same voluntary method and the same imperative to include as many members as possible and preserve external unity that prevailed in the World Zionist Organization acted in the self-governing institutions of the Yishuv to ensure the adoption of proportional representation and to protect the life of the smallest independent faction. In the case of the Yishuv, the drive towards individual party life was even accentuated because each of the units had the opportunity to implement its ideological utopia, whether in the form of a collective kibbutz, free-enterprise exploitation of orange groves, the setting up of cooperatives, or the establishment of religious colleges.

When the state was declared in 1948, the parties had been already too well established to allow for even the thought of change. Each had developed its own ideology, its own institutions, its own rhetoric, its own oligarchy, and its own vested interest, and most of them had been accustomed to living, working, and fighting with each other. When the first provisional government of Israel issued its ordinance calling for elections to the first sovereign Knesset, it prescribed proportional representation as the natural method of election.

2. INTENSITY OF PARTY POLITICS

In a climate suffused with the pragmatism of American and British politics the term "ideology" carries connotations of dogmatism, lack of realism, and fanaticism in the same way that the term "propaganda" bears undertones of lying and deception. Both terms are associated with the narrow-minded, intolerant, and violent politics of Central and Eastern Europe, which are wholly incomprehensible to the Anglo-Saxon mind. Even the British Labour Party, which calls itself socialist, endeavors to distinguish its socialism from the continental ideologies that go by that name. Its own socialism, as it continually asserts, has its roots in *British* thought and, as the leaders of the party never tire of repeating, it is eminently pragmatic and practical. When American and British parties and politicians talk about abstract ideas, they speak of "principles," never ideologies; and when they seek to spread their views, they resort to "publicity," never to propaganda, or—God forbid!—to indoctrination. For that last term, Americans have invented a very graphic expression which reflects all the horror it evokes here: brain-washing.

In Israel, a party that does not profess an ideology and does not engage actively in indoctrination is not worth its salt. It is not really considered to be a party but a group of opportunists who are only thirsty for power and self-aggrandizement. A newly established party, like the Liberal, finds it necessary to launch its career by publishing a series of ideological dissertations, even though the party is not really new but a merger of two previously existing parties, and even when the ideology professed is a rehash of the main tenets of obsolescent nineteenth-century liberal philosophy. Every party has an organ devoted wholly or in part to discussion of "fundamental questions"; it has its *idéologues,* its itinerant speakers, its school for "activists," its seminars and "study days," its cultural committees and its clubs. Old-timers in the parties bemoan today the decline of ideological fervor among the young generation and view it as a sign of a weakening of the moral fiber of Israel. Typical are the titles which a Mapai *idéologue* gave to some of his essays in a recent "soul-searching" study published by the party press: "The heroes are tired, or the decline of ideology"; "For the lack of ideological vision, the people shall be chastised"; "Let us restore the crown of socialist Zionism to its glory," and so on.

In seeking the reasons for this phenomenon, we must review our earlier considerations of some of the peculiarities of Zionism as a nationalist movement. Because Zionism was a movement that emerged among a widely scattered people who were everywhere a minority, because it lacked any means of coercion and had no substantial foothold in the territory to which it laid claim, it could only rely on persuasion and moral pressure to achieve its aims, at least until it could establish a position permitting it to use other means. It needed to persuade the persecuted Jews that its program was the only solution to their suffering, the emancipated and assimilated that it offered them the only guarantee of their security and dignity, and the traditionalists that its scheme was in the best spirit of Judaism; it had to make some world powers believe that it was in their best interest to support it, and convince all and sundry that its project was practically realizable. To accomplish all this and to answer the objections of the disinterested and the hostile among Jews and Gentiles, it had to develop a whole sociology on the nature and causes of anti-Semitism, produce a reinterpretation of the history and eschatology of Judaism, and make continual reassessments of world power realities as they might affect or be affected by Zionism and Palestine. All of these quickly built up into a general stockpile of ideology on which all parties in the movement drew, and to which they made specific additions, each according to its inclination.

Zionism did not content itself with mere expressions of allegiance and moral and political support on the part of its members. When it became apparent that Herzl's grand scheme for obtaining a charter and organizing a general exodus from Europe had failed, the movement directed its effort toward slow, piecemeal colonization work in Palestine based on the labors of small numbers of pioneers. Since conditions in the country were very difficult and life there involved great hardships and sacrifice, candidates to do the work could be recruited only through prior intensive indoctrination or ideological self-intoxication. As the Zionist endeavor progressed and succeeded, the original pioneers became the founders and leaders of most of the country's institutions and parties and left on them the imprint of their predilection for ideology.

But probably the most significant reason for the indulgence of Israeli parties in ideology lies in the circumstances in which Zionism and Zionist parties grew in Eastern Europe in the last decades of the nineteenth century and the early decades of the twentieth. Zionism reached Eastern Europe at a time when Judaism there was confronting a most severe crisis as a result of the impact of the Enlightenment and the frustrating conditions of Jewish existence. Large numbers of Jews in Tsarist Russia and Poland who had managed to acquire a modern education during the short period of relative liberalism in the sixties and seventies became convinced, like many Christians around them in similar circumstances, that their religion was obsolete, superstitious, false, opposed to progress, or harmful. The initial reaction of some of them was to abandon their faith, substitute for it one of the many current liberal, populist, or socialist philosophies, and join groups of Russians in similar circumstances in seeking to spread the principles of their favorite philosophy and in endeavoring to reform or transform Russian society in accordance with them. But the reaction which set in after 1881, and particularly the pogroms, which were often condoned tacitly by Russian "progressive" and revolutionary groups, made many of these Jews realize that their Jewishness set them apart and would make it impossible for them to live their philosophy even in a transformed Russian environment. They were thus alienated from their own still orthodox brethren as well as from the Gentiles. Other educated Jews, who were not attracted to any of the Russian reformist or revolutionary groups, had tried to establish their identity not on the basis of religion, in which they had ceased to believe, but on the grounds of an enlightened secular Jewish culture which they endeavored to create themselves. But although their effort produced the beginnings of a substantial and varied literature in Hebrew and in Yiddish, the ultimate success of their efforts seemed to be handicapped by the limitations imposed on their work by the uncertain conditions and prospects of their people. It was in this atmosphere that Zionism made its appearance in Eastern Europe, when large numbers of educated Jews had lost their moorings in traditional Judaism and had been frustrated in their attempts to find an alternative philosophy and identity. To these people, and to others who would have reached the same blind alley later, it came as a heaven-sent outlet, providing them with the opportunity to give up Judaism for their preferred philosophies while remaining Jews. Thus grew the multitude of hyphenated Zionist groups with ideologies that were not merely political doctrines, but religion-surrogates for a generation of people who had lost their inherited faith.

Because Zionist commitment filled the role of religion even for the secularists, Zionist politics assumed a total, passionate, explosive character, which was carried over into Israeli politics. Parties fought each other with a bitterness and a relentlessness reminiscent of religious controversy. Tolerance was virtually unknown, not to speak of forbearance and respect for the opponent's views. The knowledge that they all must try to preserve at least the semblance of unity vis à vis the enemies and potential supporters of Zionism on the outside set some limits upon the ultimate practical conclusions to which the parties might push their warfare; but these restraints served to heighten all the more the intensity and drama of the struggle within the vague boundaries of the permissible. Every group strove to maintain its ideological purity and viewed compromise as tainted with sin; even minor tactical differences were sufficient grounds for the

definition of a new faction and for endless haggling amidst flam-
boyant oratory.

Perhaps in speaking of Zionist politics a distinction should be
made between the attitudes of Eastern European and Western Jews
which, incidentally, would serve to underline the importance of the
coincidence between the religious crisis and the appearance of
Zionism among the Jewish communities of Eastern Europe. By the
middle of the nineteenth century Western Jews had been able to
make an uneasy adjustment to the Enlightenment by reinterpreting
their Judaism so as to enable them to live in most respects by the
light of the principles of the society around them. When Zionism
appeared, its adherents in that part of the world saw it as a strictly
political movement with a mild humanitarian and philanthropic
flavor involving them in one more commitment added to the many
others they already had. Members of the movement brought up in
the West and prominent Zionists like Herbert Samuel, Justice
Brandeis, the Rothschilds, never therefore considered Zionism as the
be-all and end-all of existence as their East European colleagues
did, and parties which had their strongholds in the West—the General Zionists for example—never quite developed the fierce devotion
of the Eastern European parties. This distinction, however, does
not bear much relevance to the politics of Israel since most of the
parties operating there were founded, led, and supported primarily
by Eastern European Jews.

Illustrations of the passion with which Israeli parties have carried
on their politics are embarrassingly abundant. As one instance, some
left-wing factions seceded from Mapai in 1946, and two years later
united with the extreme left-wing movement of Hashomer Hatzair
to constitute the United Workers Party (Mapam), which became
the chief rival of Mapai for the vote of the workers. The struggle
between these two parties became so intense that, in many kibbutzim, secessionists from Mapai and loyalists felt they could no
longer live together. Whichever group was in the majority expelled
the minority, and in some cases, sections of one and the same kibbutz had to be segregated by barbed wire. Lifelong friendships
were broken, children who had grown together were separated,
families were sometimes sundered, and all over such issues as
whether or not Mapai had sold out to the capitalists and whether or
not Mapam had sold out to the Russians. The irony of it was

that within a year after the climax of this controversy Mapam itself
was split three ways over the implications of the Prague Trial and
the Moscow Doctors' Plot (see below). Another example relates
to the controversy that flared up in 1952 over the acceptance of
German reparations. The opposition, composed on that occasion
of Mapam and Herut, lashed at the government with such fury that
the only charge missing was that of actually participating in the
murder of the Jews in Europe. The leader of Herut even saw fit
to march a mass of demonstrators on the Knesset, both leader and
followers in a state of outright hysteria. In view of the touchy background of the issue, one might have thought this an extreme example were it not for the fact that once the reparations agreement
had been signed and reparations goods began actually to flow, the
entire subject was inexplicably dropped from the agenda of party
warfare. A more recent example may be seen in the notorious
"Lavon Affair" (see below). The complete record of the ins and
outs of this issue will not be known for a long time, if ever; but
it is clear even now that the whole problem could have been resolved
at several junctures were it not for the passion and intransigence
with which the protagonists preferred to pursue their struggle. In
the end, what was basically a quarrel between a minister and his
subordinates, all of whom were members of Mapai, was turned into
an ideological and political free-for-all which lasted over a year and
paralyzed normal government and political life.

Crises such as these tell much about the temper of Israeli politics;
but the uninitiated observer from more sedate political climates can
easily read too much into them. One has to realize that Israeli
politics are *normally* keyed to a very high pitch in order to assess
the importance of outbreaks of this sort. The fact is that after each
of the crises mentioned, the parties concerned were ready to sit
together in the same government, and most of them actually did,
except for the Communists and Herut which Ben Gurion insists
on ostracizing. It is a *normal* thing to denounce the tactics of one's
opponents not as opportunistic or even sharp, but as "sins and
crimes"—to quote a recent utterance of Ben Gurion. It is *normal*
for a religious spokesman arguing against a bill to safeguard property acquired by a wife after marriage to denounce it as an instrument that is bound to lead to "the utter destruction of family life
in Israel." It is not considered unusual when a casual visit of a

German cleric to a high school class brings upon the head of the Minister of Education the charge that he is insensitive to the German massacre of his people. Hyperbole, passion, cataclysmic oratory, and occasional outbreaks of fanatic zeal against the opponent are the stuff of Israel's everyday politics. They are the burnt offerings made by the parties to their ideological deities as ritual homage, and perhaps to propitiate them for sins committed against them in a world that so insists on compromise. And, from a more distant past, the fury and splendid invective of the prophets seem to echo again in the land.

3. RAMIFICATION OF PARTY ACTIVITY

American parties are organized primarily for the purpose of capturing power during election contests. In the interim, they may issue partisan political bulletins and serve as social clubs on the local level. During the heyday of bossism, the ward politicians also engaged in some social and charitable activities, but these were clearly subordinate to the main function of vote-getting.

In Israel the elections are often less significant than other widespread activities of the party which occupy most of its energy, its staff, and its financial resources day by day. Parties have helped build agricultural settlements and industries and founded schools and clinics; they have their own publishing houses, issue newspapers and periodicals, establish cultural centers and synagogues, develop housing projects, maintain sports clubs and sponsor youth movements; in the past they have even supported their own military and paramilitary organizations. To carry on all these activities the parties employ relatively large permanent staffs, and to finance them they have founded their own banks and other credit organizations and run their own fund collections in the country and abroad. To account for this extraordinary ramification of party activity in Israel one must go, once again, to Yishuv days and to the peculiar circumstances of the emergence of the Jewish state.

Many new states have come into being in recent years when societies which had long existed as subject communities finally achieved their independence. In the case of Israel, however, the society that gained its independence in 1948 did not exist at all only a generation or two before; it was created by the deliberate action of men who had lived elsewhere. These men came to Palestine and banded together into small groups to build a new society on the basis of definite ideas which each group had as to what that society should be like. As the total endeavor progressed and central institutions endowed with funds made available by Zionists and Jews everywhere were established in Palestine, these small groups became political parties competing for influence over these institutions though all were partners in them or beneficiaries of their funds. Newcomers who did not already belong to a party were immediately absorbed into one or another, so that at the time of the establishment of the state most of the population was politically affiliated. One can say, then, that whereas everywhere else societies give birth to political parties and determine their character, in Israel it was the parties that gave birth to society and shaped its character.

The most remarkable manifestation of this tendency today is the Histadrut—the General Federation of Jewish Workers, founded in 1920 by representatives of two socialist parties. So important is this organization that it deserves separate consideration in this, as in any study of Israel (see Chapter IX). Suffice it to say here that such is its economic, social, and political power that some of its leaders have claimed for it parity with or even priority over the state. The success of the Histadrut, controlled nowadays by Mapai, led other parties to develop, in competition, similar institutions of their own. The religious Poel Hammizrachi, for example, founded the Histadrut Hapoel Hammizrachi, and the Revisionists—the ancestors of Herut—founded the Histadrut Ovdim Leummiyim, the Histadrut of Nationalist Workers. These organizations never approached the Histadrut in wealth and power, but they became strong enough to prevent members of their founding parties from being absorbed by the Histadrut and contributed in any case to reinforcing the pattern of ramification of party activities beyond the immediate strictly political sphere. Other parties, which did not or could not aspire to imitate the Histadrut in the comprehensiveness of its operations, concentrated their extra-electoral activity in selected fields. Thus the Mizrachi concentrated on building a network of religiously oriented schools; the Agudat Yisrael on founding and supporting Yeshivot— Talmudic and theological colleges; the General Zionists on general secular schools, sports, and boy-scout organizations. All parties without exception have their own daily newspaper in Hebrew and, in most cases, publish other periodicals in several languages; and all of them have at least one bank or financing institution of their own and several cooperative economic enterprises or other types of economic association.

The assumption of nonpolitical activities by the Israeli parties, together with their addiction to ideology, has had the effect of strengthening party loyalties to an extent unimaginable in America or in the West in general outside the hard core of devotees of the Communist parties. The establishment of the state and its assumption of primary responsibility in fields which had been previously in the hands of partisan organizations, such as education, social security, housing, semimilitary pioneering operations and others, together with the mass immigration of Jews who had had no previous contact with Zionist politics have done much to weaken or check the spread of this phenomenon. But even today the floating vote in Israel is extremely small, and one fourth to one third of the voters are estimated to be card-carrying party members. The number of Israelis today who implicitly equate what is good for their party with what is good for the country would probably shock Americans; but since our quantitative social scientists never checked on it at the time, nobody knows how *few* were the Israelis who *did not* think in such terms, say in January 1949, when the first national elections took place.

4. CENTRALIZATION OF PARTY AUTHORITY

In America we are used to the idea that each of the national parties is a confederation of scores of sectional and local parties which comes to life once every four years to nominate and try to elect a president. For the rest of the time, and for purposes of other electoral contests, the local party is virtually independent of any central national organization. Hence it is not surprising to Americans that sectional or local leaders in state or local positions or in Congress are able for years and years to defy the national party leadership as long as they mend their fences back home.

In Israel such independence from the party center in any position at any level is almost unheard of. There is not in Israel even the slight degree of local and individual independence that is to be found in British parties which have presented to American students of government models of centralization and discipline to be admired or denounced. In Britain, at least, the constituency parties have the main say in selecting their candidate for Parliament and, despite the proverbial docility of Members of Parliament in general, this system has consistently produced a sufficient number of strong or troublesome individuals to compel the party leadership in Parliament not to take the support of its rank-and-file completely for granted.

In Israel, the election system does not recognize even the theoretical possibility of an independent candidate. If someone wants to run for the Knesset on his own he has to constitute himself first into a party, present a "list" of himself approved by a thousand signatures, and poll at least one per cent of the total national vote before his list can be considered in figuring the outcome. In the Knesset, under the prevailing rule of proportional distribution of time, he will be allocated exactly five minutes to speak on bills and major debates; and under the rule of proportional representation in committees, is not likely to receive any assignment at all. In short, he will be virtually useless unless he "allies" himself with some faction, in which case he ceases to be independent. In the First Knesset there was one such case when the leader of the former terrorist group known as the Stern Gang was elected and tried to remain independent; it never happened again.

Thus Israel's electoral system provides the key mechanism for maintaining the central authority of the party leadership. The voters do not choose candidates but party lists; they have no right to change the order of the candidates on the lists or to write in any. Since the distribution of strength of the various Israeli parties has shown itself to be relatively stable in the course of five elections, ranking on the list is tantamount to election or defeat except for a few borderline cases. And the ranking is done in all parties by their respective central bodies.

Because the Knesset Member owes his election so entirely and absolutely to the central party authority—he has no constituency of his own to back him, he was not personally elected, the campaign was entirely financed by the party, his name was placed where it was on the list by the party—his allegiance and obedience to that authority cannot be less than entire and absolute if he cares to be re-elected. This imperative applies to his voting in the Knesset as well as to his work on its committees; it applies to his right to speak and sometimes even to the specific content of his speech.

The import of the remarks about the subjection of the Knesset Member to the party leadership must be qualified by the observation —itself of importance in understanding the power structure within the Israeli parties—that for the most part the Knesset Members are themselves of that leadership. Because the number of parties is so large and the total membership of the Knesset is so small—only 120—each party can return only relatively few members. Mapai, the largest party, has never returned even fifty Knesset Members, while the second largest party has never returned twenty-five. Such a small number of seats for each party does not even suffice to take care of all the members of the central committees which *approve* the lists of candidates, and in some cases the number of Knesset seats won is not even enough to provide for all the members of the respective party executives that *draw* such lists. Consequently the chances for candidates below the very top of the party hierarchy are exceedingly slim, and the names of old party stalwarts have in fact filled the rosters of the Knesset again and again. As a result, the Knesset has not served as a training ground for future leaders as the British Parliament and the American Congress have done, but has tended to be almost exclusively the club for the ruling oligarchies of the various parties. Little wonder that as much as 65 per cent of the membership of the Third Knesset and 56 per cent of that of the Fourth was over fifty-one years old.

These percentages point to the dim prospects for a young politician to work his way upward inside the parties to the top of the hierarchies within a reasonable period of time. A much clearer indication emerges from a study of the Mapai leadership undertaken in 1956 by the Israel Institute of Social Research. This study found that in the largest of Israel's parties and the one which disposed of the largest number of positions of leadership, more than half of the leaders in 390 top positions were past forty-five. Nearly three out of four had come from Russia or Poland as early as 1900–1910, usually as members of a youth movement; four out of five had come to the country before 1940. Twelve per cent of these leaders, or about forty-five individuals, had each held ten or more positions in party or government. Half of the leaders did not finish secondary education and only 13 per cent had finished some university. The picture that emerges is unmistakable. It is one of men with a common background and a common mentality who have struggled hard, and who have won and lost many battles together while "others" were having it easy; and now that the dream of a national state has been achieved, they are not going to let those others tell them what they should do with it. Not, at least, if they can help it.

The basic formal pattern of internal party organization resembles in all cases the structure of the World Zionist Organization and the Yishuv self-government. A party convention elects a council of party leaders and representatives of local branches to serve as a supreme body. The council elects a smaller central committee which in turn delegates authority to a small executive and secretariat. Actually, conventions have been very irregularly called, and councils have rarely met, so that real power has rested in the hands of oligarchies constituted as executives, secretariats, and central committees which now and then co-opted some new members as they were needed.

In recent years attempts have been made by a few of the parties to shift their structures a little in order to allow for greater mobility within. They were sparked by the action of a few of the topmost leaders of Mapai, headed by Ben Gurion, who had been concerned about their party's obvious loss of vitality and, above all, by its failure to produce men whom they considered fit to take over and give the country the leadership it needs under its new and rapidly changing conditions. Taking advantage of an election setback in 1955, these leaders set in motion a movement aimed at reinvigorating and rejuvenating the party through a high degree of decentralization and democratization. A party convention was assembled in 1956—the first in seven years—and adopted a new constitution which empowered two hundred district branches to nominate two thirds of the candidates to a Central Committee of 196 and two thirds of the candidates to the Knesset—measures which were obviously designed to clip the wings of the old guard reigning in the central organs of the party. The old guard fought back in several ways. It managed to have the proportion of Knesset candidates nominated by the branches reduced from two thirds to one half. It was probably behind the highly unusual phenomenon which occurred in 1958 when Mapai lost strength in the Histadrut elections but gained in national elections. In any case, the power struggle undoubtedly spread to the Histadrut and combined with other as yet unclear factors to produce the Lavon Affair. As of now the outcome of the initiative for reform has been to cause a deep breach in Mapai. The breach was temporarily bridged over by the August 1961 elections, which also gave Ben Gurion a temporary victory inside his party. Whether Ben Gurion will rest content with these results or will resume the struggle and fight his opponents to the end cannot be predicted. In the meantime, it is important to recall that the party's constitutional reform has failed so far to produce any significant change. Dayan, Peres, and Eban, the three "young" Mapai leaders who have emerged since Ben Gurion's reform drive, were not thrown up by the reformed party organization but were adopted by the old process of co-option.

5. EFFECT OF PARTY CHARACTER ON THE POLITICAL SYSTEM

In the course of our analysis of the special characteristics of Israeli parties we have indicated both by implication and by example some of the particular consequences to which they led. In the next few pages we shall consider briefly the collective impact of these characteristics on the Israeli political system as a whole and shall then venture some remarks about the future prospects of Israeli politics.

The multiplicity of parties in Israel and the wide variety of their ideological coloring offer the Israeli voter an unusual choice of programs and orientations. To that extent the multiparty system may seem more "democratic" than the two-party system which often gives the American voter, for example, few alternatives. It should be recalled, however, that having chosen the party which best expresses his wishes, the Israeli voter never has the chance of seeing that program realized in full, because under the existing system of proportional representation and firm party allegiance, no single party is able to obtain the necessary majority to put through its program. All governments must be coalition governments based on compromise, and this dilutes considerably the programs of the parties included. This is not to say that compromise in itself is bad, of course; on the contrary, it is the basic characteristic of democracy everywhere and takes place also within the two-party system. However, in a two-party system it takes place mainly *before* the election, and the voter can therefore know in advance what sort of compromise he is voting for, whereas in Israel the voter is never sure of the ultimate compromise since this will depend on the nature of the coalition that will be formed *after* the elections.

The difference in timing of the inevitable compromise has further implications of great importance for Israeli political life. Where a compromise has to be formulated after the elections it is bound to be more difficult to achieve, is likely to be less enduring, and is sure to be more repugnant to the average voter from a moral viewpoint than where it is reached quietly before the elections. For elections everywhere, and especially in Israel, stress the differences rather than the common elements among the various parties, involve bitter attacks against the opposition, impel the parties to "rededicate" themselves to their original "pure and unsullied" principles, and in general arouse to a high pitch the spirit of partisanship and belligerence. To compromise at all after the bitterness of an election is an act which is likely to cast a doubt on the sincerity of the leaders involved; to compromise easily, without giving ample evidence of a deep reluctance to do so and without standing unflinchingly on at least some points of "principle," is bound to be viewed by the recently aroused party faithful as plain cynicism. Hence, the formation of a government in Israel after elections has always been a long, painful, wearing process involving a dangerous demoralization of the public and a considerable danger to the stability of democracy in the country. Parties must agree over the prospective government's program in detail and the distribution of portfolios within it, and in the process of bargaining the two topics invariably merge into one. Thus a demand by a religious party to include in the program the enactment of a Sabbath or pork import law, for example, may be traded for a ministry or a department; and a demand for an "economic ministry" by Achdut Haavoda may be traded for a less important one plus a commitment not to sell arms to Germany in the lifetime of the envisaged government. Ministries are dismembered and their departments are shuffled around to allow greater maneuverability for the negotiators, and absurd combinations of titles and positions are made. The social security administration, for example, may be annexed to the Ministry of Labor or it may be shifted to the Ministry of Development; Tourism may remain in the Prime Minister's Office or it may be shifted to Commerce and Industry; one minister may hold three portfolios while other ministers may hold none; a ministry like Defense may duplicate the functions of several other ministries, while several separate ministries may be set up for Posts, for Information, for Police, for Religions, and for Tourism. All this is done in the glare of publicity while the public is left waiting for months and the Knesset is paralyzed; and all the while each party stresses the horrors of it all even as it throws the responsibility on the other parties. The irony of this whole situation has been that after the long agonies of birth, the governments that have finally issued have for the most part had a relatively short and contentious existence which has ended in a storm long before its formal appointed term, and necessitated the resumption of the irritating process.

In the fourteen years of her existence, Israel has had five Knessets and eleven governments. Only one of the four dissolved Knessets had come near the end of its four-year term; the other three dissolved themselves when, after the resignation of a government, complete deadlock had been reached and no new coalition could be formed. Two or three of the governments fell after the resignation of the Prime Minister for "personal reasons"; all the other cases were the result of coalition crises over various issues which included conflicts over religious subjects (three crises), conflict over deliberate leakage of information on the sale of arms to Germany, conflict over the hoisting of red flags on schools on May Day, conflict over the addition of a new ministry and the delineation of its jurisdiction.

The character of precariously constructed coalitions that Israeli governments have invariably had has led to a lack of central direction in the administration of the country and to serious deficiencies in the coordination of its development. Ministries tend to become the preserves of the various parties, and projects sponsored by them tend to receive a higher or lower priority depending on the political coloration of the minister in charge as well as on their intrinsic merit. A Minister of Labor belonging to Mapai may get the approval of the Mapai-controlled Treasury to vast housing schemes with a minimum of trouble while a development project sponsored by an Achdut Haavoda minister may have very hard going; Tourism under the Prime Minister's Office may obtain all the money it needs to develop this income-producing branch while income-producing and vital telephone development may be left to lag woefully under some minor-party Minister of Posts. Mapai's important ministries may recurit their staff more or less in accordance with the advanced civil service regulations of the country while lesser ministries and ministries of other parties may be turned into agencies to subsidize the "higher" pursuits of party members.

All the governments that have been formed in Israel have been dominated by Mapai. This is partly due to the fact that, with the average third of the Knesset seats it has been able to gain continually, it is by far the strongest party. But more than that, it is the result of the particular position that Mapai occupies at the center of the Israeli political spectrum. Mapai can draw partners for a coalition from its immediate right as well as from its immediate left, and from one and all of the religious parties. Its opponents, on the other hand, cannot muster a majority unless they all coalesce, and this they have never been able to do because they are too far flung to the right and to the left. A decisive illustration of this situation was provided by the aftermath of the 1961 elections. After the most bitter campaign in Israel's history, the main one-time partners of Mapai—the Liberals, the National Religious Party, Mapam, and Achdut Haavoda—formed a common front which vowed to punish Mapai by at least compelling it to accept parity with the four in the next government. But the fact that the front could form a government without Mapai only by drawing Herut into the partnership—to which the two left-wing parties objected —deprived it of the ultimate sanction against Mapai and, after an unusually long stalemate, the front broke up and its members filed in to negotiate separately with Mapai.

The dispersal of Mapai's opponents has another equally important consequence for the Israeli political system. For the same reason that it assures the dominant position of Mapai, it ensures the absence of a constructive and responsible opposition. As often as not the formation of a government by Mapai and its allies left an opposition which had very little in common beyond general hostility to the government. Its criticism did not therefore present any coherent pattern implying an alternative program; and since the opposition as a whole was never "in danger" of having some day to assume responsibility for making good on its suggestions, it could afford to take the most extreme positions suggested by the dictates of demagoguery. The Israeli voters thus found themselves over and again in a situation in which the majority had had quite enough of the rule of a Mapai grown fat and complacent, but had no hope of seeing any alternative materialize. The blame is of course largely theirs since they cannot agree in sufficient strength on the alternative to Mapai; but this makes the situation nonetheless ominous for Israeli democracy.

Another peculiarity produced by the Israeli system has been the unusually strong influence of the religious parties in comparison with their real electoral strength. In principle, Mapai always favored the formation of broad coalitions because this made any single one of its partners in the government dispensable and therefore more tractable. In practice, however, Mapai has had to rely a great deal on the religious parties because these confined their demands to an area to which Mapai was on the whole indifferent, while the other parties insisted on concessions in the field of foreign and internal economic and social policies which were central to its interest. For Mapai this arrangement has obvious advantages; but for the country at large it means the imposition on the majority of the population of far-reaching restrictions based on religion owing to the balance-of-power position of minority religious parties.

6. RECENT TRENDS IN ISRAELI PARTY LIFE

Although observers who have followed closely the unfolding of the latest of Israel's crises—the Lavon Affair and its aftermath—may doubt it at first, many of the underlying patterns of Israeli political behavior have been altering slowly but surely. The crucial fact about Israel is that the main features of her life (and this includes politics as well as economy, society, and culture) had been established before the emergence of the state under the impact of influences and forces which were operative at that time. As these influences and forces disappear or weaken in the new conditions brought about by the establishment and development of the state, those features of Israeli life which had been shaped by them slowly alter too. The readjustment involves the painful surrender of cherished habits and ideas and the encroachment on the vested interest of many institutions and individuals; it should not be surprising therefore that it is punctuated by many crises, of which the Lavon Affair will surely not be the last. There are indications, however, that it is nevertheless proceeding apace and that it is pointing on the whole in the right direction, at least in the sphere of politics.

One of the first impressions felt by a visitor to Israel now, after several years of absence, is the very evident decline of ideology in the political life of the country. Among the aging potentates of some parties one can still hear the old slogans and jargon; but even they recognize and bemoan the fact that theirs are increasingly becoming voices in the wilderness. As the fact of contemporary Israel replaced what had been several theoretical alternatives, and as the state assumed many tasks which could previously be done voluntarily only through ideological intoxication, many of the old issues became obsolete. But probably the chief factor has been the nature of the immigration that has multiplied by two and a half the initial population of Israel. The hundreds of thousands of immigrants from the Muslim world have brought no doctrinaire political traditions in their meager baggage; and the bulk of the immigrants from Eastern Europe have known ideology in their countries of origin as a cover for repression and as something to be suspected. Since these immigrants acquired the right to vote the moment they landed in the country, political parties have been compelled to appeal to them increasingly on matters of sentiment, the personality of the leadership, and the bread-and-butter issues so familiar to American and British voters.

Along with the decline of ideology there has been a weakening in the intensity of party loyalty. Before the establishment of the state, a man was a Labor-Zionist, a Revisionist-Zionist, or some other party-hyphen-Zionist; today this man is an Israeli *tout court,* or if a hyphen is added it comes after Israeli and is more likely to refer to his profession than to his political coloration. This development was helped by the fact that the state provides many richer symbols attracting loyalty than does Zionism and by the fact that, under Ben Gurion's direction, it has taken over many of the functions which had been previously performed by political parties. Thus education has become national, and so have social security, the labor exchanges, frontier settlement, and other services. There is even serious talk in some Mapai circles of setting up a national health service, although this might weaken the Sick Fund of the Histadrut which has been one of its chief sources of strength.

The movement away from the climate of the Zionist Organization and Yishuv politics which these developments have fostered has also led to an increasing concern with ways and means of over-coming the worst legacy inherited from those days: the excessive multiplicity of parties. Several hopeful developments in this direc-tion have already taken place in recent years. Not only were all the newcomers assimilated into the existing main parties and produced no enduring new groupings of their own, but several ethnically based lists which had been successful in the First and Second Knessets were wiped out. Another important development has been a tendency on the part of several existing parties to merge. Thus the Mizrachi and Poel Hammizrachi have merged to form the National Religious Party which is now seeking to draw Poalei Agudat Yisrael; and the Progressives have merged with the Gen-eral Zionists to form the Liberal Party, which considered for a time the question of a merger with Herut. A continuation of this tendency offers the best hope for the Israeli political system though the merger and subsequent split of Mapam and Achdut Haavoda should serve as a warning against expectations of rapid progress in definitive steps.

Some Israeli leaders, headed by Ben Gurion, have urged with an insistence bordering on obsession the substitution of constituency representation for proportional representation as the best method of remedying the ills caused by the multiplicity of parties and the concomitant necessity of coalition government. On the face of it, Ben Gurion's proposal seems sound, and the agitation on the part of Mapai for such a reform may appear as another hopeful sign. In fact, however, such a measure has small chance of adoption at present, and if it were adopted at this stage would probably raise more problems than it would resolve. Constituency representation favors parties whose strength is spread in small concentrations in all parts of the country over parties whose strength is too thinly spread throughout or too concentrated in certain areas. In the last case all the votes in excess of a plurality are wasted; in the second all those short of a plurality are wasted; whereas in the first case the economy of votes is optimal. Among the parties of Israel only Mapai's distribution of strength conforms to the optimal pattern; the other parties, except perhaps the Liberal, have their strength too concentrated or too thinly spread. It may therefore be true that constituency representation would produce one party with a clear Knesset majority; but since that party is sure to be Mapai, the other parties object to adopting that system, while Mapai alone cannot muster a majority for its adoption.

But even if Mapai were somehow able to achieve a majority to pass the reform legislation, such a step now might have disastrous consequences. Apart from the fact that it would constitute a drastic legal repression of the minority parties, it would result in installing one majority party which would be confronted by an opposition too variegated and scattered to check it or provide an alternative to it; all this in a situation in which there is no constitution to impose even minimal limits on the powers of a simple majority of the legislature. It would take a party of angels not to abuse such unlimited power.

The truth is that Israeli political opinion is as yet too divided to be ready for a two-party system or an approximation thereof. Progress in that direction can be achieved by means of mergers effected through political give and take and not by attempts to fit Israeli opinion in a procrustean bed. A real breakthrough may occur if the Liberals merge with Herut, or Mapai with Achdut Haavoda; whichever comes first is likely to precipitate the other. In that case there would be a major left-wing and a major right-wing party, each capable of forming a government alone or with the help of a unified religious bloc, or of presenting a coherent alternative program in opposition to the government. Then, but only then, can the election system be reformed to fix the new configuration and prevent it from degenerating toward the old pattern. The chances for such a breakthrough improve continually as the influences mentioned in the preceding pages continue to operate. They will be decisively improved when the present old guard in the various parties is gone, or if it is pushed aside by younger men who were not involved in fighting the old battles. In this respect, the struggle now going on in Mapai is of transcending significance. Its outcome is not yet clear.

IX

The Histadrut: Labor's State within the State

The Histadrut is the most important, most original, and most problematic institution bequeathed to the state of Israel by the Yishuv. To the outside world, the Histadrut is primarily known as a federation of trade unions. Actually, it is a huge, comprehensive organization without parallel anywhere; it is almost a state within the state. It has a trade union section which encompasses the overwhelming majority of Israel's working population; but it is also the biggest employer in the country—bigger than the government—and has vast interests extending into agricultural and industrial production, commerce, insurance, finance and banking, housing and construction, land, sea, and air transport, health, education, welfare, culture and the arts. The Histadrut is also intimately involved in politics, and not only because its extensive interests inevitably lead to its having extensive dealings with the government. It is itself governed by politics in the sense that various well-defined parties formally compete in electoral contests for the ruling positions within it. Moreover, since these parties happen to be identical for the most part with parties that compete for power in the national arena, the Histadrut finds itself directly involved in national politics. Because of its enormous actual and potential impact for good or evil on the economy, society, and politics of Israel, an assessment of the Histadrut, its role and problems, is indispensable for an understanding of that nation.

The role of the Histadrut in the development of the Yishuv and the birth and growth of Israel was nothing less than crucial. It was the most important instrument in shaping the character of the Jewish endeavor in Palestine, was an invaluable force in the struggle on many fronts for winning independence and defending and developing the new state, and was a decisive influence in the molding of Israel's welfare society. However, in the last eight or nine years, the Histadrut has presented Israel with at least as many grave problems as it has made important contributions to her development. There are many different reasons for the trouble, but they are all related essentially to the need of the Histadrut to redefine its aims and readjust its organization and institutions in the light of new and unforeseen realities, and its inability to do so. The problem is only partly a failure of leadership and intellectual acumen; it is much more one of vested interest mixed with intricate power politics and honest but oftentimes narrow ideological commitment. As with the failure to agree on a constitution, it is a case of excessive rigidity being built into the existing order. But with the Histadrut the situation is worse because there has been no indication so far of even a modest process of adjustment, as there has been in the constitutional and political sphere, and because the tensions within it seem even more relentless. The aim of this chapter will be to describe briefly the scope of the Histadrut's operations and the contributions of its activities and policies to the social order of the Yishuv and Israel, and then to analyze some of the main problems involved in the present position and role of the Histadrut in Israel.

1. THE ACTIVITIES OF THE HISTADRUT AND ITS ACHIEVEMENTS

The Histadrut was conceived and built by men of the Second and Third Aliyot. Its structure and development reflect the socialist and Zionist ideals of its founders, and their belief that the two harmonized and complemented each other. Zionism, as they understood it, provided the opportunity of building afresh the good society in Palestine, unencumbered by the unfavorable conditions of Jewish existence in the Diaspora; while the creation of a just society under socialism seemed to them best calculated to facilitate the task of recruiting and building the workers' and farmers' base necessary for creating a normal nation in Palestine. Hence, the Histadrut was from the outset not merely a trade union movement, but a comprehensive organization aimed at creating a labor commonwealth; and it was not purely a socialist movement, but also a Zionist organization committed to advancing the national cause in every respect. This multiplicity of purposes is reflected in the extremely variegated activities of the Histadrut and accounts for much of its power and influence in the past and the present. But it is also at the root of some of the most difficult problems that have troubled it in recent years.

The activities of the Histadrut and its achievements may be reviewed under five headings: production, trade union work, social services, education, and miscellaneous activities of national concern.

Production

From the time of its foundation in 1920, the Histadrut became involved in economic activities far beyond the scope of the traditional trade union. Partly out of socialist belief and partly out of the necessity of creating employment for its membership, which increased with the arrival of every immigrant ship, it encouraged its members to organize themselves into producers' cooperatives, bought enterprises that were about to dissolve, in order to save the employees' jobs, and founded enterprises of its own. Because its activities were viewed as an effective means of colonization and of absorbing immigrants, the organs of the Zionist movement as a whole provided it with many of the resources needed to finance them. In the course of time, the Histadrut enterprises have grown in size and number until they have become an economic empire employing 170,000 workers and having an annual turnover of about two billion dollars.

The production section of the Histadrut is a legally distinct entity known as *Chevrat Ovdim*—Workers' Society—which is identical in membership with the Histadrut's. This section comprises four kinds of enterprises according to immediate ownership and degree of legal control by the Histadrut's Executive. They may be classified as follows:

1) Cooperative enterprises in which the equity capital is owned by the members themselves, with the Histadrut exercising general control and providing all sorts of aid, such as credit facilities, tech-

nical advice, legal and political protection. Such enterprises include, among many others, the transport cooperatives which control 85 per cent of the country's motor transportation, and about six hundred kibbutzim, moshavim, and agricultural cooperatives which produce three quarters of the country's farm production and account for an even higher proportion of Israel's farming population.

2) Companies owned wholly or in part by the cooperatives themselves. They are under the same general control and receive the same kind of assistance as their mother-enterprises. Among such companies are Tnuva, which markets most of the country's agricultural products, and Hammashbir, which supplies the cooperatives with all their needs from shoelaces to tractors. Both companies maintain retail chain stores for the general public all over the country and have founded specialized enterprises of their own such as grain mills, seed sorting stations, packing plants, garages and repair shops, dairy processing plants, shoe and rubber factories, credit institutions, and so on. Tnuva and Hammashbir, together with their affiliates, employ about 10,000 people and have an annual turnover of about 225 million dollars.

3) Companies in which the Histadrut Executive is in partnership with the government or the Jewish Agency. Examples of this type are Mekorot, the national water company; Zim, the largest navigation company with a fleet of nearly half-a-million tons; and El Al and Arkia, the international and inland airline companies. The Histadrut often owns only a minority interest in these companies, but its influence is potentially much larger than its share because some government and Jewish Agency representatives on these companies' managing boards are themselves Histadrut men.

4) Companies owned directly by the Histadrut Executive and operating under management appointed by it. Examples of this kind are the Workers' Bank—the second largest in the country with a balance sheet of $90 million, and Solel Boneh—a three-headed contracting and industrial giant employing over 28,000 workers and having a turnover of about $120 million annually. Solel Boneh's industrial segment includes plants for cement, ceramics, glass, quarry products, rubber, textiles, ship repair, the newly built "steel town" near Acre and many others. Its foreign contracting segment has built military installations in the Middle East for the United States government and operates in ten Asian and African countries

where it employs 20,000 indigenous workers. The construction segment accounts for a high proportion—in some years over half—of the construction work in Israel.

Much of what is today part of the Histadrut production section has been added or initiated in the period since the establishment of the state. Some of the enterprises previously mentioned, Tnuva and Hammashbir, for example, have grown seventeen and eleven times, respectively, during that period. It is estimated that in the course of the first decade after the birth of Israel, the Histadrut sector in all its branches has invested close to $600 million in Israel's economy.

Trade Union

The trade union section of the Histadrut embraces today close to half-a-million members, or nearly 90 per cent of the total eligible labor force, which consists of all those who "live by their own work and do not exploit the labor of others." It includes all kinds of workers: agricultural and industrial, white collar employees and civil servants of all ranks, professional and technical people, including physicians and engineers, academicians and artists, among them university professors and musicians. Together with the non-working wives of members and their children, who are entitled to membership and have access to all the facilities of the Histadrut, the "Histadrut population" amounts to 1,100,000 persons, or nearly 60 per cent of the total Jewish population of Israel. In 1953 membership in the trade union section was opened to Arab workers and, immediately thereafter, two thirds of the registered Arab hired labor force enrolled. More recently, they have been given the right to full Histadrut membership.

This feat of organization, unparalleled anywhere in its extent and comprehensiveness, is all the more remarkable since it was accomplished under circumstances of mass immigration which doubled the population of the country in a few years and brought in hundreds of thousands of workers and employees from Oriental countries who had not the first notion about trade unionism. It is true that the Histadrut's control of the labor exchanges, the imposition of closed-shop contracts, and other advantages, such as medical insurance and housing benefits, were crucial inducements to the newly arrived workers to join; but all these institutions had been established and made effective in the first place mainly through Histadrut initiative and effort.

The trade union section includes three dozen national unions most of which are industrial and are organized in a Federation of Industrial Unions. Members are enrolled directly in the central trade union department, not in their particular craft or industrial unions. Most of the individual national unions were, in fact, created only recently as administrative units of the trade union center, which remains the decisive authority constitutionally and can take into its hands as much basic-wage and policy formulation as it desires. This arrangement is designed to allow the development of an integrated, national wage system and to prevent the emergence of autonomous centers of power. The Histadrut achieved notable success in both respects; but in recent years the existence of an integrated national wage system has provoked a great deal of restiveness and insubordination among many unions.

Bargaining is done collectively on a national basis. The Histadrut has to deal mainly with two protagonists, the industrial employers organized in the Manufacturers' Association, and the government. Despite its overwhelming power as a union vis à vis its protagonists, the Histadrut has acted on the whole with remarkable restraint. This is partly due to the fact that the Histadrut itself is the biggest employer in the country, partly due to its own sense of concern for the national economy, and partly the outcome of the continual pressure for moderation exerted by the government's economic ministers in the councils of Mapai—the party to which both the Histadrut chiefs and the ministers belong. With their great power and moderate approach, the central Histadrut authorities have rarely found it necessary to declare a strike; the strikes that have taken place in Israel have been mostly the outcome of conflicts within the Histadrut itself. Lately, such strikes have been much more frequent than heretofore, and the strikers' revolt has been precisely against the moderation and restraint of the central leadership.

The integrated wage policy of the Histadrut has been geared to providing even the lowest-paid worker with a European standard of living and has put a great deal of stress on fringe benefits and allowances. As early as 1948, it had secured for the Israeli worker an average wage equal to Central European levels, and working conditions and social benefits—including an eight-hour day, five-and-a-half-day week, family allowance, holidays with pay, contributions to medical insurance, annual vacation and provident funds—which were well advanced even by American standards. But since, in the state of Israel's economy then as now, this policy meant that the unskilled and semiskilled workers received a minimum total wage well above their productivity, the attempt was made to make up for the difference in large part by keeping the wages and salaries of the skilled workers, the technicians, and the professional people relatively low. The result was a very compressed wage structure in which the difference between the most highly skilled and the unskilled was the lowest in the world. A production engineer, a physician, a university professor, a Histadrut executive, rarely drew a net salary of more than 60 to 80 per cent above the wage of an ordinary worker. This situation has been substantially modified since then, but it is still at the root of much of the labor unrest that has gripped Israel in recent years.

Social Services

In the field of social services, the most notable achievement of the Histadrut is its Kuppat Cholim—its medical insurance system. From its modest beginnings two generations ago as an organization which gave more comfort than aid to ill members, Kuppat Cholim grew virtually into a privately administered system of "socialized medicine." It embraces two thirds of Israel's population, maintains close to a thousand clinics in addition to thousands of hospital beds throughout the country, employs 10,000 medical workers, including about half of Israel's doctors, and has a current budget of $40 million. Service covers every contingency, though small fees have to be paid for medicines, glasses, hearing aids and so on. The system is financed by a fixed proportion of the individual's total Histadrut membership dues (graded from 3 to 4.5 per cent of the member's salary) plus employers' fixed contribution and a small subsidy from the government for services to new immigrants. Unemployed members are excused from part or all of their dues.

Kuppat Cholim is not the only organization for medical aid in the country. Even before the state entered the field of public health and built its own hospitals and facilities, there was the Hadassah medical program supported completely by American Zionist women, and the Wizo Women International Zionist Organization—welfare centers which provided the Yishuv and Israel with some unexcelled facilities. There was also another group of sick funds administered by non-Histadrut bodies which embraced another 17 per cent of the population. Nevertheless, if Israel has been able to establish one of the finest public health records in the world, including one of the lowest infant mortality rates and one of the highest life-expectation levels, the credit goes very largely to the medical insurance system of the Histadrut's Kuppat Cholim.

Before the establishment of the state, the Histadrut ran the only social insurance scheme in the country covering old age, disability, and unemployment. The method for unemployment insurance, however, was not to pay relief, but to carry out projects of public work for the benefit of the unemployed. It also ran various schemes within the framework of some existing national unions for additional insurance against industrial accidents, payments during illness, compensation for dismissal, and child and vacation allowances. All these programs involved contributions by the employers as well as by the insured members. In 1952 the state introduced a compulsory national insurance program which, with later additions, covers old age, industrial accidents, maternity benefits, and child allowances for large families. It also assumed, of course, primary responsibility for relief work during unemployment. The Histadrut continued with some of its schemes after readjusting them to provide additional benefits beyond the standards assured by the national security system. Health insurance remained, however, the concern of Kapput Cholim and the other sick funds, though there has been talk of the state taking over or sponsoring health insurance on a national basis.

In addition to the programs described so far, the Histadrut runs a large number of facilities for the benefit of its members. The most important of these are its easy-terms housing schemes, organized on a cooperative basis, which have built close to 60,000 apartments housing more than a quarter of a million people. Other facilities include low-priced resort hotels, restaurants, homes for the aged, nurseries, and so on.

Education and Culture

In the field of education, the Histadrut played a central role until 1953, when a national education system was established. Since then the Histadrut has fulfilled a diminishing though still important function in certain more specialized aspects of education and culture.

In Mandatory days, the Histadrut and the settlements affiliated with it had built a network of schools which encompassed 45 per cent of the Jewish children and youth. This network served the function of providing members' children with regular primary and secondary education in the absence of a national system; but it was also a vital instrument for educating youth to value work and all the socialist ethics surrounding it, thereby contributing to the continuation of the process of creating a class of workers and farmers by voluntary commitment. In order to promote this last aim further, the Histadrut also established a network of technical and trade schools which currently produce a thousand skilled craftsmen a year, supported the agricultural schools and colleges under the auspices of the kibbutz movement which presently turn out a major proportion of the country's agricultural specialists and technicians, and set up a wide program of formal and informal vocational on-the-job training.

Complementing these educational institutions, which have now reverted mostly to the responsibility of the state, there is a very extensive network of cultural and artistic activities which continue to be directly or indirectly under the aegis of the Histadrut. The Histadrut publishes an important daily newspaper in Hebrew and several in other languages, in addition to a large number of magazines and periodicals. It has a large publishing house which prints many original and translated books annually, as well as school texts for children. It sponsors a great many lectures, concerts, and art exhibits throughout the country, maintains a vast sports organization, and supports a theater company which is reasonably good now but once saw glorious days. In addition, the Histadrut provides various kinds of assistance to the activities undertaken by affiliated organizations, such as kibbutzim, which maintain hundreds of libraries and scores of orchestras, chamber groups, choirs, and so on.

Miscellaneous National Activities

In addition to its operations in the spheres of production, trade union work, mutual aid, and education, the Histadrut devoted much energy and resources to activities of purely national concern. One of the most important of these activities was its support of the

Haganah—the underground defence force of the Yishuv which grew into the army of Israel. Many of the founders and leaders of the Haganah were prominent Histadrut men. The vast network of institutions controlled by the Histadrut throughout the country—labor exchanges, schools, workshops, kibbutzim, moshavim and others—provided convenient places for meetings, training, storing of arms, and similar activities, and its records gave the Haganah command a comprehensive picture of the manpower resources and skills it could tap. In addition, the Histadrut made direct and indirect contributions to the Haganah funds. During World War II, it provided a variety of aid to the families of men who enlisted with the British forces. In 1948-1949, it made an enormous contribution to the War of Independence by channeling into it all its human and economic resources.

Another major concern of the Histadrut has been immigration. Not only did the Histadrut deviate from the traditional opposition of trade unions to massive immigration for fear of depressing wages, but it adopted the opposite policy of actually helping by every available means to maximize Jewish immigration at all times and in all circumstances because this was the main pillar of the Zionist national endeavor in Palestine and Israel. The Histadrut gave unstinting assistance through all the phases of immigration—recruitment abroad, teaching of Hebrew, training in skills, and providing work, housing, and medical and social services. It has been said that the Histadrut could afford to encourage immigration because its unchallenged trade union power enabled it to control the consequences of mass immigration feared by trade unions elsewhere. It is at least as accurate and relevant to say that the Histadrut was able to control these consequences *because* it was engaged in encouraging and absorbing immigration. It is not difficult to imagine what the consequences might have been for the workers in Israel if the Histadrut had not been in the field, ready to absorb hundreds of thousands of immigrants from Oriental countries from the moment they set foot on Israel's soil.

For many years before and since the establishment of the state, the Histadrut has engaged in semidiplomatic activities on behalf of the national cause in the councils of the international labor organizations and elsewhere. Recently, it has moved into an exciting new kind of semidiplomatic activity by setting up its own program of technical assistance to young nations to supplement the government's own projects in this field. In 1959 it established the Afro-Asian Institute as a college designed to convey to men and women from African and Asian countries involved in the labor field the experience of Israel's workers in the areas of cooperation, trade unionism, and mutual aid. The Institute has already outgrown its birth pangs and is on its way to becoming a very important institution. Several hundred trainees have already gone through it.

All these additional activities of the Histadrut reflect more than anything else the sense of complete identity of the national interest and the interest of organized labor that its leaders have had. This sense, initially resting on substantial argumentation and contingent premises, became an unquestioned dogma in the period of the Mandate and during the early years of statehood and served to rationalize many privileges claimed by the Histadrut as well as many of the obligations it assumed. In recent years, however, the tendency has developed within the government and the Histadrut to discover certain contradictions of purpose and antagonisms between them and to dwell upon them. The reasons behind this tendency are numerous and complex. One of them has to do with the conflict between two viewpoints: the habit acquired by Mapai's leaders in the government of looking at things in a national perspective, and the tendency of Histadrut people from the same party to think of the vested interests of their organization. Another reason has to do with the need of the government to rely increasingly on its own initiative and to channel more and more of its resources through private enterprise in the face of growing evidence that the Histadrut was creaking under the burden of its own weight.

2. PROBLEMS

Any organization engaged in as vast an array of activities as those we have described is bound, in the best of circumstances, to become entangled in difficult problems of direction, coordination, and control. In the case of the Histadrut the situation is made much more difficult by the fact that its various constituent parts have expanded by anywhere from three to fifteen times in the course of twelve years, that its basic constitutional structure is complicated by the intrusion of politics, and by the fact that the social, economic, and political premises on which many of its policies and institutions were established became radically transformed within a short while. It is not surprising, therefore, to find that the Histadrut has been beset by some severe difficulties. Since the problems of the Histadrut could not fail to have important repercussions on the life of Israel, it is important to linger on the subject and consider at least the most important of them. But first a few words need to be said about the character and structure of the Histadrut.

One of the most important facts to recall about the Histadrut is that it is not a trade union organization which has extended its activities haphazardly into various extraneous spheres. From the outset the Histadrut was set up as a comprehensive institution aiming at building the Jewish National Home as a workers' commonwealth. Another important fact to recall is that the Histadrut was founded from the beginning by a number of political parties with a variety of working-class ideologies; and although the understanding was that it would not operate on a political basis, politics soon became its normal diet. The number of parties operating within the Histadrut has varied in the course of time as a result of fission, fusion, and addition. Today, there are six of them, all but one of which are regular parties operating also on the national scene. All elections to the policy-making and governing bodies take place on the basis of party lists, according to the principle of proportional representation. Party discipline is strict, and all voting in the organs of the Histadrut takes place along party lines.

Nominally, the Histadrut has a very democratic and highly centralized structure. All authority is formally vested in a Convention and a Council which delegate their authority to a large number of semiautonomous bodies and elect an Executive Committee to implement and supervise the application of their decisions throughout the Histadrut. The Convention, elected by all members, meets, on the average, every four years and elects the Council, which meets twice a year and in turn elects the Executive Committee. This Committee is composed of more than one hundred members and meets every two weeks. It appoints from its ranks a Centralizing Committee of thirteen members who are responsible for the day-to-day management of the Histadrut's affairs. Actually, effective control has throughout gone hand in hand with management and produced a fluid constellation of power which has little relation to the constitutional chart. Because the other bodies are too large, meet infrequently, and do not have the requisite information, policy determination has gravitated to the hands of the main executive organ. The Centralizing Committee, or its majority, actually initiates most policy, which is almost always assured of passage in the Executive Committee, the Council, and the Convention. At the same time, the very large size of the Histadrut's establishment, insufficient technical knowledge at the center, and the pressure of the daily routine have in fact operated to limit greatly the power of the Centralizing Committee over the large number of semiautonomous bodies formally under its control and to allow many of them to develop into organizations accountable only to their bosses or managers. This has been particularly true of the economic enterprises grouped under its production section, Chevrat Ovdim.

Until 1953, Chevrat Ovdim, though a legally separate body, had an Executive which was identical with the general Executive Committee of the Histadrut. That year, following mounting criticism about the autonomy of Chevrat Ovdim enterprises, the absence of any coordination among them, and their working in competition and at cross purpose with each other, it was decided to give this section of the federation a separate Executive of its own, composed half of members of the main Executive Committee and half of directors from the various enterprises. It was hoped that this arrangement would make possible a greater flow of information and a wider exchange of views and allow better coordination and control. But the reorganization failed to realize its objects and, five years later, Secretary General Lavon spearheaded what appeared at the time to be a sensational crackdown on Chevrat Ovdim enterprises. Big companies like Tnuva and Solel Boneh were broken up and placed under separate managers. The bus cooperatives, which had defied for years repeated injunctions to cease employing hired labor, were confronted with a plan of partial nationalization. Schemes were drawn to set up a central planning body for Chevrat Ovdim composed of experts, to control its operations and approve expansion projects. But, notwithstanding the dramatic impact of some of Lavon's moves, such as the firing of the powerful builder and manager of Solel Boneh, the whole drive had little practical effect in establishing coordination, common purpose, and regularized control. Today, the bus cooperatives continue to hold their monopoly and employ more hired labor than ever before. The central planning authority came to naught. The breakup of big concerns like Solel Boneh seems only to have added new sources of friction without at all strengthening the hold of the central authorities.

The "usurpation" of the main role in policy formulation by the central managing authorities of the Histadrut and the failure of the center to exercise effective control over the periphery may be an inevitable phenomenon in any large-scale organization, especially one that has multiplied its size over a brief period of time. Nevertheless, the realization of these pathological tendencies in the Histadrut carries important consequences for Israel's social, economic, and political order. In the first place, it sharpens the issue of the latent contradiction between the Histadrut as employer and the Histadrut as a trade union. The dual role of the Histadrut has usually been defended on the grounds that since the workers are the ultimate owners of the Histadrut's enterprises and since they choose the leadership democratically, they can check and correct the way in which it balances the goals prescribed by the two functions. But if control from below upward and from the center outward is ineffective, then the balance between the two functions is left to be determined haphazardly through clashes among various segments of the organization which not only undermine it but also have detrimental effects on the whole economy and society. Related to this is the issue of the justification of the Histadrut's economic enterprises. In the past, these have been defended on the ground that they served useful social purposes, such as encouraging cooperation and setting up high standards of wages and benefits. But if the control from the center necessary to ensure the realization of these purposes is ineffective, and if these enterprises serve instead to create a conflict of interests, then what justification remains for the Histadrut's engaging in them? The question is particularly relevant since many Histadrut enterprises were given monopolistic positions and other privileges by the Histadrut as a whole and by a sympathetic government on the grounds of their alleged social value.

Perhaps a distinction should be made between the various types of Histadrut enterprises in connection with these problems. Enterprises in which the Histadrut is minority owner seem to offer the least difficulty. These may simply be viewed as outlets for profitable investment of funds accumulated by the organization which contribute at the same time to increasing employment opportunities. The potential conflict between the Histadrut as investor in these enterprises and as representative of their employees is minimized by the fact that the Histadrut is, at least, not responsible for the management of these companies. In the case of enterprises owned and operated by the Histadrut the problem is much more difficult. No less an authority than a recent Secretary General of the Histadrut has admitted that employees of these enterprises are treated and feel no better than employees of purely private enterprises, while confessing the failure of the central authorities to guide them. These enterprises therefore lack a specific social purpose and only introduce to its full extent the problem of the conflict of interests. They do, of course, create opportunities for employment and contribute to the development of the country, but the same effects could be achieved in various other forms—through purchase of government bonds, for instance—without becoming entangled in questions of control and conflict.

Proposals that the Histadrut should dispose of these enterprises and divert the resources invested in them into other channels have been made periodically. But the likelihood of their being adopted in the near future seems practically nil. Too many people in the Histadrut are still the captives of outworn socialist clichés to make such action feasible either psychologically or politically. Instead, some of these people have been trying for some time to give a new social justification to Histadrut-owned enterprises by suggesting a scheme of joint workers-managers' direction, which they were authorized to apply on an experimental basis in a number of small plants. But what they do not see is that even if the scheme should succeed fully, it could hardly place the enterprises concerned in a better position than the existing cooperatives which pose their own very difficult problem.

The problem presented by the cooperative and collective enterprises stems from their increasing resort to hired labor, either because they find this to be more profitable than taking in new members or because they cannot find them. The Histadrut authorities have been unable or unwilling to prevent this development. If this tendency continues, the pattern already evident in the transport cooperatives and in some kibbutzim may become general and these enterprises will simply become capitalist undertakings, with perhaps a broader ownership base than usual. Such a development is likely to wreak havoc in the Histadrut. For, although its own rules would require that it should exclude from its ranks the new capitalist entrepreneurs, it will not be able to apply them politically and practically because members of the delinquent organizations themselves occupy central positions throughout its institutions. On the other hand, to continue ignoring the problem is likely before long to produce a situation wherein the Histadrut is completely dominated by employers and where it will forfeit any claim to the allegiance and obedience of the real workers and employees. The latter danger is all the more real since other problems of the Histadrut conspire to compound it.

Another problem no less severe than the future of its own and affiliated enterprises, confronts the Histadrut in the field of its trade union work. Here, the Histadrut faces the danger of fragmentation and disruption in an area which is universally recognized as being quite appropriately its own, as a consequence of its basic structure and its own policies.

We have already referred to the fact that the Histadrut had achieved for the average worker in Israel a high standard of wages and benefits well above his productivity, and that it was able to do this to a large extent by compressing the wage system and keeping the salaries of the more highly skilled workers and professional people relatively low. This policy, favored by the Histadrut on egalitarian grounds, was also necessary in order to attract people of non-working-class background to manual labor and thus build a Jewish labor force in Palestine. It was possible to make the professional and technical workers accede to it partly on social and patriotic grounds, partly because their bargaining power was weak since there was an abundance of them in relation to manual workers.

Beginning in the early fifties, the situation changed rapidly in most respects. The flow of mass immigration from the Oriental countries provided an ample supply of people who could do nothing but simple manual labor and brought in relatively few highly trained people. At the same time, the rapid development of the economy together with the establishment of a national administration, a modern army, and various new state services, created an immensely increased need for all sorts of highly educated people in general, and professional and technical workers in particular. This reversal of position between manual and brain workers occurred against the background of a situation in which inflation and several devaluations necessitated frequent wage and salary adjustments, and when the initial sense of restraint and discipline of the pioneering days gave way increasingly before an irresistible invasion of the spirit of acquisitiveness, fostered by long pent-up demand, the instability of the currency, and the flow of vast amounts of German restitution money into the hands of individual recipients.

The new situation led the more highly trained and educated groups of workers to exert heavy pressure on the Histadrut to support their demands for higher wages and salaries. But since the wage structure actually linked the high pay of the unskilled and semiskilled workers to the low pay of the skilled and the professionals, the Histadrut had either to resist the demands of the latter or else meet them in part by holding back the wages of the unskilled workers until productivity and inflation caught up with them. Political as well as social considerations at first induced the Histadrut to try to resist the higher-grade workers; but this unleashed a series of strikes, directed against it as much as against their employers, by university professors, civil servants, doctors and medical workers, school teachers and engineers. Since all these strikes proved successful, the Histadrut made a halfhearted attempt to follow the second course and restrict wage increases for the unskilled workers. But this, in turn, provoked a series of endemic wildcat strikes which set a chain reaction of labor unrest that has continued into the present. The outcome of it all was that Histadrut prestige suffered heavy damage in the eyes of member groups and the government, which is now threatening to sap the foundations of the federation's position as a trade union. Among the member groups the notion grew that the only way to protect their interests was by taking the law into their own hands; while among government officials there was a sense that the Histadrut leaders could not be relied upon to hold their members under control or to handle a strike once it has broken out. This attitude of the government was made abundantly clear when the Minister of Finance settled the engineers' strike early in 1962 without even consulting the official Histadrut leaders.

A factor adding to the difficulties encountered by the Histadrut leadership in the field of trade union work is its connection with the government. In deciding to defend the basic wage structure against the demands of the professional and technical workers, and then to hold the wage line against the demands of the unskilled and semiskilled workers, the Histadrut top leaders may simply have acted as responsible trade union chiefs. But their intimate connection with the party in power made their decisions suspect in the eyes of large groups of the rank-and-file who feared that their interests as workers were being sacrificed to the political program and exigencies of Mapai. It is true, of course, that the affiliation of trade unions to a political party is not an unusual phenomenon —witness the British Labour Party. But in that case, as in other European labor movements, the trade unions, often antedating the party, are only federated with it for political purposes, and the party leaves wage policy under their exclusive purview if only to prevent jeopardizing their position when the opposing party is in power. In Israel, on the other hand, the political parties which united to form Mapai in 1931 were *founders* of the Histadrut; and since Mapai has been in power continually and does not fear any reversal of its position in the foreseeable future, no care was taken to make a clear distinction between the process of policy formulation for the party in the government and for the party in the Histadrut. Histadrut leaders may in practice decide on wage policy and other matters without prior consultation with the Mapai authorities; but, should they adopt too independent a course, they can be brought to account in the party's Central Committee which is qualified to deal with all matters without distinction. This state of affairs, which is common knowledge in Israel, allows decisions to depend too much on the personality of the Histadrut leaders and their position in the councils of Mapai, threatens to reduce a Histadrut led by weak men into an appendage of the government, and, as a reaction, to provoke its breakup into a number of virtually independent workers' groups competing with each other in the degree of their intransigence.

All these problems point to the urgent need for a thorough redefinition of Histadrut aims and functions and a reorganization of its institutions and procedures. This necessity has been recognized for some time now by a few of the influential leaders of

Mapai in the government; but the path of reform is very difficult and dangerous as was illustrated by the Lavon Affair in 1960–1961. One of the aspects of that crisis, which rocked the foundations of Israel's political order, was precisely that its hero-victim, Lavon, who was Secretary General of the Histadrut, had almost succeeded in converting his conflict with Ben Gurion over some extraneous issues into a conflict between the Histadrut and the State. Lavon, who only a short while before the crisis talked of the need to reduce the Histadrut to essentially trade union functions on the grounds that the emergence of the state had obviated most of its other endeavors, turned around after the crisis and began to speak of the vital role to be played by a comprehensive Histadrut as the custodian of the welfare and morality of the people of Israel and the guardian of liberty and socialism against creeping *étatisme*. He hoped to rally behind him fellow-members of Mapai who had a vested material or ideological interest in the Histadrut, as well as the Mapam-Achdut Haavoda left-wing opposition which commands 35 per cent of the votes in that organization, and thus place himself in a position to impose his terms on Ben Gurion. In the end, Ben Gurion was able to foil Lavon's design and defeat him personally, but the forces and vested interests within the Histadrut which Lavon had tried to exploit remained intact and capable of splitting Mapai should its leaders make hasty or drastic attempts at reform. The consequences of such a split could be disastrous not only for Mapai itself, but also for the relative stability and continuity of government in Israel which has rested so far on the size and central position of that party.

The Histadrut's role and the balance of power within it have another crucial bearing on the political order of Israel, which was also underscored by the Lavon Affair. Lavon had ultimately failed to convert his own fight into a conflict of interest and philosophy between the Histadrut and the state; but what if somebody else should succeed in pitting the two against each other? What if Mapai should lose control of either the Histadrut or the government? It should be recalled from our earlier discussion that much of the impotence of the Histadrut is due to its being tied up by its connection with the government through Mapai. Should the snapping of that connection free it to take a militant course, it could very quickly become an immensely powerful force. Would its leaders then be able to resist the temptation to use that power to unseat the government? Would the government then resist the temptation to have recourse to extraordinary measures to protect itself against such dangers? Admittedly, all this is mere speculation at this point, since the chances of Mapai's losing its hold on the government or the Histadrut are rather slim. But the speculation serves to underscore the close connection between the problem of the Histadrut and the general equilibrium now obtaining in Israel, just as our substantive discussion of the achievements, of the difficulties encountered by that organization, and of the obstacles standing on the path of its reform should serve to underline once more the thesis previously stated: that the present democratic system and constitutional order of Israel have the advantage of resting on a balance of real political-social forces in the country, but that the rigidity of that balance gives ground for anxiety about the prospects of evolving a new, more dynamic equilibrium capable of overcoming the tensions that are undermining it now.

X

Religion and the State

The question of the relation between religion and the state is a most vexing and potentially a most explosive problem, bequeathed to Israel by Jewish history and by her own more recent background. In a somewhat simplified form, the context is that of a nation in the making needing desperately to retain and consolidate its unity, and the problem it confronts is an irrepressible opposition between two segments of itself over an issue which both consider vital. One segment, consisting of a sizable minority, wishes in effect to turn the country into a theocratic state; the other, probably more numerous, wants to make it a fully secular state. An undetermined proportion in the center is undecided but may swing now one way, now another, on specific issues. In the interest of national unity, which all desire, both sides repress their urge to seek the realization of their full aim at once and ostensibly agree to some *modus vivendi*. In fact, however, each side suspects the other of trying to build positions of strength for an eventual showdown, and uses every opportunity itself to consolidate and expand its own position. The situation leads to a great deal of friction and frequent eruptions which, however, remain localized because of extraneous considerations. But what would happen should these considerations weaken or disappear or should some eruption get out of hand? One might well ask, paraphrasing the words Abraham Lincoln used in a situation bearing striking resemblances to Israel's, how long a nation can remain half-sacerdotal, half-secular.

1. ORIGINS OF THE RELIGION-STATE PROBLEM

Practically speaking, the problem of religion and state, in anything like the sense in which it has been known in the West, did not arise for the Jews until the establishment of Israel.

Diaspora Judaism recognized no central church with exclusive authority to determine and prescribe doctrine or ritual and no office empowered to enforce the legal compendia which were universally accepted as embodying orthodox doctrine and practice. Each community developed its own institutions, which usually comprised religious courts dealing at the least, with all matters of personal status, educational institutions concerned with the transmission of religious knowledge, and various establishments necessary for the practice of the ritual. When the surrounding Gentile society separated church from state after bitter struggles, most Jewish communities needed to make few if any adjustments in the principles of their organization. The secular state may or may not have recognized the legal validity of acts performed by the communal institutions, but these could for the most part continue to dispense their services on a voluntary basis. True, the eagerness to bridge the gap between the institutions and practices of Jews and those of the surrounding society led in the case of some communities to a proliferation of styles and "denominations," but, typically, this did not produce more than verbal conflict among them. It is only with the emergence of Israel that the question of the state's relation to what had been communal religious institutions arose with all the sharpness characteristic of church-state conflicts in Western societies. And it arose because two ideological groups had for many years advocated radically opposed courses in anticipation of that moment.

The ideological conflict over the religion-state question goes back to the very origins of the Zionist movement. It assumed two forms, one of which was and still is today peculiar to Judaism. Although— or, more accurately, because—the Zionist idea of Return to the Promised Land is rooted in religion, not all religious Jews welcomed it. Opposition came from the ultra-Orthodox, who wished to await the divine Messiah to bring it about, and from some Reform Jews, who feared that the Zionist assumption of national Jewish solidarity might imperil their status in the countries in which they lived. The Reformist opposition to the Zionist idea and to the state in which it issued is largely confined today to groups like the American Council for Judaism, and bears little relevance to the religion-state problem in Israel. Ultra-Orthodox opponents, on the other hand, were to be found in fairly large numbers in Palestine when they included the Agudat Yisrael organization. They are still to be found in Israel in the group calling itself Neturei Karta—Guardians of the (Holy) City. Members of this group refuse on religious grounds to acknowledge the authority of the state, serve in its armed forces, or attend its schools; and they often engage in violent demonstrations of protest against such things as the opening of a swimming pool for both sexes in Jerusalem, motor traffic on the Sabbath, and so on. But while this group has great nuisance value, its small size and its absolute radicalism make its effect on the religion-state question only marginal.

The other, and more serious, form of ideological conflict over religion and state has its roots within the Zionist movement itself. From the beginning, the movement encompassed two conflicting visions in regard to the nature and character of the Jewish National Home it sought to promote. One group of Zionists considered the Jews a nation like all other nations, entitled to a home of its own in which it could work out its destiny in accordance with one or another of the political and social philosophies prevalent in the nineteenth century, all of which made a clear distinction and separation between religion and state. Another group continued to view the Jews as constituting "a priestly people and a holy nation" and envisaged the Jewish National Home as a holy commonwealth in which the nation could once again live fully in accordance with its ancient sacred laws. Between these two groups there was an amorphous center which included many who hoped to establish some sort of continuity between some selected elements of the ancient tradition and modern social and political philosophies, by restating these elements in a suitable secular form and incorporating them into the resurgent national life.

Adherents of all three positions came to Palestine and strove to influence the over-all Zionist endeavor there in accordance with their vision. The secularists far outnumbered the religious in the movement itself and, to an even greater degree, in Palestine. But the latter were helped by religious groups in the country who, while outside the Zionist fold, still sought to fight secularism and enhance religious life in the Holy Land. Above all, the religious were helped by the political and legal conditions that prevailed in the Palestine of the Mandate. Out of the strivings of that period both the pattern of religion-state relations that obtains in Israel today and the protagonists in the continual struggle around it became crystallized.

2. THE PROTAGONISTS IN THE RELIGION–STATE ISSUE

We have already had occasion to refer to the religious parties in our general discussion of parties and politics. It will be recalled that there are two pairs of religious parties—the Mizrachi and its workers' offshoot, the Poel Hammizrachi, and the Agudat Yisrael and its workers' offshoot, the Poalei Agudat Yisrael. The two pairs are differentiated from each other in terms of degree of religious intransigence and, perhaps more, in terms of their historical attitudes toward Zionism. The Mizrachi was Zionist from the outset and constituted before its formal foundation in 1901 the first organized group within the World Zionist Movement. Twenty years after its establishment, it gained its labor offshoot, whose main strength was in Palestine. Since the establishment of the state, the Poel Hammizrachi has surpassed its parent party in strength, and, in recent years, has in fact absorbed it into the National Religious Party constituted by their merger. The Agudah, on the other hand, was a religious organization founded in 1912 outside the Zionist movement and in opposition to it. Members of the Agudah went to Palestine partly out of necessity, partly in order to carry on their international struggle against secularist tendencies among Jews by building religious colleges and organizing strict religious communities in certain urban quarters. In 1922 it gave birth to a labor offshoot which endeavored to fight the inroads of secularism among workers and farmers and therefore found itself engaging in the same kind of activity in Palestine as the Mizrachi and its labor wing. Both Agudah groups kept aloof from the institutions of self-government of the Jewish community in Palestine and made it a point to oppose some of the basic Zionist claims before each of the many inquiry committees that descended upon the country. Since the establishment of the state, however, the two groups have become reconciled to its existence, constituted themselves into political parties, and even participated in a number of governments. For a brief time they coalesced with the two Mizrachi parties to form the National Religious Front, but then they seceded and formed between them the Torah Front. Nowadays, there is talk of a possible withdrawal of Poalei Agudat Yisrael from its partnership with its mother-party in order to join the National Religious Party.

The religious parties together have drawn on the average about 14 per cent of the total vote in Israel since 1949. This proportion does not include all the people in the country who would classify themselves as religious, but only those who presumably consider the religious issue to be more important than other issues on which the rest of the parties are divided. The religious parties thus represent the most militant religious elements and act as such. They are the activating power behind all the institutional and legal manifestations of the religion-and-state issue in the country. They continually use their power to gain concessions for religion and then exercise unremitting vigilance to see to it that these concessions are carried out and extended. They were and still are the chief opponents of the adoption of a written constitution, even one that would confirm the status quo of religion-state relations, which grants them much more than their numerical strength would warrant, on the grounds that the Torah—the entire body of religious doctrine and law— ought to be Israel's constitution.

All the other parties oppose the religious parties as far as their total aim of a Torah State is concerned. But radical opponents of any religious concession include only Mapam, Achdut Haavoda, and the Communists, as parties, plus an undefined number of leaders and members in all the other parties. In the country at large there seems to be little doubt that a large majority would oppose *on principle* most of the elements in the present pattern of religion-state relations though fewer would object to them as a temporary expedient. In any case, it seems obvious that by any criterion the religious parties exact from the community a very high price for its desire for public peace and national unity.

3. THE PATTERN OF RELIGION-STATE RELATIONS

The pattern of religion-state relations in present-day Israel includes the religious courts dealing with matters of personal status according to religious law, the institution of the chief rabbinate supported by the state, the national and local Sabbath and dietary laws, the public education system which includes religious schools, and the Ministry of Religions which is involved in all the preceding in addition to its concern with religious worship and other matters. All these elements, with the exception of the Ministry, were already established in Mandatory days, and they were established then as a result of the interplay of two factors which had little to do with the relative power of the religious groups. One factor was the need of the Yishuv to organize itself politically, and the other was the political and administrative circumstances in Mandatory Palestine as they affected this need. Soon after the first World War, the Jews of Palestine attempted to set up self-governing institutions to regulate their affairs and represent them before the Mandatory authorities. The authorities could not, however, grant recognition to such institutions without doing the same to some Arab self-government body. Since the Jews were not interested in promoting Arab political organization and did not, in any case, want to depend on what the Arabs did or failed to do, they availed themselves of an existing legal opening in order to achieve their aim. That opening was the *millet* system, continued by the British from Ottoman days, which allowed each *religious* community a high degree of autonomy in regulating its life in accordance with the requirements of its faith. The Jews built the self-government institutions they wanted as if they were appendages to the religious bodies they were entitled to set up, and so were able to obtain recognition from the Mandatory government for the whole system. The secularists among them had no choice but to swallow the religious courts, the rabbinate, and other institutions and practices desired by the religious in order to obtain the political institutions they wanted; and once the system was established it slipped almost unnoticed into the structure of the Jewish state when it was declared in the midst of war and administrative chaos.

As of today, Israel continues the *millet* system of Ottoman and British days allowing all religious communities to maintain their judicial institutions and follow their own laws in matters of personal status. For the Jews, however, this apparent continuity involves, in effect, important theoretical as well as practical changes in the position of the religious law and courts. Previously the religious courts were essentially communal institutions. The Mandatory government lent its enforcement power to these courts, but it was the community itself that chose to submit to them in the first place. Certain groups could and did opt out of the community to establish their own institutions. Moreover, the jurisdiction of the Jewish religious courts was in practice rather limited because under Mandatory law it was compulsory only for Jews who were Palestinian citizens. Foreigners and stateless Jews, who amounted to very large numbers, could either confer jurisdiction upon the religious courts voluntarily or turn to the secular district courts which applied to them the laws of their countries of origin on the matter. Not so in the state of Israel. The religious courts are an integral part of the state's judicial system supported by state funds and are imposed on everyone except foreigners. The definition of "foreigner" itself has been narrowed down to leave virtually all the population of the country within the jurisdiction of the courts.

The chief rabbinate is another institution inherited from the Mandate which has become directly integrated into the structure of the state. The rabbinate has decisive control over the training and authorization of judges of the religious courts and of religious functionaries. The major source of its power and prestige, however, derives from its position as interpreter of the religious law, sitting on the apex of the religious judicial system. Though the rabbinate, in Israel as elsewhere, cannot *make* religious law but is bound by an elaborate code of law fixed by consensus, the multitude of new problems requiring answers that crop up in the first Jewish state in two thousand years give the Israeli rabbinate in practice a very extensive power. The example of Bnei Yisrael is a case in point. These descendants of a very ancient and isolated Jewish community in India were encouraged by Zionist emissaries to emigrate to Israel, and a few thousand did. But once in the country, they encountered, besides a certain amount of social discrimination, virtual ostracism on the part of rabbis and agents of the religious courts, who would not marry them to other Jews without "conversion" on the grounds that their Judaism is doubtful. The humiliation and misery of these people who had viewed their coming to Israel as the realization of the millennial prophecy of the Return may well be imagined. Despite the fact that general opinion in the country and in the government was moved by their plight, the rabbinate took its time and after ten years produced a ruling which admitted them into the fold on principle, but still required them to pass certain tests not applied normally to other Jews.

Laws and regulations relating to public religious observance were also inherited from the days of the Mandate. On the national level, such laws were naturally limited in Palestine because of its multi-communal character. But towns and cities inhabited entirely by one religious community had the power to make regulations concerning public religious observance, and most of the Jewish ones made extensive use of it. With the establishment of Israel, the flight of Arabs from previously mixed towns, and the emergence of many new urban settlements, religious regulations were extended to most of the country's towns. Besides, the central government itself introduced a number of new "blue laws" affecting the country as a whole. As a result, on the Sabbath and holy days, all government offices are closed, interurban public transportation is halted, and military business is restricted to a minimum. Ships and planes arriving in Israel after sunset on the eve of such days cannot unload their passengers until the next day after sunset. National law requires all public institutions, including the army, to observe the Jewish dietary laws and prohibits the raising of pigs except in a limited area of the state inhabited mostly by Christians. Municipal regulations prohibit public transportation on Sabbath and holy days in most cities and towns, enforce the shutting of places of public entertainment as well as stores and businesses except for a few restaurants, and restrict the production and sale of pork.

Israel inherited from Mandate days a tradition of a fragmented system of education. The Palestine government had failed to set up a national system of public education partly for lack of sufficient means to do so, partly because the Jews preferred to set up their own schools and orient them as they wished. But the orientation the Jews chose was not uniform; various parties and local government bodies set up their own schools to ensure education according to their own ideological inclinations. Four networks of schools, known as "trends" thus emerged: a "general" network, maintained by municipalities and adhering to a General Zionist orientation; a religious network, founded and supported by the Mizrachi Party and stressing its Zionist-religious outlook; a labor network, supported by the Histadrut and promoting a Socialist-Zionist orientation; and an ultra-orthodox network, founded and supported by Agudat Yisrael and emphasizing exclusively a religious outlook. Schools thus became an important arena for carrying on the party struggle, especially the struggle for determining the character of the nation and its institutions with respect to the issue of religion and state. Promoters of the various trends fought bitterly over enrollment of immigrant children and allocation of funds, especially after the establishment of the state when the government passed a compulsory elementary education law which recognized all four trends and provided for their complete support on the basis of size of enrollment. In 1953, after several governmental crises, a law was finally passed unifying all but the Agudat Yisrael network into a single national system which specified certain schools as having a national-religious orientation and allowed parents to choose between them and secular national schools. Establishments of the Agudah network could receive financial support from the state if they complied with certain requirements of curriculum and standard. This law did much to eliminate glaring disparities in the quality and content of education and to reduce the spirit of partisanship within the schools themselves. It did not, however, eliminate squabbles and friction over the matter of secularism and religion since the religious parties continued to view the national-religious schools as their particular domain.

A new feature in the picture of religion-state relations has been added since the establishment of the state with the creation of the Ministry of Religions. Initially, this office was established for primarily international political reasons. Israel wanted to signify thereby her recognition of the importance of Palestine for the other faiths and to indicate her readiness to accord continual and prompt attention to the interests and claims of the faiths concerned. However, for various reasons, including notably the fact that the Ministry was placed at the outset under the control of a minister from one of the religious parties, the initial emphasis shifted soon to other activities. The Ministry became concerned primarily with aspects of the religious courts, Sabbath observance, dietary regulations, religious education, in addition to promoting and aiding financially and administratively religious worship. As it now stands, the Ministry has no parallel in any Western country; among Islamic states, however, similar institutions are frequently to be found. The services of the Ministry are used extensively by Jews and Muslims, but less so by Christians, who prefer to look after themselves in order to retain greater autonomy.

4. THE DYNAMICS OF THE RELIGION–STATE PROBLEM

The preceding discussion has attempted to show how Israeli institutions and practices involving a very extensive intrusion of religion in public affairs originated in Mandatory days; but it has not dealt specifically with the question why these were continued and, in many ways, expanded in the changed circumstances of the Israeli state. The answer to this question takes us into the heart of the religion-state problem confronting Israel today.

Unlike many of the new states, Israel was not born after an orderly period of transition and constitutional and administrative preparation. She came into being in the midst of war and chaos, and her first government, which was in any case only provisional, had its hands full with the task of winning the war and keeping the country together. In these circumstances, the government did what was only natural and decreed the continuation of previously existing laws and regulations until a legally instituted constituent assembly took over. When such an assembly came into existence in 1949, it confronted in matters relating to religion a set of facts already established which it could change only by initiating a *Kulturkampf* at a time when the country was surrounded by enemies, economically prostrate, and in the process of receiving and absorbing hundreds of thousands of immigrants. The wise course seemed therefore to give official sanction to the status quo and to postpone thorough consideration of the question until more normal times. Although ten or twelve years have elapsed since the matter was discussed in the context of the debates over a constitution, few responsible Israelis have felt that times have become normal enough to call for a reconsideration of the question.

Besides the desire to avoid an outright struggle over the issue of religion and the state in a difficult period for the country, internal political conditions worked in favor of maintaining the status quo and even modifying it in favor of the religious parties. The political balance of forces in Israel, as we have seen, has been such that no government could be formed without Mapai and none by Mapai alone. In its search for coalition partners, Mapai found the religious parties more convenient than any of the other parties, especially during the first years of the state's existence. Potential partners on the left and on the right insisted on far-reaching concessions in the fields that mattered most to Mapai—in economic, social, and foreign policy—as a condition for their participation in the government; whereas the religious parties were willing to let it have its way in all these matters provided it assured them that the legal status quo would be maintained, that the Sabbath and dietary laws would be strictly enforced, and granted them other minor concessions. Since the emergency conditions in which Israel found herself from the moment of her birth did not, in the judgment of Mapai's leaders, permit any drastic modification of the prevailing situation in any case, the concessions demanded by the religious parties seemed to them more acceptable than those which the other potential partners insisted upon.

From a broader and deeper point of view, the willingness to compromise on the various issues relating to religion and state at the time Israel was born was enhanced by the absence of any historical memory of conflict between the two. In Western democratic societies, the separation of church and state became a fundamental tenet only after centuries of conflict, religious wars, and civil strife which left a deep impress on their collective consciousness. Israel, on the other hand, is just beginning to experience some of the troubles involved in the injection of organized, institutionalized religion into politics and the state, because now, for the first time, after two thousand years of wanderings, Jews have a state, a semblance of a church, groups with diverse outlooks, and the possibility of genuine religious compulsion. Moreover, in the West, the modern nation-states could begin to emerge only at the expense of and in opposition to the idea of a single universal Christian community. In the case of Israel, however, the religious community of Jews everywhere has generally supported the emergence and crystallization of a national consciousness. The most radical Israeli secularists recognize that it was Judaism as a religion that preserved the national identity of the Jews and prevented them from melting into their surrounding societies as so many other faiths, races, and ethnic groups did. Even now, most of them feel particularly concerned about the Soviet drive against religion because they know that its success or failure is likely to determine largely whether the Jews of Russia will some day find their place in Israel or be lost forever to Israel and to Judaism. All Israelis know that community of religion, however formal and passive, is the link between them and Jews in the rest of the world; and although Zionism seeks to give Jewishness a national rather than a religious meaning, no Zionist group could conceive of anyone being a Jew by nationality while professing another religion.

All this is not to say that people in Israel are resigned to an indefinite continuation of the present situation or that the present arrangements work smoothly. On the contrary, since the beginning of Israel's sovereign existence, each year has brought new pressures on the status quo by the religious as well as the secularist forces. Not content with the existing situation, the religious parties have used every opportunity to extend the influence of religion in public life. After the elections of 1961, for example, when relations between Mapai and the other parties had been particularly strained by the bitter fights over the Lavon Affair, the religious parties used their enhanced bargaining position to extort from Mapai a promise to enact a national law, instead of the ineffective municipal regulations, banning the raising of pigs in most of the country, which was duly done. Next on their agenda is a plan to bring about a national law prohibiting intracity public transportation on the Sabbath—a question now left to the discretion of local authorities which in some instances have chosen to allow the buses to run. Another point the religious parties have been pressing for years is to bring about the nullification, legally or at least practically, of a statute which now subjects all women to compulsory military service or, in the case of religious women, to some other kind of national service. Besides these issues, hardly a month passes without an outcry being raised by some religious group about one incident or another, be it the opening of a swimming pool or of a Reform Jewish chapel in Jerusalem, the transfer of a child from school to school, the holding of a flower show on Saturday, or the hour at which the Minister of Foreign Affairs disembarked from a plane on a Friday night.

While the religious parties have pressed for more religious enactments and more stringent application of existing rules and laws, the secularists or secularizing parties have taken advantage of favorable political moments to push through measures which they felt were essential to the national welfare even though these ran counter to religious tradition or the wishes of the religious parties. Reference has already been made to the national education law which unified the elementary school system against strong religious opposition, and to the military service law for women. Other instances, more dramatic and significant because they bear directly on the sphere of personal status reserved for religious jurisdiction, include the Equal Rights for Women Law of 1951, the fixing of a minimum age for the marriage of girls, with authority given to secular bodies to break up marriages undertaken in violation of the law, the abolition of polygamy, and the authorization of secular burial societies. These acts have taken place against a background of a cumulative increase in public irritation as the implications of this or that aspect of the existing situation are dramatized in individual cases receiving wide publicity: cases like the plight of the Bnei Yisrael community of Indian Jews; or the example of a baby refused burial in the confines of a cemetery because it was born out of wedlock; or of men and women persecuted and tortured by the Nazis as Jews who are refused recognition as Jews by rabbinic courts; instances of divorced women unable to remarry because the prospective husband is called Cohen (signifying descent from the priestly clan originating with Aharon, the brother of Moses, whose members are enjoined to marry only virgins); the "Yossele Affair," in which a child was kidnapped by his grandfather because the parents wanted to place him in a school considered insufficiently religious, and in which many religious individuals conspired to frustrate the police efforts to recover the child for two years and a religious party used its vote on a crucial national issue to compel the government to desist from enforcing the law. These, and countless occurrences of this nature, produce among large numbers of Israelis a sense of indignation and an antireligious fervor that match the holy passion aroused among the religious parties and their followers by violations of the Sacred Law. Legislation extending the domain of religion and legislation restricting it, outbursts against too little observance of religion, and outcries against the sinister influence of religion on politics and the harshness of the archaic Judaic laws create an atmosphere of persistent tension which makes precarious the life of any compromise and presses for a radical solution. If this pressure has been contained so far, it is only because of greater outside pressure on the country as a whole, because of the newness of the problem itself, and because of calculations of internal political expediency. Whether these considerations will repress the conflict for another year, or ten or twenty years, it is hard to tell. But that a showdown is due sooner or later seems surely predictable.

PART FOUR: THE STRUGGLE FOR LIVELIHOOD AND LIFE

XI

The Economy: Development, Characteristics, Problems

Four years after Israel had been established, a prominent economist entirely without bias in favor of Israel astounded a distinguished American academic audience by suggesting that that country might be able to "make a go" of its economy in a decade or two
and that, fundamentally, its economic position was perhaps more
manageable than that of its neighboring countries. The astonish-
ment reflected the belief current at the time among all but the most
confirmed of Zionists that a complete economic collapse of Israel
was imminent. And, indeed, Israel presented a sad picture then.
Here was a country, small, half of it wilderness, that seemed devoid
of any significant natural resources with one or two minor exceptions. It was surrounded by hostile neighbors who made no secret
of their intention to wipe it off the map, and in the meantime compelled it to divert much of its scarce resources to maintain a defense
establishment disproportionate to its size and means, while inflicting on it heavy losses through an economic boycott. Since its foundation, the state had welcomed all Jewish immigrants, and now its
countryside was strewn with primitive canvas and tin hut camps in
which hundreds of thousands of them waited in misery and frustration, living on doled-out food and clamoring to get relief work.
For some time, the government had financed much of its work by
"creating" money, trying to suppress the inflationary consequences
through a comprehensive price-control and rationing system; but

the system had just broken down completely, and rampant inflation was wreaking havoc on prices, wages, and currency. Everything was short, the black market was rife, the population was utterly demoralized. In 1952–1953 emigration from the young nation actually exceeded immigration.

Today, it seems that only wishful thinking could possibly expect Israel to break down under economic strain. Going about in the country, one is struck by the apparent signs of vitality and prosperity everywhere. Hundreds of new villages and factories dot the countryside. Miles and miles of esthetically indifferent but fresh-looking apartment buildings radiate from the old cities; and new towns have grown like a mirage on desert landscapes. No trace remains of the depressing immigrant camps, and incoming groups are almost immediately housed in cheerful, comfortable, monotonous developments. Except for some isolated pockets, there are more jobs available than people to fill them; a suggestion was even publicly voiced (in mid-1962) to import labor from Cyprus to meet the manpower shortage. Inflation is still a problem for the economy as a whole, but shortages are a thing of the past. Housewives who had to stand in line for an hour to receive a ration of half-a-pound of coffee or three bars of soap can now load their carts in an American-style supermarket with a rich variety of good-quality produce mostly grown and packaged in Israel. Refrigerators and gas stoves, once an index of rare wealth, are now to be found in a larger proportion of homes in Israel than in any other country in the world outside the United States. Israelis leave their country at the rate of a hundred thousand a year; but of these only a handful are emigrants, and the rest simply go for business, study, or pleasure, and return. The American aid mission has just closed its doors, considering its business in Israel to be finished—the only such instance since the termination of the Marshall Plan. What is more, Israel is now itself in the business of aiding other countries.

Underlying this transformation, there is undoubtedly a record of solid economic achievement. But it would be as erroneous to think now that Israel is on the high road of economic development and growth as it was to think, ten years ago, that she was heading for collapse. The country still confronts some very serious economic problems which can cause enormous damage if they are not met soon and with determination. It will be our task in the next pages to analyze briefly Israel's economic development in the last ten or twelve years and to point out the chief problems still confronting her today. While doing this, there will be occasional digressions from our main subject to dwell in some detail upon related topics which seem relevant to Israel's position today or appear to be of social or political interest in their own right.

1. THE GROWTH OF THE ECONOMY

At about the time Israel celebrated the second anniversary of her birth, her economy, measured by the size of per capita income, stood close to the level of developing countries like Argentina and Colombia or of poor European countries like Ireland, Italy, and Austria, but was considerably below that of Western European countries and only a quarter that of the United States. Since then, it has grown at a very rapid rate and has reached, if not surpassed, countries like West Germany, Holland, and Finland. Reliable comparable figures for the entire period are not available; but the figures for the years 1950 to 1958, which are probably more or less true for the period as a whole, definitely indicate that Israel's output (Gross National Product, or G.N.P.) has increased by an average annual rate of 11 per cent. This magnitude represents the highest rate of development in the world outside the Soviet bloc, whose figures in any case are difficult to assess. It is more than three times the equivalent American rate and slightly less than five times the equivalent British rate during much the same period.

During the eight-year period mentioned, Israel's labor force grew by an addition of two thirds its original size; and one may point to this fact as creating some presumption that total product would rise significantly. But even when this factor is taken into account and economic growth is examined on a per capita basis, this still comes out to an impressive average rate of more than 5 per cent a year. Though no longer the highest in the world, this rate would be warmly welcomed by any nation seeking economic development. It represents somewhat less than three times the per capita rate of growth of the United States' national product during the same period, and more than twice the equivalent rate for Britain in the years 1946–1956.

The magnitude of Israel's achievement becomes all the more apparent if we recall that it took place against a background of very limited natural resources, a relatively poor economy, and several serious handicaps. The new immigrants not only included a very high proportion of children, but most of them possessed no skills other than those of artisans and small traders. Many of them needed more or less extensive aid before they could start to take care of themselves and the majority had to spend a long period getting settled or learning a trade before they could become productive. Among immigrants from Muslim countries, tradition and very large families confined women to their homes. All these factors reduced the participation of the immigrants in the labor force to a small fraction of their number and contributed to making the proportion of the working population and the proportion of those directly engaged in the production of goods in Israel among the lowest in the world.

In addition to these physical and human hindrances, Israel has labored under a political handicap owing to the hostility of the neighboring countries. The Arab economic boycott cost the country about forty million dollars annually in higher shipping costs, oil prices, and insurance rates, besides scaring away potential investors who have business in Arab countries. Much more important, the threat of military invasion forced Israel to devote vast sums in foreign currency to keeping its arsenals reasonably furnished in the face of rapidly arming neighbors, and to divert some of the best minds and energies at her disposal into military service. And although the bulk of Israel's armed forces consists of trained reserves rather than standing forces, hundreds of thousands of workdays had to be sacrificed every year to keep the reserves fit and ready. Nonetheless important for being less obvious, considerations of national security have frequently been the motive behind many costly, uneconomic endeavors which might not have been undertaken otherwise. In view of all this, the question becomes all the more urgent: how did Israel do it?

From a technical economic point of view, the answer appears simple: Israel has achieved that high rate of development per capita thanks to a very heavy investment program financed from outside sources. Indeed, for most of the period between 1950 and 1958, and probably in the years since, Israel has invested on the average the equivalent of 26 per cent of her Gross National Product every year in capital stock. This proportion has rarely been exceeded anywhere outside the Soviet bloc during those years. Put differently, Israel has invested more net dollars for every person living there, every year, than any country other than the United States. The money for this investment came overwhelmingly if not entirely from loans, grants, and contributions of sources outside Israel, including United States government grants in aid and loans, proceeds from the sale of bonds, German government reparation payments to the Israeli government and restitution payments to Israeli citizens, proceeds from various charitable funds and miscellaneous other sources. In the course of the ten years 1951–1960 roughly three billion dollars were thus transferred to Israel. The net contribution of domestic savings to the process of capital formation has been negligible if not negative.

There can be no dispute, of course, that the vast flow of money from abroad was an indispensable condition for the success achieved by Israel's economy. Moreover, there can be little doubt that this very heavy reliance on foreign aid, and especially the failure of domestic savings, confronts Israel now with very severe problems, as we shall presently see. But, while we are speaking of economic achievement we must mention at least two important points which qualify the simple explanation just given.

The first point is that the growth of national product achieved by Israel was far from being entirely attributable to heavy capitalization. Reliable calculations seem to indicate that one third to one half of the increase in per capita output was due to greater productivity. This degree of improvement in "efficiency" is roughly equal to that attained by many other advanced countries. But since Israel has an unusually large service sector which is not susceptive to rapid advances in productivity, her over-all per capita advance signifies an unusual degree of improvement in industry and agriculture.

The second point is that the vast inflow of capital from abroad, though a necessary condition, is not a sufficient one for achieving the economic advance generally attributed to it. Such an inflow involves many complex adaptations and adjustments which cannot be taken for granted, and have not, in fact, been achieved by other countries with the consequence that large amounts of foreign aid were dissipated. It involves, among other things, the setting up of a reasonably efficient over-all economic administration, the assimilation of new techniques over a wide range of industries and the adaptation of human skills to them, making many internal adjustments in the structures of consumption, production, and distribution, and rearranging the network of external relationships.

Both the increase in productivity and the making of adjustments must be largely credited to the Israeli human factor; and, indeed, a look at the human resources with which Israel started shows her to be exceptionally well endowed. To the extent that formal education can be used as a criterion, Israel's population in 1948 seems to have been the most highly educated in the world. According to comparative data assembled from United Nations sources, Israel had that year a higher proportion of people who had completed their university education than the United States, and twice the proportion of the next highest country. A similar picture emerges with regard to the proportion of people having completed secondary education, where Israel ran ahead of the United States, particularly with respect to people past middle age. This large volume of very high-quality "human capital" provided a valuable foundation for subsequent development, especially since much of it was under-utilized before the state was established. Its diminution since then by the arrival of massive Oriental immigration, though still leaving Israel among the highest-ranking in the world, poses some problems for the future of the economy which will be discussed later.

To summarize, then, in the course of her fourteen years of existence, Israel was able to increase her national product to about three and a half times its original size and to raise the per capita product by about 90 per cent. She has realized this impressive growth while absorbing into her economy almost twice as many people as the state had at the beginning, while maintaining a large and ever more expensive defense establishment, and while raising the standard of living of her population to its present Western European level. It is worthwhile to note that Israel has been able to accomplish all this without infringing upon her democratic institutions and procedures, and without invoking any extraordinary powers, that is, powers not practiced by free governments elsewhere. This remarkable record was attained thanks to a combination of extremely generous assistance from friendly powers and exceptionally high-quality human resources. In other important respects, however, Israel has not done nearly so well and has suffered a number of failures. Before looking into these, we shall turn for a moment to some features of Israel's economy.

2. THE ROLE OF THE GOVERNMENT IN THE ECONOMY

One of the most important features of Israel's economy is the central role played in it by the government, understood as including local government, the Jewish Agency, and the National Funds. From the outset, the government has owned and operated directly certain enterprises, such as the railways, the post, telegraph and telephone services, which are publicly owned in many other countries in the world, and has carried out typical public works such as road construction, irrigation and drainage schemes, afforestation, conservation, and so on. These undertakings are financially integrated into the national budget. In addition, the government has itself established more than one hundred public corporations not integrated into the budget, of which it owns more than 50 per cent of the shares. Among these are enterprises engaged in the production of electricity, potash, bromine, phosphates, fertilizers, copper, ceramic materials, and so on, most of which operated at financial loss until 1956. Altogether, the government and its various undertakings generate about one quarter of the national product. Adding the similar share of the Histadrut to it, this would leave private enterprise as the source of approximately half the national product.

Large as it is, the share of the government in total national product does not exhaust the extent of the government's role in the economy. Throughout the first ten years of statehood the government has been responsible for financing capital investment in the country to the extent of 50 to 80 per cent of total investments. This level contrasts rather sharply with the share of the government in capital formation in a country like France, which was only 11 per cent in 1954. Even in Britain, where many big industries are nationalized, and in India, a developing country, the share of the government in total capital formation in that same year was 29 and 30 per cent respectively.

The disparity between the Israeli government's share in investment and its share in the national product is mainly explicable by the fact that the government has awarded large amounts of its investment funds to Histadrut and private undertakings in the form of loans. In 1954, for example, nearly 70 per cent of the investment in such enterprises was financed by the government. This policy, which has been used in very recent years to stimulate the private sector and foreign investment more than the Histadrut, has had the effect of reducing the government's role in direct production below what it might have been. On the other hand, since the government insisted in most cases on the participation of additional funds from private sources as a condition for its investment, this policy gave the government an even greater influence on capital formation throughout the country than its share might indicate.

In addition to its direct and indirect investments, the government has exerted a very great influence on the economy through other means. It has, of course, used the fiscal and monetary controls employed by governments everywhere to guide the general course of the economy; but it has also supplemented them with a vast array of direct controls, subsidies, and allocations designed to achieve specific purposes such as promoting exports, encouraging agriculture, keeping down the price level of essential commodities, and others. Moreover, it has used its political relation with the Histadrut leadership to influence the wage structure and level and has affected the entire economy through its immigration policy. All these factors together make governmental activity the axis of the economy and endow it with the means of affecting the everyday life and well-being of citizens to a degree unusual in other free countries.

The extraordinary involvement of the government in the economy has very little to do with the domination of all the governments of Israel since her establishment by the mildly socialist Mapai party. Had nonsocialist parties been in control all that time, they might have been more lenient on certain controls; they might have used a different order of priority in making allocations, and they might have decided to stimulate private enterprise sooner than the government actually did. But essentially, they would have altered very little the fact of the government's predominant role and position in the economy because this has rested mainly on three factors: 1) the Zionist conception of the state; 2) the poverty of the country's resources; and 3) the particular defense requirements of Israel.

The Zionist view, which considers the state as an instrument for solving "the Jewish problem," implies, among other things, that the state should open its gates to unrestricted immigration of Jews who want to come. This principle was expressed in Israel's Declaration of Independence and was embodied in a fundamental law of the country by unanimous agreement. In the economic sphere, this view meant that all governments, regardless of political orientation, were bound to intervene in the economy on a large scale in order to increase its capacity to absorb new immigrants and to channel them and fit them for productive work. The experience of Western governments in the 1930's, to whom intervention in the economy was more repugnant on principle than to any Israeli party, points out that the absorption of masses of unemployed into the economy necessitated extensive public measures even when the question was not one of creating new capacity, as it is in Israel, but of making full use of existing resources.

But even without a continual massive immigration, any government of Israel was bound to assume a leading role in the economy for many years in order to insure its growth at a satisfactory rate. This is because Israel's natural resources are poor and the financial means of the Yishuv were modest; and these two factors, together with the Arab boycott, ruled out private local as well as foreign investment as significant immediate sources for financing economic development. The only other resources available to Israel were foreign public and nonprofit funds, and most of these could be tapped only by the government. With the bulk of investment money coming from these sources into its hands, it was inevitable that the government should play the central role in the economy.

Finally, Israel has faced from the outset a continual military threat to her existence and territorial integrity. In view of her almost infinitesimal size and numbers in comparison with her enemies, Israel could hope to resist this threat successfully only by a continual centrally directed planning of her defense potential. This means not only a high level of military spending, but the orientation of the whole economy in accordance with the strategic requirements of the country as well as economic considerations. Such a task requires a high degree of intervention and planning in the economy, and these would have been undertaken by any government of Israel.

3. THE PATTERN OF PRODUCTION

One of the most striking features of Israel's economy, and one of the principal hindrances today, is the exaggerated size of its service sector. Commerce and banking, transport and communications, personal and government services, occupy fully one half of Israel's labor force and account for close to 58 per cent of her national product. These proportions have been little affected by the great changes in the size and composition of the population and by the very considerable growth of the national product; within the limits of one or two percentage points, they are the same today as they were in 1950. An idea of the inflated size of these services may be had if it is recalled that West Germany, with an economy now at the level of Israel's but higher for most of the last ten years, employs only slightly over one third of its labor force in the same occupations. France, with a more advanced economy and with the residues of an empire, employed in 1957 only 40 per cent of her working population in the service sector. Even Switzerland, the land of banking and tourism *par excellence,* employed perceptibly less of its labor force in service occupations than Israel.

Numerous and varied reasons have been given for this phenomenon. One of these has to do with the unusually large size of the defense establishment that Israel has to maintain; but this could only be a small factor since most of Israel's forces consist of trained reserves and only a moderate number is at any time under arms. Another explanation points to the enormous excess of imports over exports, which excess consists mostly of commodities, and maintains that this has necessitated a compensatory shift of the domestic resources toward the service sector. But internal evidence—the "normal" size of the transport and communications areas within the service sector, for example—seems to give this argument only a limited validity. Other partial explanations include the small size of the settlements and the productive units making for duplication of service functions and a simple inflation of the civil service. But the decisive reason seems really to be the occupational background of the immigrants, who constitute the bulk of Israel's labor force, to which we have alluded in several previous contexts. Despite great and partly successful efforts on the part of the government and the

Histadrut to induce the new arrivals to change their traditional commerce and service occupations, habit and predilection have continued to assert themselves whenever the opportunity presented itself.

Of the other half of the working population, which is engaged in the goods-producing sector, nearly one fifth is occupied in construction. This, again, is an exceptionally high rate, but it is understandable in view of the pressing need for housing to meet the large immigration, and for plant and roads to meet the demands of an expanding economy. As a matter of fact, construction is one of the fields which has suffered recurrent shortages of workers, particularly skilled ones, and this has sometimes led to the suspension of licenses for building projects deemed "unessential." One consequence of the manpower pressure has been that construction has made considerable progress in technique and productivity in recent years. In 1958, construction accounted for about 7.5 per cent of the national product.

Agriculture employs nearly 18 per cent of the total labor force of the country and is responsible for 11 to 13 per cent of the national product, depending on the fluctuations of prices and weather. These proportions have remained more or less constant during most of the years since the establishment of the state. But to maintain them in the face of the rapidly growing population the government had to make enormous investments of money and effort. The typical unit of production remained the collective and cooperative village, and a few hundred new ones were established during the last thirteen years; recently, however, a few large-scale, heavily mechanized farms have been founded by private companies and the government. The area under cultivation has increased by two and a half times since 1949, but the ratio of cultivated land has remained about the same—half-an-acre per person. At the same time, however, the area under irrigation was increased fivefold, doubling the initial proportion of irrigated to non-irrigated land.

Thanks to improved methods, irrigation, and heavy capital investments, Israel's agriculture has developed to the point where it provides today virtually all the food needs of the country on a very high level with respect to quantity, quality, and variety except for grains, fodder, and certain oil seeds. Meat and sugar, of which large quantities had to be imported until two years ago, have now been added to the list of products locally supplied. Israel's agriculture also provides a surplus for export which is more or less equivalent in value to the food imports, so that, directly or indirectly, it can be said that it provides or pays for the entire diet of the country. In addition, a successful effort has been made in recent years to introduce and expand industrial crops which substitute for imports or provide the basis for additional exports. Chief among these are cotton, groundnuts, and beets. Of Israel's agricultural export, citrus fruits are the main item though other farm products are also being exported at an increasing rate.

Industry employs about 22 per cent of Israel's working population and generates about the same proportion of the national income. Here, as in the case of agriculture, both proportions have changed little in the course of the last twelve years, though, in view of the great increase in population, the constancy of the proportions represents a great absolute growth. Israel's industry includes a wide range of products. Between the food industries, with a total production estimated at close to $200 million a year, and the budding electrical equipment industry with an output valued at $25 million in 1960, there is a long list which includes, in descending order, an important and rapidly growing textile industry, a clothing industry, metals, chemicals and pharmaceuticals, wood and furniture, non-ferrous metals, motor vehicles, paper and printing, diamonds, leather and leather goods, machinery and precision instruments, rubber and plastics, mine and quarry products. Many of these branches produce an amazing variety of commodities which testifies to great vitality and enterprise. However, the entire Israeli industry is organized on a rather small-scale basis. Of the more than 9,000-odd industrial establishments in the country, less than half employ 25 workers or more, and less than 2 per cent employ more than 100 workers.

Most of Israel's industry runs on imported equipment, is powered by imported fuel, and uses predominantly imported raw materials. These facts, together with the limited internal market and the high costs of labor, have often led observers from well-endowed countries like the United States to question the foundations and prospects of that industry. Actually, the theoretical foundations of a prosperous and expanding Israeli industry are evident even now in some of the more successful products of the country, such as chemicals, diamonds, and citrus products. These products demonstrate that despite all the handicaps mentioned, Israel can reach out for the world market and have a comparative advantage based on making maximum use of her endowment in resources and climate, and stressing products that involve skilled labor and distinctive techniques, for which her manpower is eminently suited. It is true that these principles have not been consistently followed in practice. The recent launching of an elaborate, complete heavy steel industry—the "steel town" near Acre—for reasons of sentiment and prestige, where Israel has virtually no comparative advantage, provides only one example of the many considerations which have directed and can direct important resources into economic dead ends. But such failures, and others of which we shall speak in a moment, are faults of judgment; they do not negate the possibilities still available for building an expanding, viable industrialized economy.

4. FOREIGN TRADE

Israel is a very active participant in foreign trade. With a total trade movement of about $1,100 million in 1960, she exhibits an extremely high level of per capita participation, typical of small economically advanced countries like Switzerland and Norway, which compensate for their limited resources and markets with intensive economic activity on the international plane. However, unlike these countries, Israel's role in the international market is much more that of a buyer than a seller: she imports more than twice as much as she exports, and pays for the import surplus from funds she receives in loans and assistance from abroad.

Israel's exports of goods and services have increased about twelve times in the period between 1949 and 1960, amounting in that last year to $357 million. Of that total, services accounted roughly for two fifths and goods for three fifths. A little less than half the value credited to the export of services is accounted for by earnings of Israel's international commercial airline and merchant fleet. Both have been undergoing a program of expansion and renovation designed to keep them in the forefront among competitors in respect to quality of equipment. The merchant fleet has passed the mark of half-a-million tons capacity consisting of vessels with an average age of four years, which makes it the most modern in the world. Besides transport, insurance contributed 15 per cent and tourism 18 per cent to the earnings from services in 1960.

Of the $210 million of goods exported in 1960, 26 per cent were agricultural and the rest industrial. These proportions practically reverse the relative shares of the two sectors that obtained ten years before and thus testify to Israel's new vocation as an industrial country. It is also important to notice the trend toward increasing diversification in both sectors. In agriculture, citrus fruits continue to provide three quarters of the export, but a large variety of products such as eggs, groundnuts, poultry, fruits, and vegetables has been added to the list in recent years and accounts for the remaining quarter. In the industrial exports sector, 38 per cent covers polished diamonds which, in Israeli terms, are a "traditional" export by now; but the remaining 62 per cent includes a large selection of goods which have only recently broken into the export field. The most important of these products, listed in descending order after diamonds, are chemicals, tires, textiles, machines and cars, processed food, plywood, cement, and paper products. The entire export picture reflects Israel's economic posture as a country in transition from the typical underdeveloped economy relying on a few export items to a modern economy producing a large variety of merchandise, capable of shifting emphasis according to circumstances and market conditions.

A similar effort to achieve greater maneuverability through variety is detected in the search for markets, but with less success so far. Israel's clientele includes more than seventy countries, most of which are in Asia, Africa, and Latin America. But in terms of value of exports, her main customers consist of the six Common Market countries and the seven members of the European Free Trade Association plus the United States. The two European groups buy 55 per cent of Israel's exports and the United States buys another 15 per cent. All the exports to other countries, with the exception of Turkey, Yugoslavia, South Africa, and Hong Kong (diamonds), are significant more for the potentialities spelled by the establishment of commercial connections with them than for any actual business done with them. This very heavy dependence on Europe confronts the Israeli government with one of its main problems today, as the Common Market becomes more and more of a reality and as other European countries rush to join it.*

In their structure, Israel's imports reflect the already familiar pattern of the economy's production and growth. The bulk of the import bill—65 per cent in recent years—covers raw materials and fuel and lubricants for industry, agriculture and construction. Another 25 per cent consists of the costs of investment goods, and the remainder of consumers' goods. The most important single source of Israel's imports is the United States, which accounts for 29 per cent of the total. It is followed by West Germany, with 14 per cent, Britain, with 12 per cent, and then by France, Holland, Switzerland, Italy, Belgium and Turkey. The foreign trade of Israel is thus oriented overwhelmingly toward the advanced Western countries, the Soviet bloc and the less developed countries accounting for only a tiny proportion of it.

5. PROBLEMS AND PROSPECTS

Despite her impressive record of economic achievement in the last twelve years, Israel still confronts today a number of difficult problems which seriously threaten her future welfare and development. Among these problems are to be found the kindred troubles of inflation, excessive consumption, and low saving, high labor costs and distortions in the allocation of resources. But overshadowing all these troubles and lending them a particular urgency is the issue of Israel's excessive dependence on foreign assistance as reflected in an import surplus of enormous magnitude, and the more recent threat and challenge presented to her economy by the development of the European Common Market. The critical emergence of these two issues at this time presents Israel's government and people with an economic test more severe than any they have undergone so far.

The problem of economic dependence now confronting Israel is

* This observation was made before President de Gaulle's emphatic NON to Britain, which was declared while this book was in press. The exclusion of Britain and of other prospective candidates weakens but does not cancel altogether the points made here and at other places in this chapter in connection with Israel and the Common Market. After all, the six Common Market countries by themselves still account for about 30 per cent of Israel's exports and constitute the largest market for Israeli products. Moreover, the Common Market is apt to affect Israeli goods in other markets through the use of its bargaining power to obtain favorable conditions for its own competing products in those markets.

twofold. The question is where to get foreign assistance in the years ahead, and, even more, how to insure that forthcoming aid resources should be used more effectively than in the past to reduce the country's dependence on them. While the use of the vast inflow of capital to realize a very high rate of growth of aggregate and per capita national product was an eminent achievement on the part of Israel, her failure to use this growth in order to reduce significantly the degree of her dependence on foreign assistance was a signal shortcoming on her part. The record of this failure is quite clear despite all innocent and deliberate attempts to befog it. Reliable studies for the years 1950–1958 show that, despite the growth of the Gross National Product in that period by about 140 per cent, the proportion of the import surplus in relation to it remained the same at the end of the period as at its beginning, if it did not, in fact, increase. Moreover, the same studies show that no significant portion of the expanded Gross National Product went into new net investment, the whole Gross National Product in 1958 being just about equal to total consumption plus depreciation.

In other words, the facts indicate that as the economy expanded, all the increase in production went for consumption, and the increased need of the economy for investment resources was supplied by an enlarged import surplus financed from the outside. And while it is true that the expanded economy also permitted an increase in exports at a much faster rate than imports, still, because the starting point was one of very slight exports and very heavy imports, the end result was that the absolute size of the import surplus increased. Thus it was that between 1950 and 1958, the ratio of exports to imports increased from 14 per cent to about 42 per cent, yet the size of the import surplus grew from $282 million to $333 million. Between 1958 and 1961, the ratio increased to about half, but the absolute size of the import surplus grew to $375 million. The point is clear, then: Israel's failure to finance her own economic growth not only perpetuates her condition and level of economic dependence, but makes it more and more difficult to find the increased absolute amounts of resources needed to finance further development. As it happens, the next few years not only do not promise any increase in foreign assistance, but offer the certain prospect of a very substantial reduction in the receipts from the sources of capital of recent years.

Israel's foreign capital inflow in 1960 came from the following main sources:

	Millions of Dollars
United States grant-in-aid and technical assistance	9.7
Reparations from Germany	79.7
Restitutions from Germany	97.8
Remittances by charitable institutions	69.8
United States Government loans	28.5
Independence Bonds	29.1
Direct private investment	50.3
Total	364.9

These sources had been the principal ones in the preceding five years too, though the size of the contribution each of them made has varied over the years. The size of United States grants-in-aid and technical assistance in 1960 represents a great decline over previous years; this type of aid is likely to disappear altogether within the next three years—say by 1965. German reparations have come in at a steady rate of between $70 million and $80 million since 1952; but they will stop completely by 1964, when the agreement with Germany by which they were effected comes to an end. Individual restitution payments have been increasing steadily in recent years and will probably continue to flow in for some time to come. Just how much longer they will continue is difficult to know because these payments, unlike reparations, do not constitute part of a determined sum, but come along as a result of specific decisions by German courts on cases pending before them. It is probably safe to assume that payments on a high level will continue for another three to five years if German-Israeli relations continue to be friendly. Remittances by charitable institutions have been steady over the years at between $60 million and $70 million annually. The collection of these funds has become so integrated in the life of Jewish communities in the United States and elsewhere that there would be little risk in assuming they will continue indefinitely at more or less the same level in normal times. Loans from the United States are, of course, unpredictable. In the past twelve years, they have averaged about $30 million annually, and it is likely that they will continue at this rate, or somewhat less, taking one year with another. The sale of Independence Bonds has averaged between $40 million and $50 million a year since they were launched nine years ago; but already the proceeds of new sales have to go mostly for redemption of past purchases so that little can be expected from this source in the years ahead. The figure for foreign private investment represents a major breakthrough in comparison with previous years. Whether that rate will be sustained or increased in coming years cannot be foreseen, though the government of Israel is making great efforts to stimulate it. This brief review shows that by 1965, one third of the outside resources available to Israel in 1960 will certainly have disappeared, and if the flow of restitution payments dwindles or stops, which cannot be too long in coming thereafter, then half of these resources will have gone. What can be done to compensate for this drastic reduction in the means of obtaining the imports needed to provide the economy with the raw materials, the fuel, and the capital goods necessary for its operation and growth?

First of all, the government cannot escape any longer the need to pass measures to restrict the rate of growth of per capita consumption and increase the rate of growth of domestic savings in order to provide more of the sinews of growth domestically. This will require an increase in the burden of taxation in order to diminish the proportion of disposable to national income and a determined effort to establish greater monetary stability in order to encourage more private saving. These measures will be exceedingly difficult to apply politically in a country in which the public feels it is already over-taxed, in which governments depend on coalitions, workers are accustomed to having their way in wage demands, and employers are accustomed to passing the costs on to the consumers without fearing foreign competition; this is why, incidentally, they have not been effectively applied so far. But failure to do this now is likely to entail disaster later.

Secondly, the extent of investment activity will probably have to be reduced and the relative structure of the economy's production will have to be changed in favor of import-substitutes and exports. The first of these steps is relatively easy to achieve in view of the preponderant role of the government in financing investments; but the second entails major shifts in the allocation of resources with all the concomitant social consequences, and will encounter greater and sharper difficulties the shorter the period over which it must be accomplished. While all these adjustments are being made, measures must be taken to improve in quality and price the competitiveness of Israel's products in the world market through rate-of-exchange adjustments as well as through greater productivity and improved skills.

The realization of these measures with all they entail runs so much against the inertia of habit and expectations and involves so many difficulties and political risks, that one would have expected the government and the authorities concerned to concentrate their effort on devising stopgap arrangements to meet the forthcoming payments crisis rather than to tackle resolutely now the basic issue of economic dependence. Indeed, since Ben Gurion's meeting with Adenauer in New York in 1960, there have been continual whispers that Israel might be bailed out of her expected difficulties, at least temporarily, by a half-billion dollar German loan spread over a few years after the end of reparations, by another round of restitution payments, or by the government's plans to mobilize $300 million a year in foreign investment by 1965. Whatever may come of these hopes, it is probably fortunate for Israel in the long run that she must undertake some of the very same measures needed to promote her economic independence because of another severe challenge which bears little hope of postponement: the emerging European Common Market.*

Israel now sells almost all her agricultural exports and most of her industrial exports to the Western European countries already in the Common Market or likely to join it in the near future.* Moreover, since her poverty in natural resources compels her to specialize increasingly in processing products requiring a large proportion of skilled labor which have their largest markets in rich economies, she is bound to depend on the European market rather more than less for her future development. The full realization of the projected abolition of restrictions on the movement of goods and resources among the member countries and the setting up of a tariff wall against outsiders may spell disaster for Israel if no special arrangements are made with her. And while such arrangements might be expected, given Israel's particularly friendly relations with some of the leading countries of the Market, these would in any case require her to make drastic readjustments in her economy and

* See footnote, p. 176, above.

policies. It is, for instance, certain that any concessions made to facilitate the access of Israeli products to the Market will have to be reciprocated by a corresponding abolition of restrictions, obvious or disguised, on the access of Market goods to Israel. If Israel's products are to win an expanding position in the reinvigorated market of Europe and to hold their own at home against the competition of the Common Market's products, nothing short of a revolution in Israeli economic thinking and practice is required. Industries which have so far flourished in the hothouse of very heavy protection and subsidies will have to go. The prices of domestic goods will have to be put in an advantageous position in comparison with European products by changes in the rate of exchange, greater productivity, and relative reduction of labor costs. To accomplish this, inflation must be curbed, the pressure of demand must be reduced, wage increases must be restrained, and new investment must pass more stringent economic tests. Each of these and many other necessary measures have an array of ramifications which will put to the test the ability of Israel's administration and the maturity and discipline of her people. The entire reform will be all the more difficult because it will have to be done quickly, as there is little time to spare.

On February 9, 1962, the government of Israel devalued the country's currency from 1.80 to 3.00 Israel Pounds per dollar and proclaimed a comprehensive new economic policy designed to prepare the country's economy for the impending double challenge of drastic reduction in foreign aid resources and the full realization and extension of the European Common Market.* Except for the extent of the devaluation, which is viewed as insufficient by some, the measures specified in the new program are well conceived and have met with general approval from economists. The question is how effectively they will be realized. Events since that decision do not permit the formation of any clear judgment as yet.

* See footnote, p. 176, above.

XII

National Defense: Threat, Response, Implications

National defense has been the supreme preoccupation of Israel from the moment of her birth. Minutes after the Jewish state came into existence at midnight on May 14, 1948, armies of five neighboring Arab countries had already crossed the Palestine borders and were rushing forward to destroy it and scatter its people. The valor of its fighters, the ineptitude and disunity of the Arabs, and international pressure enabled the young state to withstand its assailants, push them back, and eventually compel them to sign armistice agreements which left under its control one and a half times the territory that had been allocated to it by the United Nations partition resolution. But the Arab states remained unconvinced of the ultimate ability of the victorious Zionist state to fend for itself. They knew they had an overwhelming advantage over it in numbers of population, financial resources, size of territory, strategic posture, and international political bargaining power; and their pride and self-esteem would not allow them to accept as final the verdict just imposed on them. They were convinced that, with better management of their assets, they could one day reverse that verdict, avenge their humiliation, and crush the intruding little state and its people. Accordingly, though governments and regimes came and went in the various Arab countries, all but one of them (Jordan) refused even to consider transforming the armistice agreements into final peace settlements and most of them set about rearming and expanding their armies in preparation for what they frankly called "the second round."

For her part, Israel did not need much convincing to realize how perilous her situation was. She was fully aware of the potential advantages of the Arabs and of the temptations these offered, and she would have been impelled to do her utmost to guard against them even if the Arab states had been talking peace instead of war, if the borders had been calm instead of troublesome, if Egypt had not been courted so zealously by some of the big powers and had not embarked on sensational rearmament programs. Israel felt certain, moreover, that the risks of war were grossly uneven as between herself and her opponents; for if they launched a war and were defeated again, they might lose some territory and suffer some political and economic consequences; whereas if she were defeated, she would lose her sovereign existence, her people, her property — everything. It would be for her a destruction as total as Sennacherib's elimination of the ancient Kingdom of Israel twenty-eight centuries ago. Outsiders may, of course, take a less tragic view of Israel's risks and chances, and may therefore often judge general and specific reactions of hers as too harsh or nervous. But in matters of national defense, the countries directly concerned seldom look at threats and dangers with the same eyes as outsiders, even when these are firm friends and allies (witness De Gaulle's France and Adenauer's Germany); and in the light of the recent historical record, it would be somewhat presumptuous to say the outsiders are necessarily the better judges.

Be that as it may, Israel assessed the challenge of Arab hostility as total and lasting, and she endeavored to respond accordingly by harnessing all her wits, will, and resources both internally and in the international arena to the struggle for national survival. Internally, she geared the basic planning of the country's development toward defense requirements and developed a military establishment which instituted on a permanent basis the concept of the nation in arms. Internationally, she geared her foreign policy toward the twofold task of securing the requisites for her internal effort and achieving a diplomatic posture that would prevent another war, or at least give her the political-moral advantage in fighting one. The elaboration of the Arab challenge, an analysis of Israel's *internal* response to it, and a brief consideration of the effects of

that response on Israel's regime and national character will constitute the subject of this chapter. Israel's response in the *international*
arena will be discussed in the following chapters.

1. THE CHALLENGE OF ARAB HOSTILITY

Ever since 1950, when efforts made by Israel, on her own and
through the United Nations, to convert the armistice agreements
into permanent peace treaties failed, Israelis, regardless of party,
have been convinced that the Arab states do not wish to liquidate
the Palestine problem except in terms of liquidating their pain-
fully won state. Although the Arab states have outwardly modified
their initial objection to the existence of Israel as such and, with
the exception of Jordan, have formally expressed their readiness to
accept the original United Nations partition boundaries, Israelis
have regarded this "concession" as a political stratagem not unlike
the one Hitler used in the case of Czechoslovakia and the Sudeten-
land. It has the appearance of making a legitimate and moderate
demand—restoring partition boundaries—which, once granted, would
so fragment and weaken Israel as to put the Arabs in a position
simply to help themselves to anything else they want without much
trouble. In support of their view, Israelis point to the unbridled
campaign of threats and fomenting of hatred which the Arab
governments have continually waged, and they argue that any
territory they might reasonably be asked to relinquish could be of no
possible value to the Arabs except for its strategic use against Israel.
Westerners who invent theories to convince themselves that the
Arabs might be persuaded to make peace if Israel made sufficient
concessions to allow them to "save face," say the Israelis, are playing Chamberlain's Munich game, whether they know it or not.

This is not the place to question whether the Israeli assessment
of the Arabs' designs may have had an element of self-fulfilling
prophecy, like the Communists' assessment of the "capitalist"
world's intentions. The relevant point here is that the Arab states
have undoubtedly shown nothing but hostility toward Israel from
the moment of her birth and that they would certainly like to
destroy her if they could. These realities have confronted Israel with
a truly formidable challenge which has so far tended to become
more rather than less formidable over the years. A complete picture
of this challenge would require a separate study; but an idea of it

may be gathered from a few facts and points. Leaving aside the members added to the Arab League in the last fourteen years, the six Arab states that had actually sent military contingents to Palestine in 1948 number today, after all the massive immigration to Israel, twenty-five times as many people as Israel. Egypt alone has thirteen times as many people as Israel, and increases her population annually by a quarter of the total present Israeli population. Granted that there is a qualitative difference in militarily relevant characteristics between Israel's people and the people of even the most advanced of the Arab countries which discounts somewhat the meaning of the disparity in manpower, nevertheless, the numerical gap is so large to begin with that even after every allowance has been made, the Arab countries, or even Egypt alone, still come out with a crucial advantage over Israel. Egypt may have such low standards of health that she may have to reject 50, 60, or 70 per cent of those who are annually called up for military service, while Israel may be able to take practically everybody; yet, even then Egypt would still be able to enroll at least three times as many recruits as Israel. A standing army of 40,000 means for Israel withdrawing at least 7 per cent of her labor force into essentially unproductive use; an army four times as big represents for Egypt barely 1.5 per cent of her labor force. Israel may have a per capita budget five times higher than Egypt, but the Egyptian government still has at its disposal twice or even two and a half times the revenue of Israel's from which to draw for military expenditure. These examples show that even if Israel took the risk of discounting drastically the extent of the help that Egypt might get from other Arab countries, the challenge confronting her would still remain overwhelming.

Although Israel sensed from the outset the basically disadvantageous position she was in, her situation in the early years of her career as an independent state seems idyllic in the light of developments that have taken place since. In those early years, Egypt was hamstrung in her effort to realize her power potentialities by a most unmartial, corrupt, and inefficient regime; since 1952, Egypt has been ruled by a military regime of young officers untrammeled by internal obstacles, for whom the upbuilding of the army is a foremost and natural objective. For several years after 1948 a large British army was encamped along the Suez Canal and exercised a practical veto power over possible Egyptian adventures eastwards; since 1955 the Egyptian army has been free to move and has acquired the first-rate British facilities and stores of the Canal base in the bargain. Above all, from 1948 to 1955, Egypt and the other Arab countries could not make much use of their superior financial and manpower resources because of the limitations on the supply of arms to the entire area imposed by the traditional Western suppliers; since 1955, Egypt and some other Arab states have apparently been able to obtain at bargain prices from Soviet Russia all the arms they could buy or use, in addition to all the instruction they cared to get. In short, until 1955 Egypt and other Arab states were prevented from realizing even their immediate potentialities; since that time all the obstacles have been lifted—up to the point of their absolute capacity. Prior to 1955, Egypt and the Arab states presented a potential threat for some indefinite future; since then the danger has become much more real.

Intensifying the challenge confronted by the Israelis is the political and physical geography of their country. Israel is surrounded on all sides but her western seashore by enemy countries. She has almost 600 miles of frontier to defend, and her territory is so small and so shaped as to give her little or no depth for defense. There is hardly a point of strategic importance in Israel which is removed from Arab positions by more than thirty miles. Along the coastal plain, where most of Israel's population, economic life, and industry are concentrated, the country is only nine to fifteen miles wide; a slight enemy advance from any point in the Arab bulge westward can split Israel at the waist and deprive the southern part of the country from access to the outside world through Haifa, the only deep water port of Israel. Connections between Tel-Aviv and Jerusalem depend on a corridor which narrows down to ten miles at some points; the capital itself is within the range of light enemy weapons and is surrounded on three sides by enemy territory. Sea access to Eilat can be easily blocked by Egyptian batteries posted at the southern tip of the Sinai Peninsula; the land reach to it can be cut by the convergence of enemy forces from Arabia, Jordan, and Egypt across the narrow, uninhabited triangle that constitutes its hinterland. In the far north, the jutting finger of eastern Galilee is exposed to enemy position on three sides, and further down, Syrian batteries sit on top of the Israeli settlements on the left bank of Lake Tiberias and control the surrounding country. The only saving element in this otherwise nightmarish position is that the most threatening geographic-strategic feature, the central Arab bulge, is occupied by Jordan, presently the weakest of the Arab states. This area offers a determined enemy so many possibilities for a quick, devastating thrust that its control by any other Arab army would be likely to drive Israel into "preventive war" immediately. Indeed, the signing of an agreement establishing a unified command of the forces of Jordan, Syria, and Egypt in October 1956 was one of the main reasons that moved Israel to strike against Egypt in Sinai a few days later.

All these factors give only an idea of the magnitude of the problem confronting Israel in seeking to defend her very existence. In addition, Israel has had to face the task of dealing with day-to-day security problems resulting from her exposed frontiers and Arab hostility. Immediately after the signing of the armistice agreements, Israel was plagued by waves of infiltration of her borders and by sporadic armed disputes over the local application of the terms of the agreements. Newspaper readers the world over have been continually reminded of the Palestine conflict through such incidents and their frequent eruption into full-scale local battles; but probably very few of them realize to what extent these incidents are an integral part of the brink-of-war situation in the area. Many border crossings were undoubtedly made by miserable refugees walking over to steal a few pieces of pipe, a sheep, or a sack of watermelons; but others were undertaken by organized Palestinians bent on provoking a fight between the Arab states and Israel while robbing and killing the hated Jew. Some incidents were due to the *bona fide* conviction of an Arab government that Israel had infringed upon the armistice agreements in a demilitarized zone; but others were the outcome of deliberate action by one or another Arab government designed to pin down some of Israel's forces, harass and demoralize her people, score some political points at home or in the arena of inter-Arab politics, promote fifth-column work among the Arab minority, or carry out sabotage and intelligence activity. Israel has confronted the need to develop the means to deal effectively with an agitated border, or risk the sapping of her people's morale, which has been one of her main assets so far in her contest with the Arabs.

2. ISRAEL'S RESPONSE

The magnitude of the Arab challenge led Israel to make defense considerations the central concern in her international and internal endeavors. Internationally, Israel's chief aim has been to secure an alliance with one or more of the major powers or to obtain a firm international guarantee of her existence and integrity. Failing that, she has sought to assure for herself reliable sources of heavy military equipment that she cannot manufacture herself, and to gain friends and influence in the councils of the world that might be involved in the Palestine question. This phase of her effort will be considered in a different context. Internally, Israel tried to counterbalance the growth of Arab power and to compensate for her weak geographic-strategic position by adapting every relevant aspect of her life to considerations of defense and war. The nature of the present study precludes entering into all the details of Israeli life so affected; we shall attempt to give only a general notion of the extent to which defense has impinged on the economic activity and planning of the country and shall devote more attention to an analysis of the defense establishment itself.

Defense and the Management of Civil Resources

According to published data, Israel's defense expenditure in recent years has amounted to about 29 per cent of the government's current budget and to about 6.5 per cent of her total available resources, that is to say, her Gross National Product plus all the foreign capital and aid she received. These figures are lower than those of countries like the United States (about 51 and 14 per cent respectively) and Britain (about 29 and 10 per cent) which are much richer than Israel and carry a vast burden of international responsibilities and commitments; but they are almost twice as large as those of countries of Israel's economic class which carry a heavy defense burden such as Sweden (16 and 3.8 per cent) and New Zealand (12 and 3.7 per cent). Moreover, Israel's figures do not include certain classified defense expenditures, and understate the real direct cost of defense by evaluating imported military equipment at an artificially low rate of exchange. Were the appropriate adjustments to be made, Israel would probably appear as spending the same proportion of her resources on defense as Britain with all her imperial and global commitments.

Impressive as these figures are, they hardly give a true idea of the scope of Israel's defense effort. For, besides the direct defense activities reflected in these figures, Israel has adapted many of her normal economic and social programs to military considerations, sometimes at no extra cost, often at an enormous price which does not appear on the defense bill. This fact in itself may not be unusual in today's world; what is unusual is the relative scale on which Israel has done it. As a country that began to be built in recent years in circumstances of ceaseless and violent hostility, Israel has had the chance to build national defense into her very foundations. In the years since the 1948 War alone, when the enmity of the Arab neighbors became fixed in the mind of every Israeli, the authorities of Israel have had the chance to direct or influence the use of fifteen times more land, twice more population, and perhaps ten times more national wealth than existed at the birth of the state, with an eye to the defense problem. Few other modern states have had such an opportunity and none has made as much use of it as Israel.

The most important illustration of the incorporation of defense considerations into the foundations of the country is provided by Israel's agricultural settlements. From the early days of the Zionist endeavor in Palestine, the agricultural colonies, whatever their type, were not viewed solely as economic enterprises or as a way of life for their members, but were considered also as outposts spearheading or consolidating the Zionist conquest of the country. Initially, the enemy was the lawless beduin, who had previously made settled life impossible for anyone; in the twenties and thirties, it was the organized, politically directed guerilla bands bent on destroying the settlements to check the progress of Zionism in the country. In these latter years, many of the settlements assumed the physical shape of early American frontier forts, with stockade and towers, and their semimilitary exploits became part of the national mythology. During the War of 1948, practically all the settlements became full-fledged military bastions. Many of them were converted into formidable little hedgehogs with trench networks, prepared fire positions, rows of barbed wire, minefields, underground shelters, hospitals, and stores. The principal function of the settlements then —a function that has since become fixed in Israel's defense planning—was that of holding back enemy advance while the country mobilized its striking forces, or while these forces concentrated on particular chosen targets; and they acquitted themselves of their task brilliantly with few exceptions. Deganiah, on Lake Tiberias, blocked with its hundred or so armed men, reinforced by a regular platoon, the main Syrian advance. Gesher, further south, on the Jordan, prevented a junction of Syrian and Iraqi forces. Yad Mordechai and Nitzanim, in the northern Negev, slowed down the advance of the Egyptian army and caused its commander to pause and hesitate at the critical moment; while Negba, with 150 men, blocked decisively the advance of the Egyptian storming brigade toward Tel Aviv. Other settlements pinned down forces of the enemy and caused it to waste much of its effort, served as bases for commando raids in its rear, or provided jumping-off points for large-scale operations of the regular army which broke down the Arab fronts.

After the war, the acquisition of vast land areas by the state, the inflow of hundreds of thousands of immigrants, and the availability of hundreds of millions of dollars for development work enabled Israel to establish hundreds of new villages, planned, more than ever before, with a view to their role in the country's defense. Sites for the settlements were chosen by the authorities concerned in consultation with the General Staff. Their organization and the armament and training of their members were continually adjusted to cope with the advances achieved by the Arab armies and with the added security duties imposed on them, such as helping to check infiltration. Very often, the sites chosen for new settlements were not the best from an economic point of view, and their selection for military reasons involved a masked military expenditure in the form of greater and longer support for the villages from the settling authorities. In many cases, where defense requirements prescribed the setting up of a settlement in certain areas but where conditions did not permit any livelihood to be derived from them for some time, special sections of the army went on the land and took upon themselves the task of gradually improving it until it could be made to yield a livelihood for permanent settlers. The whole endeavor of colonization combining military and economic purposes was developed into a fine art which Israel is now imparting to some friendly countries in Asia and Africa confronted with comparable problems.

Immigration provides another example of Israel's shaping basic policies of the state to defense purposes. The "ingathering of the exiles," or the return of the Jews to their homeland, has been, of course, of the essence of Zionism and of the state to which it gave birth. But while Israel's authorities might have chosen at least to regulate the rate of immigration in accordance with the need of distressed Jews and the country's economic capacity, they chose instead to throw the gates of the state wide open and to take measures to persuade the hesitant and the reluctant to come, in complete disregard of economic considerations. This policy involved enormous waste as hundreds of thousands of people sat idly in reception camps in the early years of statehood eating the country's substance without producing anything; but the urge to increase the manpower pool for military purposes as quickly as possible prevailed over other calculations.

Similar considerations have affected every decision concerning the country's basic development. Israel's agriculture, for example, is now capable of feeding the country's population, including a steady, moderate stream of immigration; yet the government and the agencies concerned continue to make great efforts to lure people into new farming settlements because of their military importance. In planning the over-all distribution of the masses of immigrants and the location of the thousands of new industrial establishments, economic reasoning alone would have prescribed encouraging people to go where there is water, and industry to go where there are people, power, markets, and other facilities. Instead, Israel's planners have endeavored to guide people and industry to areas chosen for their strategic value though they might be barren, and to bring water, power, roads, and other facilities to them by means of enormously costly national schemes. Industries chosen for special solicitude have not been only those that promised to make the quickest or greatest contribution to the economy and those that happily combined reasonable prospects of economic viability with potential defense use; they also included many that required prolonged assistance and much protection at great immediate cost before they could become solvent—if, indeed, they ever could—because they were deemed militarily important. An aircraft industry, for example, was established on a large scale in Lydda though Israel had no qualifications for such an undertaking and was therefore bound to pay a heavy running-in cost before the enterprise could pay its way; but the price was accepted in order to build a local reserve of technicians and repairmen for the air force, reduce the country's dependence on foreign suppliers of parts, and perhaps eventually produce war planes locally. Tens of millions have been poured into building more and more cargo ships though many of the available ones often left Haifa half-empty or had to operate on charter entirely between foreign ports. But the urge to keep Israel's only supply route open, and the unwillingness to rely on foreign commercial shipping in emergencies overrode short-run economic considerations and impelled the young state to launch on a naval vocation regardless of cost. Much the same thing can be said about the recently built shipyards and large-scale integrated steel industry, about the automotive industry, and about a very large number of smaller enterprises, not to speak of a vast array of industries manufacturing military products, from canvas to explosives and from nets to machine guns, mortars and bazookas. In all these cases, desirability from a military point of view was decisive in getting the industries established, and economic calculations had to go on from that point.

The Military Establishment

Israel's defense planners sought to organize the country's armed forces in accordance with several principles prescribed by her overall strategic position. To counter the vast Arab numerical superiority in manpower, they sought to tap every man and woman who could be of any use for military service. To allow the country to support indefinitely a military establishment commensurate with its needs, they tried to organize the armed forces in such a manner that their size could be kept at reduced levels during peaceful intervals and yet be capable of very rapid expansion to meet the various degrees of emergency. To allow the armed forces to respond quickly to any grave threat that might develop at any point on the long and vulnerable front, they attempted to build an operational structure that would permit maximum mobility of large military units and great flexibility in their composition and power. To counter the fundamental geographic-strategic weakness—lack of depth for defense—they strove to gear the armed forces in every possible way to offensive warfare, relying for the static defense on the hedgehog-settlements system. How these men went about realizing their aims and to what extent they succeeded should become evident from what follows.

All three branches of Israel's armed forces—army, navy, and air force—are controlled and guided by a single General Staff, the chief of which receives his orders from the Minister of Defense, a convenient and economical form of organization which avoids duplication and interservice rivalry. The General Staff has the usual four departments—operations, manpower, supply and intelligence—which service all three branches. In addition to the central command, there are three permanent territorial commands under it known as "Fronts," one in the north, one in the center and one in the south. The Front Commands are responsible for troops in their territory with respect to mobilization, training, and administration, and are also in charge of directing military operations in their sectors and beyond the frontiers facing them. General Headquarters moves troops from one Command to another; each Command must therefore be ready on short notice to administer and feed large influxes of men, and to fuel and service their vehicles. This arrangement enables the permanent staffs of each Front Command to familiarize themselves thoroughly with the particular enemy and problems of their sector and to assimilate and array promptly large additions of forces, at the same time that it allows General Headquarters to move troops quickly from one front to another without too much concern about their supplies.

The basic formation of Israel's army is the brigade, which is more or less the equivalent of the American regiment. A brigade has 5000 men or less. The strength and organization of its sub-units are not rigid and depend on the availability of weapons and vehicles. Brigades have their own mortar and reconnaissance companies and their own signal, engineering, and antiaircraft platoons, each capable of expansion according to task. They do not have their own artillery; this is allocated to them according to requirements and availability. Any number of brigades can be temporarily grouped together for a special purpose into a "task force." Within each Front Command, the commander takes over any Task Force that may be formed from troops within his area. A skeleton Task Force Headquarters is maintained for this purpose.

Israel has no regular army as such. Her armed forces consist of a relatively small professional cadre plus conscripts and reserves. The professional cadre includes about 12,000 officers and N.C.O.'s who provide leadership, man the permanent framework, and "activate" the conscript and reserve brigades. Conscription applies to every male and female, to men for two and a half years and to women for two years. Some exceptions are made for women, but none whatsoever for men other than physical unfitness. Call-up age is eighteen, but immigrants arriving after that age are still conscripted and required to fulfill a period of service if they are subject to reserve liabilities. These liabilities are applicable after conscription up to age 49 for men and 34 for women and include up to 31 consecutive days a year plus one day per month. Officers are subject to an extra seven days a year of reserve service. Reservists are assigned to reserve brigades on a territorial basis; all reserve brigades are activated in turn either to train conscripts or to exercise their members on their annual call-up. Arabs of military service age are registered but only the Druzes (members of a Muslim heretic sect numbering 20,000 in the country) are called up.

The size of the active army at any time varies with the size of the call-up for conscription and with the security needs of the moment. Conscription brings in between 40,000 and 50,000 a year; total mobilization of trained reserves would raise, it is thought, up to 250,000 out of a population (Jewish) of two million. Mobilization of various units in turn is frequently practiced and has been developed into a fine art. Israelis boast they can mobilize twelve brigades in twelve hours and can have total mobilization in forty-eight hours. During the Sinai campaign in 1956, it was five days from the time the first reserve units were called up to the moment Israeli forces started their operations across the Israeli-Egyptian frontier; on that occasion, less than total capacity was mobilized. Whatever the exact size of the total mobilized strength and the precise time it would take to marshal it, there is little doubt that reserve duty is taken very seriously in Israel, that everybody who can be of military use is on call and knows it, and that partial mobilization can be achieved almost instantly and total mobilization very quickly.

A remarkable feature of Israel's armed forces is their very high ratio of combat-to-noncombat strength. It is said that up to fifty per cent of Israel's forces are "teeth" as compared with the twenty: eighty "teeth"-to-"tail" ratio of other large armies. This means roughly twenty-five fighting brigades plus an additional five brigades of home guard and static defense formations; Israelis say more. This achievement is made possible to a large extent by the small size of the country, which obviates the duplication of military installations, and by a very heavy reliance on civilian facilities in case of extraordinary "activation." All civilian vehicles, for example, are subject to call at any moment; during the Sinai campaign, 80 per cent of the infantry transport consisted of buses and other commandeered civilian vehicles. Civilian hospitals are prepared at any moment to turn sections into military hospitals. Garages and garage men can be taken over as working units. The Public Works Department with its depots, garages, sheds, equipment, specialized vehicles, engineers, and trained men are ready to be utilized when needed. Personnel of the sanitation, electricity, and water works are on call.

All these arrangements make for vast economies and liberate the maximum number of soldiers for fighting duties, though they cannot be very efficient in a protracted war. Their adoption reflects, in fact, two fundamental assumptions on which Israel's armed forces are built. One is that the Israeli army would not be called upon to fight an expeditionary war—an assumption based on the deliberate choice of Israel's authorities. The other is that, excepting a global war, any war in which Israel might be involved is bound to be short, calling for a maximum concentration of fighting force to achieve a favorable political-strategic posture before the imposition of a cease-fire through international intervention. This last assumption and the strategy based on it derive from an assessment of international political conditions and rely heavily on Israel's experience in the War of 1948. Fighting was then repeatedly interrupted by the United Nations to allow a mediated settlement, and the terms of the various settlement proposals invariably reflected the change in the military posture achieved in the previous stage of fighting. The 1956 War did not quite conform to this pattern in that Israel was denied most of the fruits of her victory. But the Israelis proved to be right on the question of duration. The Israelis further believe that the failure of the Anglo-French intervention confirmed their belief in the crucial importance of a quick, forceful action making do with the minimum of logistics and services. Had the two powers adhered to this principle, Israelis feel, they might have routed the Egyptian army and overthrown Abdel Nasser in the few days that were available to them between the time they issued their ultimatum to Egypt and Israel and the climax of international intervention. The cease-fire might then have found them in a position of having attained some of their main objectives and in a condition to insist on securing the remaining goals.

Another basic principle of Israel's armed forces is that in any hostilities with the Arabs they must take the offensive as soon as possible and carry the fighting into enemy territory. In the case of a full-fledged war, this principle is easily understandable in view of the obvious lack of depth for defensive maneuverings. But Israel has applied this principle even to counter Arab sabotage and harassing operations by carrying reprisal raids by large army units against targets beyond her borders. This type of action has brought Israel many condemnations by the Security Council and friendly governments, but these have never caused her to desist from undertaking the same type of action again. The reasons for Israel's defiance are many, but chief among them is probably her fear that if she respected frontiers, Arab operations might develop into large-scale guerilla warfare in which the enemy would have several "sanctuaries" to sally from and withdraw to beyond the armistice lines. Such warfare would compel her to use continually very large forces and would be frustrating, demoralizing, and costly. When, in 1956, Egypt seemed determined to carry out extensive *fedayeen* operations against Israel despite reprisal raids, Israel took all the military and political risks and launched a large-scale campaign in Gaza and Sinai.

The orientation of Israel's army is reflected in its training programs and in its general appearance. Primary emphasis is put on field action and combat, with a minimum of spit and polish. Stress is laid on speed, aggressiveness, and, above all, initiative. Officers beyond subaltern must complete toughening courses in parachuting or commando operations in addition to long training in combat leadership. Assumption of responsibility by lower echelons is encouraged, and commanders are instructed to lead their men into battle even though this might involve heavy casualties among officers as indeed was the case in the Sinai campaign. Relations between officers and ranks are easy and barrack regimentation is relatively casual, compelling officers to establish their ascendancy through competence. Promotion in all but the topmost ranks is based strictly and exclusively on proved experience and attainments in the field. During the period of frequent reprisal raids in 1955, reserve units were tested by deliberately entrusting such operations to them rather than to units of the standing army.

The air force and the navy are reared on the same principles as the army as far as being based on a professional core and a body of recruits and reserves, cultivating an offensive spirit, and maintaining close coordination with the relevant civilian enterprises and installations, such as the merchant marine, the shipyards, the commercial airlines, the aircraft industry, and the Ports Authority. Both arms are controlled directly by General Headquarters. Air and naval liaison officers are attached to the Front Commands each of which also maintains one or two "air tentacles" for direct ground support when necessary. Because of the relative dearth of equipment at their disposal, the air force and navy train many more men than they can readily use in order to make room for rapid expansion in case of need. The same policy is followed by all other technical arms such as the armored corps, the airborne battalions, and the artillery regiments.

An unusual feature of the Israeli armed forces is the *Nachal* (Hebrew initials for Pioneering Fighting Youth). This is an army corps designed to combine fighting with agricultural work. Men and women conscripts may choose to serve with Nachal for part or the whole period of their service. The main purpose is to found frontier settlements to supplement and help existing ones in insuring the static defense of the country until the army is able to mobilize or while it is occupied with offensive operations. Members of Nachal may stay on in the settlements they help to found if they choose, and many of them do. Another unusual institution sponsored by the armed forces is the *Gadna* (Hebrew initials for Youth Battalions). This is a voluntary organization for boys and girls aged 14 to 17 for the purpose of promoting patriotism, physical fitness, and premilitary training. Gadna maintains branches in all secondary schools and in the cities and towns, and has its camps and training sites. Youngsters engage in sports, judo and hikes; they play, learn how to handle weapons, and become acquainted with military affairs generally. There are air and naval, as well as army, Gadna units which help orient youngsters toward the respective arms in anticipation of their reaching induction age. While the purpose of the Gadna in normal times is mainly social and educational, in emergencies Gadna members can be useful in secondary military tasks as runners, guards, and so on.

Women serving in the armed forces is not an unusual feature in modern armies; but it is unusual to submit them to compulsory service and to reserve duties in peacetime as does Israel. Women constitute over 40 per cent of the mobilized strength of Israel's armed forces at any given time. This is much more than needed, but women are kept on for educational purposes, to broaden their outlook, teach them to look at themselves as equal to men, break their bondage to tradition, and so on. During the 1948 War, women often served in fighting units; now they are mainly used as clerks, typists, drivers, signallers, in supply depots, clinics, and hospitals, for parachute packing, in education and social welfare tasks. By filling these and similar jobs, women allow the maximum number of men to be available in the "teeth" units. In an emergency they can be used in static and civil defense tasks.

3. IMPLICATIONS OF ISRAEL'S DEFENSE EFFORT

With so much of her effort engaged in defense, with so many of her people involved in the armed forces, and with war so much at the center of her life, Israel, it has often been said, is doomed to become a militaristic nation, a nasty modern Sparta, even if she could manage to survive Arab hostility indefinitely. In their extreme forms, such prophecies have generally come from people who do not like Israel. But there are some observers who, while sympathizing with Israel and even admiring her determination and ingenuity in meeting the challenge of Arab hostility, are deeply concerned about the impact of the massive defense effort on the character of the nation that is being built and on the future of its democratic institutions and liberties. To what extent is this concern warranted, if at all?

Nothing in the record of Israel's experience so far seems to justify any sweeping prediction of total militarism. On the other hand, that record contains enough spots to make any outright dismissal of the issue somewhat hazardous. Let us look at the issue of civil liberties first. Justifiably or not—the question is not relevant here—most of the Arab minority, amounting at present to one ninth of Israel's population, have been subjected since 1948 to more or less stringent restrictions under military government on the ground that its members were security risks. The Arabs have not lacked very active and vocal champions among some of Israel's parties. On several occasions these parties, in alliance with others who opposed military government because they suspect Mapai of using it to extort Arab votes for itself, have come close to putting through a law abolishing it. But the fact remains that nervousness about defense, real or feigned, has led the Israeli government to impose a wholesale curtailment of liberties on a large portion of the population. As far as the Jewish population is concerned, the only important restriction imposed on security grounds has been the application of censorship to the press and to private correspondence on matters relating to defense. Opposition newspapers have complained sometimes that defense has been interpreted too broadly so as to protect the government against disclosures and political attacks that might damage its position; but there is no evidence that such practice, if it has taken place at all, has been frequent or widespread. As all governments in Israel have been precariously balanced coalitions of several parties, collusion to abuse the censorship for political purposes was bound to be very difficult, if not impossible. But as long as censorship exists, it is liable to misuse under circumstances that cannot be foreseen.

In regard to the relationship between the civilian and the military authorities, Israel's record has been clean so far of any intrusion of the military in politics in any form remotely resembling the recent ventures of the army in the politics of Argentina, Brazil, and France. No government has been toppled by military pressure, open or discreet, and no decision, as far as is known, has been forced on the government by the army. An important test was the withdrawal from Sinai and the Gaza Strip after the 1956 campaign; public opinion generally, including probably the bulk of the armed forces, was known to dislike it; nevertheless, the army heeded the government's decision to pull back without so much as an officer's publicly voicing his discontent. Conversely, despite the incursion of politics into most aspects of Israel's life, partisanship has been successfully kept out of the armed forces since the early years of statehood. This is no mean achievement if we recall that at the outset of the Palestine War, there were four distinct armed groups, three of which were closely associated with political groupings having distinct political philosophies. The Haganah was essentially nonpartisan, but the Palmach—the "shock troops"—though an arm of the Haganah, was closely identified with the extreme left-wing parties while the Irgun and the Lechi were avowedly and openly dissident armed political groups. At the beginning of the war, all four forces agreed to cooperate on the basis of a common central command and autonomous field units; but when in the summer of 1948 the Irgun attempted to land a shipload of arms and volunteers in violation of the spirit of that agreement, Ben Gurion ordered Haganah and Palmach forces to open fire on the ship and dissolved the separate military organization of the Irgun. Somewhat later he forcibly dissolved the Lechi after its members assassinated Count Folke Bernadotte, the United Nations' mediator, and not long after, he gradually merged the Palmach peacefully into the unified and single Defense Army of Israel. The brutal determination of Ben Gurion to eliminate anything resembling private armies in Israel is among the most notable of the many momentous services he has rendered his country.

Yet Israel's record of insulating the army from party politics and keeping it under civilian control has not been entirely free from blemishes. The outcry raised in the course of the Lavon Affair that the military chiefs had become too independent of civilian authority may have been exaggerated; but the affair did, nevertheless, reveal certain secondary pathological tendencies which might become very dangerous in the future. It revealed, first of all, that members of the top echelon of the Ministry of Defense and the army could and did obstruct the work of a Minister of Defense they did not approve of and were able to bring about his resignation. Secondly, it showed that grave sabotage and espionage operations were undertaken by the defense-military establishment without clear authorization from the Minister of Defense. Thirdly, it disclosed that for years it had been assumed that the Minister of Defense could order localized military operations that could compromise the country without previous reference to the cabinet or to some other authority. That these problems did not arise as long as Ben Gurion was Minister of Defense and became apparent only when, for the first time, someone else took charge of that post makes them all the more ominous by adding the implication that the men at the top of the defense establishment may have been reared too much on personal loyalty to one chief rather than on loyalty to the bearers of legitimate authority as such. To be sure, problems of a similar nature are often encountered in an established democracy like the United States; but their impact there is reduced by the existence of strong correctives deriving from the country's constitution, tradition, size, and power. Since the Lavon Affair, an effort has been made to meet some of the structural defects it revealed by the creation of a ministerial committee on defense which is hopefully intended to acquaint part of the cabinet with details of defense matters and to provide a body that could smooth out difficulties that might arise between the Defense Minister and his staff before they became magnified into crisis. But the real test of these or any other measures to consolidate legitimate civilian control of the defense establishment will probably not come until after Ben Gurion has withdrawn from the scene, and several successors have managed the Ministry of Defense.

The question of the impact of the defense effort on the character of the emerging Israeli nation is obviously much more complex than the topics just touched upon, and is more apt to be variously interpreted. We may perhaps confine the limits of possible controversy by drawing an artificial but useful distinction between the impact of defense on the process of nation-building as such, and its influence on the moral orientation of the nation. In the first respect, there can be no doubt that the defense challenge and the response to it made an enormous contribution to the consolidation of the Israeli nation and its political system. If the Irgun surrendered its private army without serious struggle, if a *Kulturkampf* did not break out between secularists and the religious, if the political warfare among the parties was not extended into an open social conflict, and if the antagonisms among the various communities, particularly the Oriental and the European, were not inflamed and made the basis of bitter "ethnic" hostilities, thanks are due largely to the general awareness of the foreign enemy at the gates and the imperative need for unity in confronting him.

In a more positive vein, the armed forces have acted as a highly effective melting pot and have assumed educative and social functions not undertaken normally by armies anywhere else. Military service has brought together Sefaradim and Ashkenazim, Sabras and new immigrants, religious and secularists, men and women, in a proximity which is not easily given outside the confines of the army. It allowed them to know each other and overcome some of their prejudices and stereotyped ideas, to learn and speak the same language, to share a certain amount of common knowledge of the country, its history, its terrain, its towns and cities beyond the confines of one's area of residence. It helped them to acquire some common ethics, values, folklore, habits, manners, and to achieve a basic common understanding of the nation's condition and its aims. Before the establishment of the state, commitment to the national cause was built up through many years of indoctrination and practical work in the branches of the various Zionist groups throughout the world and in their movements in Palestine itself. Since then, the army has become the most important instrument for fulfilling that function wholesale among the masses of immigrants who had had no previous acquaintance with Zionism. Although the army's work could not equal that of the Zionist groups in intensity and thoroughness, it has the advantage of embracing all the population in the prime of life and of emphasizing a national rather than a partisan or sectarian point of view.

Turning to the impact of the defense effort on the moral orientation of Israelis, the most important question we need to look at is whether or not that effort has turned or is turning Israel into a militaristic nation. If we take militarism to mean the extension of the outlook conventionally characteristic of army people to the whole population, and the projection of attitudes and dispositions typical of a war situation into peacetime, then the answer is a strongly qualified yes. If, however, we understand by militarism something akin to what Germany is reputed to have lived and practiced for long periods in this century, then the answer is no, perhaps slightly qualified.

One of the crucial facts about Israel is that she has had no tradition of a military establishment separate from the rest of society. In Yishuv days and since the establishment of the state, the bulk of the armed forces consisted of armed citizens clustered around a small core of permanent officers. The absence of a clear-cut separation between civilian and military and the lack of a specialized professional army have so far prevented the emergence of a caste-like military group with a distinct way of life, a particular collective consciousness, and its own way of looking at things. An attentive tourist can observe that Israel's men in uniform of all ranks outside of their barracks look and act less military than most military men elsewhere. On the other hand, the fusion of military and civilian in a popular army based on reserves has meant that Israel's citizens become involved in military matters more deeply and for longer periods of their lives than most citizens elsewhere; they therefore acquire the habit of looking at certain issues from a functional military perspective to a much greater degree than is usual among civilians in societies with a stricter division of tasks between soldiers and civilians. In other words, the comprehensiveness of Israel's defense effort had the effect of substantially "civilizing" the military at the same time that it led to a considerable militarization of the cilivian.

The absence of a militaristic ethos akin to Germany's is perhaps reflected among other things in the fact that Israel has developed no special or popular ideology glorifying war as such and seeing in the ability to wage it well a mark of inherent national superiority. The Israelis' desire for peace is genuine and universal regardless of what one may think of the effort they have made to secure it. At the same time, however, Israelis generally often take special satisfaction in saying or hearing it said that the Jews in their homeland have proved themselves to be as good and tough in warfare as any people on earth, and they take a quiet pride in the fact that they have inflicted many defeats on the Arabs and have been able to hold them at bay. Israelis, depending on age and background, may exalt their countrymen's achievements in one field or another—in science, pioneering, piety, learning, enterprise, the arts, and so on; but all Israelis without distinction are particularly impressed by military achievement and valor. With fierce partisanship and complete abandon, Israelis criticize everybody and everything; but the Defense Army of Israel, as the armed forces are officially known, is sacrosanct. This admiration of military prowess and this veneration of the armed forces is not entirely due to what we have called the "militarization of the civilian." It is also largely the result of the realization on the part of Israelis that their security and survival depend on their army and may have something to do, too, with an urge to compensate for the humiliating powerlessness of Europe's Jews in the face of their Nazi gaolers and executioners. If this last point is true, it may also account in part for a certain conspicuous toughness and proneness to violence on the part of Israelis, as if they were continually engaged in proving to themselves and to the world that Jews can no longer be "pushed around."

Israel has not developed any self-image depicting the nation's destiny or genius as lying in conquest, domination, or expansion. On the contrary, the traditional Judaic notion which views the Jewish people as the bearer of a spiritual light to the nations survives strongly in Israel, although in essentially secularized and muddled forms. Nevertheless, the militarization of the civilian has injected among Israelis a sense of *realpolitik* to an extent that is only rarely seen in the traditional Western democracies. Of course, the United States and Britain have always had their advocates of a foreign policy of strict national interest and power calculations; but these countries never lacked influential voices favoring altruism, moderation, idealism, nonviolence, adherence to international law, and so on. In Israel, on the other hand, the "realistic" line holds indisputable sway in certain matters pertaining to national defense. For instance, not a single Israeli outside the ranks of the Communist Party is likely to suggest the return of any significant portion of the territory conquered during the War of 1948. Only a small minority of Israelis vote continually for Herut, which formally advocates expansion beyond the Jordan; but should Israel be involved in war with the kingdom bearing the river's name, there are few Israelis who do not expect at least the western part of its territory to be annexed. For many years before the establishment of the state, the Yishuv rejected the Irgun's symbol of an arm holding a rifle with a caption underneath reading: "Only Thus" and even today the overwhelming majority of Israelis would reject that idea as a general proposition; but ever since the War of 1948, Israelis have learned to look at their position with the eyes of soldiers and to believe that they can keep only what they hold, and have to get what they want to keep. United Nations resolutions, they never tire of explaining, did not prevent the Arabs from attempting to annihilate them, nor did they stop Count Bernadotte from suggesting appeasement of the Arabs by granting to them conquered territory which had been allocated to Israel. They did not prevent Egypt from denying passage to Israeli ships in the Suez Canal and blocking the Gulf of Akaba. Only their armed resistance, Israelis contend, saved them from obliteration, and only their determined armed action secured for them the present boundaries and free passage through the gulf.

Israel cannot be accused of cultivating deliberately a cavalier attitude toward human life—another mark of militarism. Nevertheless, the constant exercises in fighting, the frequent actual armed clashes, large and small, and the need to keep army and reserves always ready for war physically and mentally could not fail to foster a certain objective recklessness toward life—one's own as well as others'. All nations are familiar with this phenomenon in wartime; but Israel has had to live with it continually. An exceptionally shocking manifestation of this tendency occurred in the tragic Kafr Kassim incident when, on the eve of Israel's invasion of Sinai in 1956, an Israeli officer ordered his men to open fire on some Arab inhabitants of that village, killing forty-three of them, for violating a curfew they did not know had been imposed. The Israeli authorities were alarmed by the event, brought the officer and his men to trial, and gave the proceedings wide publicity in the hope of countering the spirit it reflected. The court rejected the plea of the accused that they had acted under specific orders from their superior and asserted the principle, very daring to apply to an army, that soldiers obeying patently unlawful orders would be criminally responsible for the consequences. In the final account, however, one wonders whether the nature of an army's concern, and the particular environment and conditions of Israel, are not bound to undermine the sense of the value and sanctity of life despite any corrective the government may dare to apply while trying not to damage the readiness of its soldiers to fight.

Other aspects of the impact of defense—notably the impact of what we have termed "the militarization of the civilian" on the development of Israeli culture in general—are too intricate to allow us to do justice to them within the scope of a work of this kind. Even with all the space and time one could wish for, it would be exceedingly difficult to isolate the influence of this factor on Israeli culture from the multitude of other forces that have affected it.

The only thing that can be said on that subject here with a degree of certainty is that the defense endeavor has absorbed in its military and civilian establishments a very high proportion of the best minds and energies, as well as much of the economic resources, of Israel, and that to that extent the cultural potentialities of the country have not been realized as fully as they might have been. No one can blame Israel for caring first and foremost about her survival and defense and giving her best to them; but it is a tragic irony that, instead of the dream of many a Zionist that "from Zion the Law shall come forth and the word of God from Jerusalem," the most successful product that has come from Israel since her foundation has been the Uzi submachinegun.

Considering in its entirety the record of the internal consequences of Israel's defense endeavor, it would seem that one would need to be either a perfectionist or naive not to be favorably impressed with the survival of civil liberties and the functioning of democracy in the country so far, despite fifteen years of persistent and pervasive hostile pressure. Equally impressive is the fact that failures and blemishes in both respects did not go unnoticed or uncriticized, and that remedial action was taken to alleviate the restrictions imposed by military government on the Arab minority and to check the tendency of the Ministry of Defense to excessive secretiveness and autonomy. This testifies to the vitality of the democratic spirit in the country and to the responsiveness of government to criticism on defense issues, however belated or insufficient the response might be considered by some. On the basis of that record, there seems to be no ground for fears of a wanton and massive suppression of liberties in the foreseeable future under the pretense of defense necessity, nor does it seem likely that the military might some day take over the government as they have done in so many nations, both new and old. The troubling question about the future pertains not to any deliberate or obvious violations of democracy, but to the insidious influence of widespread concern with war and defense on the mind and moral attitudes of Israelis and on the character of the culture they are creating. That influence may in the long run undermine democracy and stunt spiritual and cultural growth.

PART FIVE: ISRAEL, THE MIDDLE EAST,
AND THE GREAT POWERS

Introductory

In a world bound together by modern means of communications and subjected to a common fate by the instruments of mass destruction, it has become common for governments of small as well as big powers to concern themselves with developments and events in parts of the globe which only a few years ago might have been as removed from their attention as the moon was then from the earth. Yet even by these new standards, the scope and intensity of Israel's interest in the field of international affairs are amazing. This is not merely due to the alleged habit of Jews, satirized by generations of Jewish comedians, of looking for "the Jewish angle" in such news as Eisenhower's latest golf score. Nor is it a reflection of an extraordinary nervousness about the fate of the world—Israelis have been generally too busy with their immediate problems to worry excessively about this. It is mainly that Israel does objectively have a stake, big or small, in an unusually large number of areas and problems. Her Zionist vocation, her involvement in the fate of Jewish communities everywhere, morally and as a recipient of aid and immigrants from them, her exceptional reliance on various kinds of foreign economic assistance, her involvement in continual hostility with the Arab states, her defense needs, and the fact that she is located in a seething area which is caught up in a bewildering tangle of conflicts involving the struggle between East and West, jealousies among the Western powers, clashes and tensions within and among the surrounding countries—all these factors, in addition to the usual grounds for international intercourse such as trade, cultural relations, friendship, concern for world peace, and so on, cause her to take an active interest in a range of questions which is far out of proportion to her size and her power-standing in the world.

To say that Israel takes an active interest in a very wide range
of questions does not, however, mean that she can bring any significant influence to bear on them. As a small power in a world
dominated by giants, Israel can do very little in most instances to
shape the course of events affecting her, and can rarely afford even
to *react* to them meaningfully. It is only in the area nearest to home
and in matters affecting her vital interests that she is impelled at
least to react, sometimes in a manner that can compel worldwide
attention as in her invasion of Sinai in 1956.

This basic position has three implications for our approach to the
subject of Israel's international relations. First, since our concern
with this question is mainly functional rather than academic, we
shall have to confine our discussion almost entirely to questions that
fall within the sphere of Israel's *vital* interests, where her moves can
be significant from an American or an international point of view.
Secondly, since Israel's moves even in that sphere have been more
often than not *reactions* to the initiatives of others, we can properly
understand them only by dwelling at least as much on the policies,
actions, and motives of those others. It also follows that we cannot
expect our examination to disclose any articulate, comprehensive,
and consistent Israeli policies, but rather a series of goals, positions
and dispositions which may yet be of help in gauging likely Israeli
reactions to future initiatives and events.

Israel's vital interests are involved in her relations with the countries of the area in which she is located and with the big powers of
the world. Her position in these two spheres is in turn affected by
the relations among the neighboring countries themselves, the relations among the various big powers, and the meshing of these
two sets of relations. Looking back at Israel's foreign relations over
the last fourteen years from this perspective, we can discern three
distinct periods of more or less equal duration. The first period,
lasting from the end of the war in 1949 to the spring of 1953, is
characterized by the evaporation of the theoretical alternative
courses and possibilities that seemed to exist for the newborn state,
and the crystallization of most of the basic facts that were destined
to rule its relations with the Arab countries and the big powers
directly or indirectly. The second period, extending from the beginning of 1953 to the end of 1956, is characterized by the rapid
deterioration of Israel's position as a consequence of the intensification of the big powers' struggle and the particular way in which it

meshed with the conflicts within the area itself, which impelled Israel to attempt to reverse the process by resorting to war. The third period, lasting from early 1957 to the present, has witnessed the emergence of a precarious balance in the relevant relations of Israel as a result of a temporary stalemate of the big powers' struggle in the area and the conflicts among the Middle Eastern countries themselves. The next three chapters will examine successively these three periods.

XIII

The First Period:
Crystallization of Factors

Israel, more than most new nations, began her sovereign career with a clear knowledge of the broad aims in foreign relations that were most important for her future. She knew that settling the conflict with her nighbors and consolidating her friendly relations with the giants of the world were crucial for her security, well-being, and development. But she was not overly concerned about her ability to achieve these aims and even looked beyond them to more ambitious goals. In the euphoria of the great historic moment of independence, everything seemed possible; and the facts of her early history tended to confirm this. Had not both the United States and Soviet Russia supported her at crucial moments in the struggles accompanying her birth? Did not the Arab states finally acknowledge her existence, however reluctantly, by concluding armistice agreements with her? Did not Great Britain, the only big power whose interests had placed it on the side of the Arabs against her, finally give up her earlier policy and signify this by recognizing her? Israeli thinking about foreign affairs in the first year or so therefore tended to soar to the realm of imagination, seeing the Jewish state as having a world historical role to play by virtue of certain unique endowments. Debates between the parties on foreign relations tended to be concerned with theoretical possibilities and alternative roles according to the ideological predilections of the participants, as if the only important question were the deliberate choice of the country.

All this changed rapidly under the impact of events in the few years following independence. Peace with the Arabs failed to materialize, and with this failure went the prospects of Israel's being able to maintain a policy of neutrality in her relations with the big powers. A greater involvement of the United States in the heartland of the Middle East presaged the introduction of the Cold War into the area on a larger scale than before; it also put a limit on the extent of support Israel could expect from a country now compelled to give more weight to Arab sensitivity, even as fear of Arab *revanchisme* and the deterioration of her relations with Russia impelled Israel to seek greater American support. The initial high-sounding idealism quickly gave way to a thoroughgoing realism based on a hard-boiled conception of the national interest, which was to be the overriding consideration in Israel's foreign policy.

1. THE ISRAELI VIEW OF THE NATIONAL INTEREST

Soon after the establishment of the state, Israelis came to recognize three basic objectives which they agreed were to be the supreme determinants of their foreign relations. First and foremost was the need to ensure the security and integrity of the state, in the immediate present and the longer-range future. All Israelis without exception have been in agreement that the most important measure to achieve that objective is genuine peace with the Arab states. In the absence of peace nearly all believe that the security and integrity of the state should be protected by a combination of national armed power and international support capable of deterring Arab aggression and crushing it should it occur. Such a combination, the Israelis believe, should also persuade the Arabs that Israel's existence is unshakable and thus convince them that by making peace they would not be conceding to the Jewish state anything it could not get by itself. The nature of the international support to be sought has been subject to disagreement among Israelis according to circumstances and party affiliation, but that the national armed power depends on access to heavy equipment and that this equipment should be secured from any source is generally acknowledged.

The second national objective recognized by Israelis is the urge to promote massive immigration of Jews from all parts of the world. This objective has its rationale in Zionist ideology; it is the *raison d'être* of the Jewish state. Perhaps only a few Israeli leaders still believe today that Herzl's conclusions about the inevitability of large-scale anti-Semitism and the hopelessness of the Diaspora apply to United States' Jewry; but probably most of them still think that these conclusions apply to most other countries in which Jews live and, at any rate, they are all convinced that a meaningful Jewish life can be lived only in Israel.

In addition to these ideological promptings, immigration is also fervently sought because of its close connection with the security of Israel and her prospects of survival. This may seem naive at first sight in view of the certainty that the Arabs will have an over-whelming numerical superiority under any conceivable circum-stances; but actually a substantial increase in Israel's population can be a crucial factor. In the first place, it should not be forgotten that in modern wars, the economic aspect is all-important. Should Israel's population reach the four million mark in the next fifteen years of her existence and should her economic performance ap-proximate in any way her achievement in the last fifteen years, she would then be able to marshal nearly half-a-million people for her defense and would have at least three times the present national product and twice the present per capita income from which to support and equip them. No reasonable forecast of Arab economic development during that period can be made to yield sufficient re-sources to provide for the minimum general economic and social progress needed to maintain internal stability, and at the same time to provide for training, arming, equipping, and supporting the gigantic armies that would be needed to crush such a force, much less to crush it quickly. Even now there are signs that Egypt is beginning to feel a strain on her resources in her effort to maintain her present military establishment while trying at the same time to push through programs of economic and social reform calculated to achieve only minimum goals in employment, income, health and education.

Even if these calculations should prove wrong, a substantial in-crease in Israel's population would still be crucial because it would make it very difficult for the Arabs to blot out the Jewish state even if they should defeat it. When Israel had a population of one or one-and-a-half million Jews, the Arabs could hope that if they could break through her defenses quickly, they would let the masses of refugees swoop in and, together with the Arabs already in Israel, swamp the Jewish population and dispossess it in a matter of days. Once this was done, it would be extremely difficult for international intervention, by the time it materialized, to unscramble peoples and to restore any semblance of a viable Jewish state. The question for the world would then be perhaps to organize the evacuation of those Jews who had survived the fire of the soldiers and the knife of the returning refugees. Today, with two million Jews in Israel, such a plan would be more difficult to realize; with three or four million Jews it would probably be impossible. Defeating Israel might in the latter case gain some concessions for the Arabs but it would not enable them to destroy her; and since the reward would be utterly disproportionate to the effort, the attempt might not be worth making at all.

In terms of Israel's international relations, promoting mass immigration has several important implications. It means, in the first place, the injection of a complicating issue in the Arab-Israeli conflict, since the Arabs fear that immigration might lead to Israeli expansion and Israel insists that the issue of immigration is not negotiable. It means, secondly, that Israel has to maintain an apparatus for the promotion and direction of immigration in all countries of Jewish concentration, having to take certain risks, sometimes, to do so. It means, thirdly, the injection of the immigration issue and considerations relating to the condition of Jewish communities as crucial factors in the relations between Israel and the countries concerned. Israel had, for instance, maintained cordial relations with Peron's Argentina largely out of regard for the half-million Jews living there, while her relations with Russia and some Soviet bloc countries have been soured to a large extent by Israel's attraction for their Jews, on the one hand, and on the other, by the prohibition or restriction of Jewish emigration and Jewish cultural life imposed by these countries.

The third national objective recognized by Israelis is rapid economic development. This goal bears its own, self-evident justification and is nowadays a universal aspiration. In the case of Israel, however, it assumes an added importance because it is a necessary condition for being able to absorb a massive immigration and is related in this way, as well as more directly, to the supreme objective of national security and survival. The implications of this objective for international relations derive from the fact that Israel has from the beginning been heavily dependent on outside aid for her economic development. Insofar as this aid comes from foreign government sources, its meaning for Israel, as for all countries dependent on outside aid, is that policy calculations have to take into account in greater or lesser degree the dispositions and interests of the helping countries. And insofar as this aid also comes from private Jewish contributions the implication is that Israel has to manage her relations with the countries in which the contributing communities live with this factor in mind. Just how far should Israel subject her foreign relations to these considerations in concrete instances has often been the ground for bitter controversy. But that the need to secure the means for economic development has a very high priority in all policy decisions is generally conceded. A dramatic illustration of the extent to which the government was willing to be influenced by this consideration is provided by its conclusion of the reparations agreement with Germany in 1951, despite the fact that it knew perfectly well the depth and bitterness of the popular feeling against Germany at that time.

2. THE FAILURE OF PEACE AND ISRAEL'S ARAB POLICY

Immediately after the conclusion of the armistice agreements with her neighboring states, Israel's main foreign effort was directed at an attempt to convert these agreements into final peace. The prospects for such a consummation then looked fairly promising. The Arab governments of the time seemed to have been impressed by the vigorous diplomatic and practical support Israel was getting from both the United States and Soviet Russia and by her ability to protect herself. Though embittered by their defeat, they showed signs of resigning themselves to it while putting the blame for it on the next Arab government, on the big powers, or on the United Nations. The common front they had attempted to put up on the Palestine question had patently broken down; and since Egypt led the way in signing a *separate* armistice agreement, it looked as though each Arab state was going to look after itself and try to live with Israel on the best terms it could work out with her. After those early months of 1949, there was never again to be such an opportunity for true statesmanship to apply itself fruitfully to the

Palestine question. Unfortunately, the opportunity was missed, partly through the fault of United Nations agents.

Even as the armistice agreements were being negotiated, the United Nations General Assembly had appointed a Conciliation Commission, composed of representatives of the United States, France, and Turkey, to follow them up by helping the parties to convert them into a final settlement. Instead of following the procedure which had just proved successful in the armistice negotiations and attempting to bring each Arab country face to face with Israel, the Commission made the fatal mistake of assembling all the Arab delegations together as one party and thus put them in a position in which none of them would dare make any concession for fear of being accused by the others of being soft on Israel. The first result was that the Arab delegations refused to sit with the Israelis and insisted on dealing with them through the Commission. Eventually, the Commission succeeded after months of effort in getting the parties to agree on the agenda and the basis for discussion in what came to be known as the Lausanne Protocol of May 12, 1949. The two sides agreed to take the United Nations partition resolution as a basis for discussing the boundaries question, and Israel, for her part, announced her willingness to take back 100,000 refugees as a good-will gesture prior to any negotiation of the whole refugee question. But this was the limit of the Commission's success; from that point on negotiations bogged down beyond retrieving and the two sides tried thereafter to qualify away the Lausanne Protocol.

As the Lausanne negotiations seemed to be heading toward deadlock, the Israelis made an effort to conclude peace with one Arab country separately. In March and April of 1949 the Israelis had already made secret contact with King Abdallah of Jordan during which the terms of the Jordanian-Israeli armistice agreements were actually worked out, while the world looked to the island of Rhodes, where the official armistice teams met. Now, after Lausanne, the two sides got together again and thrashed out slowly but steadily the terms of a peace treaty, which the king undertook to get his government to sign. The agreement was crucial for Israel since it involved a state which had under its control the most threatening strategic feature, the Arab bulge, and contained the majority of the refugees. But by the time negotiations had come near to conclusion,

the other Arab states had recovered from their initial resignation and were able to deter an Jordanian leader from putting his signature to a peace treaty. Contacts between the king and the Israelis continued sporadically, but on July 20, 1951, the courageous Jordanian monarch was shot dead in the old city of Jerusalem by a henchman of the former Mufti of Palestine, and with him went all prospects of an early peace.

Not since those years has there been any serious discussion between Arabs and Israelis aimed at achieving peace. On several occasions, when changes within one or the other of the Arab countries or in the relations among them indicated that there might be an opportunity for a fresh start, Israeli agents made contact with Arab agents to explore the prospects; but these attempts got nowhere. The sad truth is that the Arab governments have had very little incentive to make peace, and weighty reasons to oppose it. They had concluded the armistice agreements only because of the implied threat of military action to follow if they did not, and they were disposed for a brief while to go further and negotiate peace only because they thought this to be inescapable. But once they sensed that Israel would not dare resume hostilities to compel them to make peace, and once they realized the weakness of international pressure, they procrastinated for a time, and then balked altogether. The one exception of Jordan really proves the rule. Jordan was the one Arab country that expected to draw important benefits from peace by consolidating her territorial annexation, injecting into her economy large amounts of refugee compensation money, and gaining an outlet to the Mediterranean through free port rights at Haifa; even so, the attempt to make peace cost the king his life. Egypt and Syria, on the contrary, had reason to fear Israeli competition in their attempts to industrialize. Lebanon would have had to share Beirut's transit trade with Haifa, and she and Syria would have had to share with Israel the benefits from providing passage to oil pipelines. Besides, the Palestine question had become so embroiled in internal Arab politics and inter-Arab rivalries that the Arab governments had become the prisoners of the intransigent public opinion they had contributed to arousing.

Once the Israeli government realized that the Arab states were unwilling or unable to make peace, it directed its main foreign policy effort elsewhere, confining itself to an Arab "policy" which amounted to the sporadic assertion of a few principles and an attempt to convey by word and deed certain impressions of its attitude. It reiterated endlessly its readiness to discuss peace with no prior conditions, and at the same time it sought to impress the Arabs with Israel's strength and determination by reacting fiercely against any "encroachment" upon the security and territorial integrity of the country. It made the gesture of allowing over 30,000 refugees to reunite with their families in Israel, released blocked bank accounts of former Palestinians, and declared its readiness to pay compensation for refugees' property and to take back an unspecified number of them in the framework of a general settlement; but it endeavored to stress unequivocally that the bulk of the refugees would not be allowed to return and would have to be resettled elsewhere. It expressed its neutrality in the inter-Arab struggle for unity, but it made it plain that it would go to war to prevent the Jordanian bulge from being reinforced by the movement of other Arab troops into Jordan. It declared its opposition to "preventive war," but launched a war in Sinai to "destroy *fedayeen* bases" and warned that it would go to war to reopen the Gulf of Akaba if it were blocked again. Thus, the prevailing attitude of the Israelis seems to be: "Talk peace as if you were not acting tough, and act tough as if you were not talking peace." Whatever sense this attitude might make to Israelis, to the Arabs the toughness seemed the essential and the peace talk mere eyewash. The outside observer cannot doubt Israel's earnest desire for peace, yet he cannot help being puzzled by such gaucheries as Ben Gurion's inviting Nasser to talk peace on November 2, 1955, while Israeli troops were preparing to attack an Egyptian outpost in Sabha, which they wiped out the next day.

3. RELATIONS WITH THE POWERS: THE BRIEF VENTURE IN NEUTRALITY

While she was still working on a peace settlement with the Arabs, Israel tried to adopt a policy of neutrality in the struggle between East and West and of friendship with the United States and Soviet Russia. Such a policy was not just a reflection of Israel's gratitude for the help she received from both great powers but seemed also to be the line best calculated to promote her national interest. It was designed to ensure the continuation of the flow of immigration that was pouring from Eastern Europe and perhaps to win Russia's consent to the emigration of her own Jews, and aimed at the same time at making possible the continuation of the contributions of America's Jews and perhaps getting loans and aid from the American government itself. In the enthusiastic moments to which they were particularly prone in those days, Israelis had visions of their state blissfully immune from the conflicts of the world, quietly gathering its "exiles" from all corners of the globe, developing with the aid of Western Jewry its material and human resources, mending the scars of past hostility with its neighbors and bringing to them and to humanity at large the home-ripened fruits of the Jewish genius, uniquely enriched by centuries of universal experience. Such visions, alas, did not leave much of a trace once the Israelis woke up to the reality of the Arab states' unwillingness and inability to make peace; the Israelis not only engaged in marshaling their resources for the "second round" of which the Arabs began to speak, but started on a rapid process of whittling down the neutrality policy in an endeavor to ensure their national security through some diplomatic arrangement with the West.

The prcoess began early in 1950 when Israel's government requested the American government to sell a quantity of arms to it in order to counter the shipments that were being made by Britain to some of the Arab states by virtue of outstanding treaties. The pleas of Foreign Minister Sharett for approval of the request promptly evoked charges from the Soviet Union that he was "cringing" before the United States. The American government was sympathetic to Israel's needs but feared the development of an arms race in the Middle East which might lead to renewed war. Consequently, it made an effort to coordinate arms sales with Britain and France, the area's traditional arms suppliers, which was reflected in the Tripartite Declaration of May 25, 1950. The Declaration, however, went beyond the subject of regulating arms sales to an attempt to lay a basic policy of the three powers regarding the chief problems of the zone. It proclaimed their determination to act within and outside the United Nations to oppose any attempt to modify the armistice boundaries by force and, while declaring their intention to prevent the creation of any imbalance in armament, promised to supply Israel and the Arab countries with enough weapons to meet their legitimate needs for self-defense, and "to permit them to play their part in the defense of the area as a whole."

The guarantee of her frontiers and the promise to supply her with arms on the basis of a balance of forces between her and the Arab states could not fail to please Israel immensely. The idea of possible participation in a regional alliance, hinted at in the bracketed phrase, was somewhat problematic since it was likely to antagonize Russia. But this disadvantage seemed to be balanced by the prospect of being included with the Arabs in one defense organization, and by the realization that a worse problem would result if she remained outside an organization that promised to reinforce the Arabs militarily. Consequently, Israel's government welcomed the Declaration, promptly rejected a warning from the Soviet government against forming any Middle East bloc, and was as promptly denounced as having sold out to the imperialist Western powers.

A few weeks after the Tripartite Declaration, the Korean War broke out. From the beginning of the conflict and throughout its course, Israel supported the United States in every move in the United Nations, including the decision to authorize the forces fighting under the United Nations' flag to cross the thirty-eighth parallel and reunify Korea by force. In the world forum and at home, Foreign Minister Sharett explicitly renounced the neutrality policy in favor of a line that, he said, would not align Israel permanently with either bloc. But in December 1950, after the Chinese intervention in Korea raised the specter of general war, the Israeli government, fearing the disruption of the country's supplies and its isolation in the face of its enemies in such an eventuality, was reported to be studying the possibility of an outright alliance with the West. The outcome of this study and whether or not it led to any diplomatic initiatives is not known; in any case, the necessity for the move faded as the fighting in the Far East reached a stalemate the following summer and the shadow of world war receded. But Israel's new tendency toward an alignment with the West became increasingly apparent. This tendency was confirmed when in November 1951 the Israeli government was unofficially reported willing to join the Western-sponsored Middle East Defense Command, a proposal which had been submitted to Egypt the previous month.

From the perspective of recent years, when neutralism has become fashionable and expedient, many who have Israel's interest at heart have criticized her government for surrendering the neutrality policy and seeking to ally itself with the West or with the United States alone. Looking at the matter from Israel's point of view, one may well agree that her government erred in its estimate of the United States' readiness to meet its wish for such an alliance, and therefore made some premature and badly conceived moves. But basically Israel's neutrality policy was untenable once peace with the Arabs failed and the Cold War encompassed the area. She could not remain indifferent to the efforts of East and West, using weapons as a lure, to win over her declared enemies. Sooner or later she was bound to turn to one of the two camps in search of some guarantee of her security. That she actually turned to the West was not only a logical outcome of the affinity of regimes, the many connections she has with Western Jewries, and of the economic aid she obtained there, but was also a matter in which the Soviet government left Israel little possibility of choice.

4. THE UNITED STATES' INTERVENTION IN THE MIDDLE EAST

The Tripartite Declaration and the proposal of a Middle East Defense Command signalized an extension of America's involvement in the Middle East from the Greek-Turkish fringes to the heartland of the area. The extension was of the utmost consequence since it converted what looked like a rearguard British action into a new drive aiming at integrating that part of the world into the global Western containment belt against the Soviet bloc. This necessarily brought the Cold War into the area in an intensive way and thereby complicated all its politics. For although the specific proposal of a Middle East Defense Command submitted to Egypt in October 1951 was almost stillborn, attempts to draw the area into the Western defense system in one way or another and America's full involvement in Middle East politics have continued to the present, and so, of course, have their implications. In order to understand this crucial event and subsequent developments in the Middle East we must pause for a moment to consider its background.

At the root of the American intervention in the heartland of the Middle East there are three factors: the failure of Britain's postwar policy there, the particular interest manifested by America in Palestine, and the intensification of the struggle between East and West. At the conclusion of the second World War, Britain emerged as the sole dominant power in the Middle East after having ejected the Italians from Libya and helped ease the French out of Syria and Lebanon. Some time before the end of the war, the United States had begun to show interest in Saudi Arabia and shortly after it she began to exert pressure in support of Jewish demands for resumption of mass immigration in Palestine; but these attentions of the American government seemed to be in the nature of lobbying on behalf of some interests of its citizens and did not question Britain's hegemony in the area as a whole. Even after the Truman Doctrine committed the United States to the defense of the Greek-Turkish fringes of the Middle East and to a policy of containing Communist expansionism everywhere, the American government was, on the whole, quite content to let the British take care of the hinterland by themselves. For Britain's interests in the area were known to consist essentially of protecting her vast oil interests, on which she depended heavily for the reconstruction of her economy, and of ensuring the security of her imperial lines of communications; and insofar as these interests required Britain to work for the stabilization of the area as a whole and for its defense against outside attacks, they were basically in harmony with America's global policy as enunciated in the Doctrine. The trouble between the two countries over Palestine developed out of the complete inflexibility of Foreign Secretary Bevin's stand on the question in the context of his varied policies to realize Britain's broad objectives.

Britain's position in the Middle East at the end of World War II rested on treaties of alliance with Egypt, Iraq, and Transjordan and the Mandate she held over Palestine, and on troops and bases she maintained in all these countries by virtue of those agreements. But even before the war was actually over, nationalists in Egypt and Iraq had begun to agitate for the termination of those treaties and the evacuation of their country, and Jews in Palestine had launched a campaign of terror and other illegal activities to bring about the repeal of the White Paper of 1939 which restricted Jewish immigration and colonization. Transjordan seemed quite content with her treaty with Britain but she, together with all the other Arab countries, was anxious about the future of Palestine. Britain herself, it should be added, was economically exhausted by the war, and her government was under very heavy pressure to reduce the country's overseas commitments as quickly as possible.

All this made it quite obvious that Britain needed to revise her entire position in the area.

In going about this task, Foreign Secretary Bevin had one primary object in mind, and that was to secure a few viable bases in the region from which the Suez and overland routes to the East, and the Iraqi and Persian Gulf oil could be protected. Just where and how these bases should be sought was a relatively flexible question, since the Foreign Secretary had in fact several plans. It might be possible to induce the Arab League to sign a collective treaty to replace the hated treaties Britain had with some of the League's members. It might be possible to help some of the Arab statesmen realize old dreams of a Fertile Crescent or a Greater Syria in exchange for an alliance and bases. It might be possible to induce some Egyptian government and some Iraqi government to sign new, more liberal, agreements to replace the old, while still retaining access to the bases Britain occupied in these countries. There were still other possibilities but two things were quite clear to the Labour government's Foreign Secretary and these were that any bases that could serve the purpose, if they were to be viable and be held cheaply, had to be held with the consent of the Arab governments concerned, and that the consent of these governments would depend largely on the kind of policy he adopted in Palestine.

We need not concern ourselves here with Bevin's successive attempts to achieve his purpose except to highlight some relevant facts. He endeavored, against mounting Jewish defiance and violence and increasing American pressure, to maintain the status quo in Palestine by all means until he could explore with the Arab governments the various possibilities of achieving his purpose. But, in the two years during which he was able to withstand the pressure before surrendering the Palestine question to the United Nations, he failed in all his negotiations with the Arab governments, although he had not budged one inch from the White Paper of 1939. Throughout, he saw only shady motives in American pressure on behalf of the Jews and expressed these views in harsh words, thereby permitting a gulf to develop between American and British positions on Palestine. Finally, by early 1948, after the Baghdad mobs had torn up a new treaty he had just signed with the Iraqi premier, and after the United Nations had already decided to partition Palestine, he was ready to play his last card. This aimed at taking advantage of the chaotic situation in Palestine in order to gain for his only reliable ally, Transjordan, access to the Mediterranean. Such a move would make that country suitable for the relocation of the bases then in Egypt and Iraq. Accordingly, on May 15, 1948, as the Mandate in Palestine formally came to an end, the British-led Arab Legion of Transjordan moved in to seize at least the territory allotted to the Arab state by the partition plan, and perhaps to improve on it by capturing some areas that would make access to the sea more secure. This time, however, Arabs, Jews, and Americans coalesced fortuitously to frustrate Bevin's plan. The intervention of Transjordan provoked other jealous Arab countries to send in their armies to block her expansion as much as to fight the Jews; the Israelis offered unexpectedly successful resistance to all the Arab armies and barred Transjordan's path to the sea; and when the British tried in the United Nations to promote the Bernadotte plan, which was to give them by diplomacy what their ally had failed to obtain by force, the American President blocked their effort.

The failure of Bevin's endeavors left Britain in a shaky position as the Middle East entered upon an era of turmoil unequalled even in its own long disturbed history. The British still retained bases in Iraq and Suez, but they were clearly on the defensive in both places, especially in Egypt, where a new government led by the veteran nationalist party, the Wafd, was soon to begin the most reckless agitation and guerilla campaign against them. In all the Arab states, governments and political leaders succumbed to waves of assassination, street riots, and military coups. The peace talks between the Arab states and Israel had failed, and the brief moment of sobriety in their relations that followed the war quickly gave way to mutual fears and threats, sharpened by Britain's resumption of arms deliveries to Jordan, Iraq, and Egypt under the terms of her treaties with them. It was clear that Britain alone could no longer take new initiatives to stabilize the situation, just as it was clear that such initiatives were crucially needed. For even as the Palestine conflict reached its climax in the War of 1948, the Cold War between East and West had reached new heights as a result of the Communist coup in Czechoslovakia, Tito's defection from the Soviet bloc and Moscow's threatening reactions to it, and the Berlin blockade. The tensions generated by these conflicts made a general war seem very likely and drove the Western powers together in the North Atlantic alliance at the same time that they impelled Washington to seek to strengthen weak spots at the periphery of the Soviet bloc. Among these, the Middle East heartland seemed so unstable as to invite aggression or encroachment; and since Britain alone could no longer cope with that instability, there was no alternative for the United States but to intervene herself. The first result was the Tripartite Declaration of May 1950.

The immediate aim of the Tripartite Declaration was to freeze the Arab-Israeli conflict after the failure of the peace negotiations and to prevent it from degenerating into another armed clash. But it was also a preparatory step to another measure, forecast in the Declaration itself, aimed at suggesting an outlet for the British-Arab impasse and strengthening the defense of the area by bringing all the parties together into a regional defense organization. The submission of specific proposals for this next measure was delayed by the outbreak of the Korean War a few weeks later which preempted the attention of Washington and the world; but once that war reached the point of stalemate, the need to provide for the defense of the Middle East became more urgent than ever. On the one hand, the Korean War had demonstrated that Soviet leadership was ready to resort to open aggression to break through at vulnerable spots along the periphery of the non-Communist world; on the other hand, the situation in the Middle East had deteriorated gravely as the Wafdist government broke off negotiations with the British and prepared to abrogate the 1936 Treaty unilaterally, and as Iran was thrown into turmoil as a result of the nationalization of the British-owned Iranian Oil Company. Consequently, on October 13, 1951, the United States, Britain, France, and Turkey put forward the proposal for a Middle East Defense Command. The proposal was submitted to Egypt first because the crisis there was nearing its climax, because plans for the defense of the area rested on the Suez Canal base, and because Egypt's acceptance was thought essential to pave the way for acceptance by the Arab countries. When Egypt peremptorily rejected the offer, the Middle East Defense Command died. However, other reincarnations of it were still to haunt the area for many years and the United States was henceforth to be actively associated with them.

THE DETERIORATION OF
ISRAELI–SOVIET RELATIONS

Contrary to earlier expectations, it had become clear to Israel in the course of the many-sided *pourparlers* concerning the Middle East Defense Command that the proposing powers, while wishing to include her in the envisaged organization, were not going to make her participation an essential condition for starting it if the Arab states objected to her inclusion. Therefore, Israel's government was relieved to see the proposal collapse as a result of its rejection by Egypt, and tried now to repair some of the damage suffered in its relations with Russia since it had given its welcome to the Tripartite Declaration. In February 1952 it gave its assurance to the Soviet government that Israel would not join any aggressive alliance against Russia, after having previously rejected several specific Soviet warnings not to join any Western-sponsored regional organization. But the Israeli gesture was futile, and relations between the two countries moved soon afterward to the breaking point with dizzying speed.

Sometime in the middle of 1952 a wave of anti-Semitism and anti-Zionism erupted throughout the Soviet bloc which, in its emotional fervor and violence, was comparable only to the hysteria that accompanied the Great Purges of the 1930's in Russia. The incredible frenzy soon provided its own justification in a series of sensational events. In December 1952 came the Prague Trials of Communist boss Rudolph Slansky and his associates which linked the Jewish Secretary of the Czech Communist party with Zionism, Israel, and the "American warmongers" in an unspeakably wicked conspiracy. In the following January came the Moscow Doctors' Plot in which four Jewish physicians were linked with the Joint Distribution Committee, the "well-known agency of the American intelligence," in a satanic scheme to assassinate top Soviet leaders. In February, anonymous infuriated Israelis bombed the Soviet Legation in Tel Aviv and provoked Moscow to retaliate immediately by breaking off diplomatic relations with Israel amidst a barrage of vituperation against her government unusual even in the Soviet tradition.

The origin of this frenzied outburst has found no explanation to the present day unless it may be attributed to the failing mind of Stalin just before his death. Khrushchev's revelation of other instances of Stalin's odd behavior in his last days, the fact that the fury continued until his death in March 1953 and then stopped abruptly, and the subsequent admission by Soviet authorities that the Doctors' Plot had been contrived seem to point in that direction. But leaving aside the exceptional emotional violence of the eruption, one could think of a few "understandable" reasons as to why the Soviet government should have changed its initial friendly and helpful attitude toward the Jewish state into one of hostility.

First of all, it should be understood that Soviet support of the United Nations' partition plan and of the Jewish state had come against a background of nearly three decades of unrelenting hostility to Zionism. This hostility had been founded on ideological as well as tactical grounds. Ideologically, Soviet doctrine maintained that anti-Semitism, a chief *raison d'être* of Zionism, was the outcome of the capitalist system and could be eliminated only by the elimination of that system everywhere. Zionism, by looking for a solution to that problem in the return of the Jews to Palestine, appeared to be a reactionary movement which diverted the attention and great revolutionary potential of the Jewish toiling masses and intellectuals from the class struggle to the pursuit of a romantic idealist dream. Tactically, the Soviet Union opposed Zionism because of that movement's alliance with British imperialism through the Balfour Declaration and the Mandate, and its serving as a whip in the hands of that imperialist power to perpetuate its dominion over the Arab peoples.

After the conclusion of the second World War, the conflict between the Yishuv and the British on the one hand, and the apparent rapprochement between the British and the Arabs, which rested largely on the anti-Zionist Palestine policy of Bevin, suddenly reversed the tactical situation: now it was the Jews who were fighting British imperialism and the Arabs who were lending themselves to its machinations to maintain itself in the area. The coming of the Palestine question before the United Nations just at that time gave the Russians the opportunity to lend a helping hand to the Jews in their effort to rid that country of British rule. Ideally, the Russians would have preferred to support the federal solution recommended by the minority of the United Nations Special Committee on Palestine, which would have achieved the same purpose of evicting the British without antagonizing the Arabs as much as the partition plan. But a quick survey of the distribution of forces in the United Nations indicated that partition was the only plan that had a chance of getting the required two-thirds majority; consequently, Soviet Russia and her satellites cast their votes for it. When the British and the Arabs made common cause to nullify this decision by force, the countries of the Soviet bloc did everything to help the Yishuv and the Jewish state frustrate their effort.

While the Soviets thus supported the Jewish state on tactical grounds, their basic hostility toward Zionism on ideological grounds remained unchanged, or almost unchanged. In his historic speech in the United Nations supporting partition, Soviet delegate Gromyko went so far as to say that the failure of the capitalist Western powers to protect their Jews against the brutal Hitlerite onslaughts entitled those who survived the massacres to look for protection among their brethren in Palestine in a state of their own. But he left the clear implication that the Jews living in the socialist camp had no need of any Jewish state or any Zionist help. This view was spelled out somewhat later as clearly as it could be for the benefit of the Soviet-bloc Jews by the prominent Russian Jewish writer Ilya Ehrenburg. Writing in *Pravda* of September 21, 1948, at a time when the Soviet government was still giving practical help to Israel, in answer to a question about the attitude of the Soviet Union toward Israel, Ehrenburg noted that the U.S.S.R. had always supported *all* the oppressed in their struggle against imperialism; after paying tribute to the soldiers and toilers of Israel, he went on to remind his readers that the Jewish state was no heaven, that it was already beginning to be invaded by American capital, and, above all, that the solution of the "Jewish question" did not ultimately depend on Palestine and military victories, but on the triumph everywhere in the world of socialism over capitalism. "The citizen of a socialist society . . . ," he concluded pointedly, "looks upon the people of any bourgeois country, including the people of the state of Israel, as upon wayfarers who have not made their way out of a dark forest . . . Soviet Jews are rebuilding their socialist motherland together with all the Soviet people. They are not looking toward the Near East; they are looking to the future."

What happened, then, after the establishment of the Jewish state was that the tactical reasons for supporting it disappeared and were even reversed, and the ideological reasons for opposing it reasserted themselves with more urgency than ever. The tactical reasons disappeared when Israel fulfilled her purpose in Soviet eyes by helping to throw the British out of Palestine and fighting successfully to keep them from re-entering it through the back door in the wake of the Arab Legion. They began to be reversed when Israel seemed to be helping to have the "old British imperialism" replaced by the "more youthful and vigorous American imperialism." To Soviet thinking at that time, Israel started to become the tool of American imperialism even before she welcomed the Tripartite Declaration, supported the United States on Korea, and showed her eagerness to join in a regional defense organization; she moved toward the enemy camp when she sought American economic aid and when she adopted a policy of neutrality. For at that time Soviet foreign outlook was guided by the "Zhdanov Doctrine," reminiscent of the later view of Secretary Dulles, which considered neutrality in the East-West struggle as tantamount to tacit support of the enemy. Naturally, Israel's actual surrender of neutrality and her gradual movement toward the West made matters much worse.

The reversal of the initial tactical grounds for supporting Israel would have been sufficient reason for the reassertion of the ideologically motivated hostility to the Zionist state. As it was, this reassertion was made all the more urgent by a completely unforeseen development of great moment: the reawakening of Zionist sentiment among large numbers of Russia's Jews. In explaining the reasons for Russia's support of the Jewish state, Gromyko may have expressed all sorts of implicit caveats about Zionism, but these subtle qualifications were lost on the large number of Russian Jews who had repressed their love for Zion for decades and who now took their government's support of Israel as a license to express their emotions and as a glimmer of hope that they might be permitted to leave for the Promised Land. Was not their government allowing and even encouraging tens of thousands of Jews from the satellite countries to go and join in the defense and development of the new state? Ilya Ehrenburg's letter was designed precisely to warn against such illusions; but so strong was the feeling aroused among Jews that a visit by Israeli ambassador Golda Meir to a Moscow synagogue on the Jewish High Holidays a month later became the occasion for a spontaneous demonstration by thousands of Muscovite Jews expressing their affection for the state she represented. The whole phenomenon of Russian Jews' showing concern for Israel was not merely an intolerable identification with a foreign state; it also reflected, three decades after its enunciation, the fallacy of Soviet doctrine and policy on the "Jewish question" which envisaged its solution by assimilation through the triumph of socialism. Infuriated, Stalin decided to strike back by terrorizing his Jews, by launching a campaign against "rootless cosmopolitans," by destroying all remnants of Jewish culture and eliminating Jewish writers who retarded the process of assimilation, by depicting the state of Israel—the object of his ungrateful subjects' love—in the blackest terms and leaving no shred of doubt as to how the Soviet government felt about it.

After the death of Stalin in March 1953, the convulsive attacks against Israel calmed down to more routine hostility and, in July of that year, diplomatic relations between the two countries were resumed after Israel had given renewed assurances that she would not join any aggressive pact against Russia. But a few months later the new Soviet leadership, having given up the "Zhdanov Doctrine" for a more flexible policy, was engaged in the beginning of a drive to win influence in the Middle East by espousing Arab causes against the West and backing the Arab states against Israel. This was to reach its first climax in the Soviet-Egyptian arms deal in the late summer of 1955. For its part, Israel's government became convinced that there was nothing it could do to improve the Soviet attitude toward Israel, and resigned itself to taking for granted a relation of subdued hostility between the two countries until a change in the tactical situation in the Middle East or a modification of Soviet policy toward Russia's Jews created more favorable circumstances for friendlier relations.

XIV

The Second Period: The Road to Sinai

After four years of statehood, Israel's government and people may have looked back upon their achievements in the field of international relations with only qualified satisfaction. Israel had gained international recognition, secured American aid, received masses of immigrants from Eastern Europe and the Muslim countries, and was covered by the Tripartite Declaration. But her effort to make peace with the Arabs had failed, and so had her endeavor to consolidate her security position through an international engagement more binding than the Tripartite Declaration; just then, too, came the icy gusts forecasting the storm that was to blow from Moscow. Yet, from the point of view of Israelis, so bad were the four years following, that from the perspective of the eighth anniversary celebrations the first four years must have looked to them idyllic by comparison. From 1953 onward, event seemed to conspire with event to corner the young state and wreak its ruin until, in 1956, its government seized a fleeting opportunity to strike a daring blow in an attempt to reverse what appeared to be fate's course.

1. THE FOUR LEAN YEARS

The fact that the four lean years of Israel's foreign relations corresponded with the first term of the Eisenhower Administration was not entirely coincidental. The Middle East policies and measures adopted by the new Secretary of State had much to do with Israel's misfortunes. It was not that Secretary Dulles sought to alter in any fundamental way the American government's moral commitment to the existence and integrity of Israel, as expressed among other occasions in the Tripartite Declaration. In fact, even at the lowest point in Israel's fortunes, he refused to associate the American government with a publicly voiced suggestion by Britain's Prime Minister Eden that Israel should make some territorial concessions as a price for peace with the Arabs. Rather, Israel's troubles stemmed indirectly from the implications of policies that the United States attempted to pursue vis-à-vis various Arab states. Israel's government saw grave dangers in Dulles' attempt to woo the Arab states into an alliance with the West without due regard for the repercussions on the Palestine issue; it was convinced that the Arabs would use their increased military capacity resulting from the alliance only against Israel. The Secretary of State, however, believed that if the Arab states were in the Western fold, they could be prevented from taking any warlike initiative against Israel. In effect, Dulles was, as it were, asking Israel to entrust her security to the United States without any formal commitment. This, the Israeli government was unwilling to accept if it could help it, especially since the Secretary of State, in the course of his efforts to woo the Arabs, tended to speak and act in ways that were bound to arouse misgivings among Israelis.

Israel's apprehensions were aroused by a declaration made by Secretary Dulles as soon as he assumed office, to the effect that the United States was henceforth going to pursue a policy of friendly impartiality between Israel and the Arab states. For just as the Secretary of State was to assert later that neutrality in the conflict between the free world and Communism was immoral, so the Israelis felt that impartiality as between Isreal and the Arab states unjustly and dangerously blurred the distinction between the potential aggressor and his potential victim.

The apprehensions of Israel were reinforced when a request for a $75 million loan was promptly turned down. They became confirmed when, in October 1953, the American government withheld the disbursal of economic aid earmarked for Israel because of her noncompliance with an injunction of the United Nations' Truce Supervision Commission to halt work on a hydroelectric project on the river Jordan pending consideration of the issue by the Security Council. These incidents seemed all the more significant to the

Israelis since the American government was at the same time making a special effort to be demonstratively friendly to the new government of Egypt and had already outlined the idea of a new regional defense organization which left Israel out of the picture from the outset.

In the spring of 1953, Secretary of State Dulles went on a fact-finding expedition that took him to all the principal countries of the Middle East, preparatory to formulating a New Look in foreign policy. The conclusions he reached confirmed the aim of the Truman Administration of trying to reinforce the area against Communist pressure and possible aggression through a regional defense organization linked to the West, but introduced important modifications in the method of pursuing this aim. Instead of trying to build a defense organization encompassing all the area at once, he suggested doing the job piecemeal, starting with the countries of the "northern tier," and then gradually drawing in the others. This approach seemed to the Secretary of State to offer the advantage of allowing a start to be made toward the creation of the desired alliance among those countries that had shown some awareness of the Communist danger, without having to wait for a solution of the Anglo-Egyptian problem and the Arab-Israeli conflict. It was probably the hope of the Secretary of State that once the organization got going in the north, it would constitute a pressure on the Arab countries of the south to join it.

The first step toward the realization of the "northern tier" alliance was taken early in 1954, when Turkey and Pakistan signed a mutual defense agreement which received the blessings of the United States and a promise of military and economic aid. This was of no particular concern to Israel. Two months later, however, the United States awarded military and economic assistance to Iraq with the view of facilitating the effort of her government to bring that country into the alliance. Israel protested both directly and through her friends in the United States that arms to Iraq endangered her security since that country, which had participated in the War of 1948, had not even signed an armistice agreement with her. But she was only given verbal reassurances that the military aid given to Arabs would not lead to an arms imbalance or to renewed aggression. At the beginning of 1955, Iraq formally joined the Turkish-Pakistani alliance, in June Britain followed suit, and toward the end of the year Iran too came in, thus converting the Turkish-Pakistani alliance into CENTO, or what came to be known informally as the Baghdad Pact. The United States, which originated the idea, stayed out of the Pact and contented herself for the time being with supporting it economically and militarily. This was hardly a consolation for Israel who knew that the American government's reserve was due to its desire to continue wooing Egypt, whose government was opposed to the Pact, and to avoid any premature embarrassment that might result from Congress choosing to delve into the implications of the Pact for Israel. Therefore, as soon as Iraq joined the alliance, Israel's government applied to the United States, Britain, and France to include Israel in the Western defense system through NATO or in some other way; and when this initiative failed, the Israeli government urged the United States formally and openly to conclude a bilateral mutual defense treaty. As Israel herself undoubtedly expected, the American government could not meet her request since this would have doomed its efforts to draw the Arab states into a regional alliance. In August 1955, Secretary of State Dulles announced the United States' readiness to provide large-scale aid for the repatriation or resettlement of the Palestine refugees and the development of regional irrigation schemes, and her willingness to guarantee any frontiers on which Israel and the Arab states might agree. This generous plan reflected the eagerness of the United States to see the Palestine conflict settled to the satisfaction of all concerned; but from the point of view of Israel and her immediate concern for her security, it only begged the question.

Israel's anxiety about her security prospects in the face of these developments was sharpened by the simultaneous deterioration of her position through aonther chain of events connected with Egypt. In July 1952, a new regime had come into existence there in the wake of a military coup which brought to power a junta of young officers. The new rulers, fearful of British intervention on behalf of the deposed king, had sought to secure the good will and restraining hand of Washington from the outset, and the United States had gladly responded. Relations between the two governments further improved when the new administration in Washington began to turn a sterner countenance toward Israel and exerted a steady "friendly pressure" on Britain to be more accommodating to the Egyptians in the negotiations on the future of the Suez Canal base. The British had wanted to make the surrender of their treaty rights to the Suez base conditional upon the Egyptians' entering into a new defense agreement; but the United States was willing to gamble on the hope, skillfully nurtured by the new Egyptian rulers, that once the Egyptians saw that their country was truly and fully independent, they would then turn around and join a Western-sponsored alliance of their own accord. In July 1954, an Anglo-Egyptian agreement was finally reached envisaging the evacuation of the base mainly on Egyptian terms, and in the following September the agreement was ratified by the British Parliament.

The developments in Egypt were of grave concern to Israel for at least two reasons. One had to do with the fact that the evacuation of British troops from the Canal base would remove an important buffer between her and Egypt and also place the Egyptians in a better position to enforce a strict blockade of the waterway against Israeli ships and goods; the other had to do with the fear that the elimination of the Anglo-Egyptian dispute would indeed lead to Egypt's joining an American-sponsored alliance that would leave Israel out. So deep was their suspicion by then that the Western powers were bent on going ahead with their scheme to draw the Arab states into their defense network without any regard for the attendant perils to Israel's security, that the Israelis began to react in a reckless manner.

Before the ratification of the Anglo-Egyptian agreement, Israel sent the *Bat Gallim,* flying the national color, through the Suez Canal in an attempt to test her right of free passage through the waterway. This was the first Israeli ship to seek passage since 1949; in the interim, Israeli cargo had been allowed only in foreign bottoms. By timing the operation as they did, the Israelis sought to accomplish one of two things: if the Egyptians let the ship go by, Israel would have established a precedent of her right to pass; if the Egyptians prevented the ship from going through, then opponents of the new Anglo-Egyptian agreement in Britain might use the incident as evidence that the Egyptians could not be trusted with the physical control of the Canal, and might marshal enough forces to withhold ratification of the agreement. In fact, the maneuver failed utterly. The Egyptians impounded the ship and imprisoned its crew, but the treaty was ratified, and Israel reaped only the resentment of the British and American governments for seek-ing to "embarrass" them. Not long afterwards even Israeli cargo on foreign ships was prohibited.

The maneuver with the *Bat Gallim* was awkward, but it was at least legitimate, since Israeli ships had the right, confirmed by a United Nations Security Council resolution in 1951, to pass through the Canal. But another Israeli reaction, the true nature of which was not disclosed for several years, was much less innocent. Toward the end of 1954, the Egyptian authorities announced that they had uncovered an Israel-led ring of spies and saboteurs who allegedly engaged in bombing and arson attempts against American installa-tions in Cairo with the aim of poisoning relations between Egypt and the United States. The story was generally thought at the time to be a fabrication; Israel declared so explicitly. When the Egyptians hanged two of the thirteen persons involved, Israel retaliated with a raid on Gaza in which nearly forty Egyptian soldiers were killed. Almost six years later it became known unofficially in the course of the Lavon Affair that the spying-sabotage adventure had in fact been mounted by Israeli intelligence, if without the authorization of the responsible minister.

Although Israel's efforts to sabotage the prospects of Egypt's join-ing a Middle Eastern alliance sponsored by the West boomeranged pitifully, Egypt in fact did not join the emerging Baghdad Pact. President Abdel Nasser, by that time the real boss of Egypt, had come to oppose the Pact violently because, while he was busy negotiating an agreement with Britain, the United States had given Iraq military and economic aid and allowed her rulers to become, as it were, the recruiting agents for the Pact among the Arabs, pushing Egypt to the sidelines. But Egypt's self-exclusion from the Pact was to prove more of a curse than a blessing for Israel, at least in the short run. For Abdel Nasser sought to counter Iraq's gains in power and prestige through her alliance with the West, and to remedy his own weakness as revealed by the Israelis in their raid on Gaza by turning to Soviet Russia and concluding with her an arms-for-cotton deal, which set in motion a momentous chain reaction in the area and placed Israel in a most perilous situation.

The conclusion of the arms agreement was announced in Septem-ber 1955, and by then Russian ships ware steaming to Alexandria and Port Said carrying the first deliveries. The deal included planes, tanks, guns, war ships, submarines, ammunition, and other military equipment of a quality and in quantities hitherto not dreamed of in the area. Russia's purpose coincided largely with Abdel Nasser's desire to undermine the Baghdad Pact and deal a blow to the prestige of its Western sponsors. In addition, Russia sought to have a voice in the future of the area and acquire influence among the Arabs as their loyal friend in their struggle against the Western "imperialists" and their "client" Israel. The first consequence of the deal was that Abdel Nasser's prestige in the Arab world rocketed overnight. The masses of Arabs everywhere delighted in the Egyptian ruler's defiance of the West, his gaining a powerful ally for the Arabs, and his acquisition of the instruments of revenge against Israel. The other Arab governments, though fearful of Abdel Nasser's rising star, could at first only bow to the pressure of their peoples, join in the applause, and think of the best deal they could make with him.

Israel's reaction to the arms transaction was at first one of qualified alarm. Because of the obvious anti-Western implications of the Soviet-Egyptian deal, Israelis half expected the United States to react vigorously against Abdel Nasser and, among other things, to reinforce them as a counterweight to the anticipated increase in Soviet influence next door. In any case, there was certainly a widespread confidence among them that the United States would provide them with enough arms to counter Abdel Nasser's new acquisitions. One can therefore imagine the Israelis' dismay as they watched the initial shocked reaction of the West give way to a frantic endeavor on the part of the United States and Britain to appease Abdel Nasser by offering to help him finance the building of the Aswan Dam, at a time when their own request to purchase arms in the United States and other Western countries was meeting with deferment month after month. By the end of February 1956, when Secretary Dulles told the Senate Foreign Affairs Committee that Israel should rely for her national defense on "collective security" and the United Nations, not on arms alone, Israel's mood had become one of heavy, brooding, desperate determination. On March 18, Ben Gurion warned that war within a few months could not be avoided unless Israel got the arms she needed to counter Egypt's new weapons. Three days later he repeated the warning, and in the next month he reiterated it from the forum of the Knesset. In the meantime, the Israeli-Arab frontier flared up continuously as Arab raiders made deep sallies into Israel to sabotage installations and terrorize the population, and as Israel countered with massive murderous raids against Arab positions.

Thus, as the eighth anniversary of Israel's birth drew near, her government and people might have looked back wistfully at the position they were not too well satisfied with four years before. In the intervening period they had met nothing but heartaches and failures in their efforts to buttress their security through their foreign relations. Not only were they not able to obtain any firm guarantee or alliance, but several props bolstering their security had been knocked down even as the perils to their country's existence became magnified and immediate. The buffer provided by British troops along the Suez Canal was gone. The arms balance established by the Tripartite Declaration was shattered. Russia was playing a deep game with Israel's most dangerous enemy. Britain was engaged in rebuilding her Middle East position on the foundations of the Baghdad Pact, and her Prime Minister had considered it opportune, after Abdel Nasser had concluded the arms deal, to advise Israel publicly to concede some territory in order to make peace with the Arabs. The United States' relations with Egypt continued to be impelled by the momentum engendered by the early hopes of winning that country's rulers to the Western plans for the Middle East, even after Abdel Nasser had made it his mission to destroy what little of these plans had already been realized in the north, and had opened the door to Soviet influence in the area. Even France, which had a deep grudge against Nasser for his aid to the Algerian rebels, sent Foreign Minister Pineau to Cairo after the arms deal to try to reach an understanding with the Egyptian ruler so as to avoid his dumping his obsolete arms into North Africa. In the sullen mood that wrapped the country, the ancient Jewish view of the world as divided between the two hostile camps of Jews and Gentiles surged from the subconscious depths of many Israelis who thought they saw the Christian nations getting ready to look away once more while the Arabs undertook to make the Middle East "Judenrein." The general reaction was a fanatic determination that, whatever happened, the Jews in their own homeland were not going to allow themselves to be tricked into remaining passive.

2. THE SINAI-SUEZ WAR

The low point of Israel's four lean years had been reached in the late winter and early spring of 1956, when Abdel Nasser's arms deal and its repercussions in the Middle East seemed to conspire with the attitude of the big powers to place Israel in mortal peril. Subsequently, from April–May on, the worst of the crisis from Israel's point of view had passed as the Western powers, one after the other, became embroiled with Egypt and mollified their attitude toward Israel, while one of them—France—even began to sell Israel the arms she desperately needed. But the problem created by the repercussions of Abdel Nasser's deal in the area and by his later initiatives continued and became aggravated, so that in the fall Israel confronted a serious and immediate military challenge. Taking advantage of her somewhat improved military position and a favorable temporary international conjuncture, Israel decided to strike to remove the military threat facing her and launched her invasion of Sinai.

As far as her relations with the Western powers were concerned, the ice had begun to break by about April. The first to come to her aid were the French who, after failing to dissuade Abdel Nasser from helping the Algerians militarily, started selling to Israel fairly large quantities of weapons matching, at least in quality, the arms received by Egypt. The Israelis welcomed this help, of course, but continued to press the United States to sell them some arms, mainly because of the political significance of the act. Washington did not quite respond to Israel's demand; but in April and May, partly in response to pressure at home and partly as a reaction against Abdel Nasser's continued war against the Baghdad Pact, the State Department let it be known that the United States agreed to relinquish NATO priority over some French military equipment to permit their diversion to Israel. The political results were almost the same as if the United States had sold arms to Israel directly, except that they took a little longer to materialize. For Abdel Nasser reacted to the American move by withdrawing recognition from Nationalist China and recognizing Communist China, and this gave the State Department pause. Early in July it was announced that American Ambassador Byroade, whose name had been closely associated with the policy of trying to cultivate Abdel Nasser's good

will, would be recalled from Cairo. Later in the month, the doubts
that had been accumulating for some time about the efficacy of that
policy, together with complaints from the Turkish, Iraqi, and
British allies against the favors shown by Washington to the
Egyptian ruler in the face of his continued war against the Baghdad
Pact, mounting pressure from Congress, and intelligence that the
Russians, contrary to Egyptian claims, did not envisage assuming
the costs for the Aswan Dam project combined to induce the
Secretary of State to withdraw in a demonstrative manner the
American offer to help build the dam. A few days later, Abdel
Nasser retaliated by nationalizing the Suez Canal.

The Suez Canal had been built by a French-promoted international company owned for the most part by French and British
shareholders. It was the main passageway for most of Western
Europe's oil and had been considered by the British, ever since its
construction ninety years before, to be the jugular vein of their
empire and commonwealth. An international treaty dating from
1884 had prescribed that the Canal should be open to the traffic of
all nations in peace as in war; but the British, who held physical
control of it until 1954–1955, had previously blocked it in wartime
against enemy traffic, and now the Egyptians had blocked it against
Israeli shipping. One of the main issues in Abdel Nasser's nationalization of the Canal was the fear that he might use this vital waterway as an instrument of his politics against the West as he had
used it against Israel, and as the British had used it against their
enemies.

Abdel Nasser's action, which had come in direct retaliation for
the American withdrawal of the Aswan Dam offer, seemed to
throw the three big Western powers together against him. In seeking to evolve a concerted response, however, Britain and France,
while ostensibly trying to devise with the United States guarantees
against interference with free movement in the Canal, pursued in
fact an additional aim which the United States wished to avoid.
The British, who had lost their control over Jordan the previous
March as a result of Abdel Nasser's agitation and who resented the
trouble Cairo-Radio was creating for them in Iraq, the Arabian
coast principalities, and Africa, were determined to use the Suez
crisis as an excuse to crush, or at least humble and thus render
harmless, the Egyptian dictator. So also were the French who had

been embittered by Abdel Nasser's defiant assistance to the Algerian rebels. Both the British and the French governments had convinced themselves that the Egyptian giant stood on feet of clay and would be easy to topple quickly without any serious consequences in the Arab world. The American government, on the other hand, wedded until very recently to a policy that had estimated highly Abdel Nasser's influence among the Arab peoples and had sought to ride on his particular brand of nationalism, was fearful of the repercussions of the Franco-British policy and was disinclined to associate itself with the two "colonialist" powers in any nineteenth-century style gunboat diplomacy. Though wishing to see Abdel Nasser go, Secretary of State Dulles rather sought to meet the Suez Canal problem on its own merits, and then work discreetly and slowly to isolate Abdel Nasser and render him harmless. The incomplete agreement on aims among the allies made it impossible for them to follow a common course; and although the Secretary of State had managed by ingenious maneuvering and a good deal of ambivalent talk to divert the angry partners for a time from the warpath to a diplomatic labyrinth, the difference between them eventually asserted itself and led the French and the British to turn away from Washington and take the road of armed intervention in Suez.

Before the nationalization of the Canal, when they started supplying arms to Israel, the French must already have considered and approved the possibility that Israel might use these weapons to fight a war against her Egyptian enemy. At that time, however, the French could expect Israel to fight such a war only if the Egyptians took the initiative to attack, since they were well aware of the weak international position of the Jewish state. In the fall of 1956, the international situation had changed considerably after the Aswan Dam and Suez Canal episodes had clearly thrown the United States and Britain into the anti-Abdel Nasser camp, and as the Soviet Union became involved in trouble with her own satellites. Just who approached whom in that fateful October is not known; but Israel was in any case ready to act for her own reasons. During the preceding few months the cruel thrusts and counterthrusts of Egyptian-sponsored fedayeen and Israeli army units had been resumed after a brief respite arranged by the Secretary General of the United Nations and had cast a shadow of violence and terror over the area. Jordan, which had been seething since March, when King Husayn dismissed the British commander of his army, was on the verge of falling completely under Egyptian control. Syria had already placed her armed forces under Egyptian command. Abdel Nasser, carried away by the momentum of his enormous popularity with the Arab masses after his arms deal and his Suez coup, boasted about the exploits of his fedayeen and seemed bent on bringing his career to a climax by turning against Israel. The Israeli government seemed, then, to face the alternative of allowing a belligerent Egyptian chief, commanding the combined armies of Egypt, Syria, and Jordan and controlling the Jordanian bulge, to choose the moment of attack, after assimilating the enormous quantities of arms he had received, or to avail itself of the opportunity of Franco-British support, America's involvement in the last stages of a Presidential election and Russia's preoccupation with Hungary, and risk an immediate military action to remove the impending threat. Given the recent background of Israel's failures to move the powers to pay heed to her security needs, and the super-realism and toughness exhibited by the men in charge of Israel's national defense, there could be no doubt about the choice. After many long months of uncertainty and tension, it was with a patent sense of relief that the citizens' army of Israel broke forth into war.

Of the torrent of events that burst in the wake of Israel's attack we need only recall the following as basic to an understanding of the situation and of subsequent developments:

1. The Israeli invasion of Sinai began on October 29, 1956; the next day the French and the British used it as an excuse for intervening against Egypt.

2. By November 5, Israel was in occupation of the Gaza Strip and the entire Sinai peninsula but the French-British forces had occupied only Port Said and a small strip to the south of it.

3. The United States assumed the leading role in marshaling United Nations opposition to the Franco-British-Israeli action, which expressed itself in a series of quick and overwhelmingly adopted resolutions calling for a cessation of the fighting and for an immediate withdrawal of foreign forces from Egypt.

4. The Soviet Union, while seconding the United States' efforts in the United Nations, sent a series of notes to the attacking powers culminating in one to Israel which questioned her future existence,

and one each to France and Britain brandishing the implicit threat of using rockets against them if they did not desist immediately and withdraw their forces.

5. On November 6, Britain and France agreed to cease fire and withdraw as soon as the United Nations Emergency Force, decided upon on November 4, could take over, and by Christmas the Anglo-French forces were out of Egypt.

6. On November 8, Israel, too, agreed to withdraw and had evacuated all the occupied territory by February, except for the Gaza Strip, which she did not consider Egyptian territory, and the tip of the Sinai peninsula facing the Strait of Tiran, from which the Egyptians had blocked the entrance of the Gulf of Akaba.

7. A movement developed in the United Nations for adopting sanctions against Israel to force her to evacuate the previously mentioned positions. The United States was about to join that movement but finally succeeded in inducing Israel to give in after assuming a moral commitment to stand by her right of "innocent passage" through the Gulf of Akaba, and to see to it that the Gaza Strip was not used as a base for renewed fedayeen attacks on her.

The reasons for the United States' active opposition to her allies and Israel, which has been generally credited with bringing about the ceasefire and the restoration of the *status quo ante,* are not perfectly clear. Even those who partook of the relevant decisions have given different accounts of the motives behind them. The available evidence seems to suggest that in the immediate sense, the American government's reaction was largely governed by a strong urge to dissociate itself *actively* from the action of the three attacking powers in order to prevent the rest of the world from drawing what would seem a natural conclusion that it was in collusion with them. This urge was all the more compelling because it was supported by resentment on the part of the American government at the fact that its allies had kept it in the dark about their plans, and Israel had flouted its warnings. Underlying this almost impulsive reaction, however, there had been an American predisposition against the type of action undertaken by the French, the British, and the Israelis resting on substantive calculations made months before. These were based on the fear that a direct open attack against Abdel Nasser might set the entire Middle East aflame and imperil all the Western positions and interests in the area, even as

it would give Russia a unique opportunity to pose as the sole de-
fender of the Arabs. From such a conflict a general war might
ensue.

The results of the military intervention were an unmitigated disaster for Britain and a more qualified one for France. These two once-
great world powers were dramatically depicted before the world as
incapable of taking action to protect their vital interests against the
challenge of an infinitely weaker power without the support of
their giant ally. They not only failed to topple Abdel Nasser but
helped him win a great political victory. They did not secure guarantees of free navigation in the Canal but lost whatever concessions
to their demands had been proffered before. They did not protect
the waterway from Israel-Egyptian hostilities but provoked its complete blocking and the cutting of the oil pipeline from Iraq, which
plunged Europe into a prolonged oil shortage. The collapse of their
prestige encouraged the intensification of pressures against their remaining interests in the area. Thus Britain's 1954 treaty with Egypt
was denounced, her installations and depots in the Suez base were
seized, and her position in the Arabian coast principalities and in
Iraq was shaken. France, already out of the Middle East, had less
to lose; nevertheless, her cultural influence and institutions in Egypt
and Syria, built over many generations, were practically wiped out.

As for Israel, the outcome of the war was quite different. In the
immediate sense, Israel gained only few and limited advantages;
but these were sufficient to place her in a position in which she
could afford to leave the center of the stage and let the other actors
in the Middle East drama fight each other to a conclusion which
has suited her tolerably, at least so far. To understand Israel's position fully, we must pause for a moment to examine the unfolding
and conclusion of the power struggle that took place in the area as
a whole in the months and years following the Sinai-Suez War.

XV

The Third Period:
The Emergence of a Balance

Even before the rubble from the Sinai-Suez War had been cleared away, the United States was impelled to take the final step in the process of her involvement in the Middle East and to assume practically the sole responsibility for defending the Western position in the area. That position seemed at the time to be challenged by a formidable double threat. One was the threat presented by the tremendously enhanced appeal of Abdel Nasser and his brand of Arab nationalism which appeared then to be firmly committed to an anti-Western line. The other was the threat of further Soviet penetration powered by the credit that Russia had gained among the Arab masses through her energetic and drastic interventions on the side of Egypt. With the loss of British power and prestige in the Middle East, Washington feared that the last friendly Arab governments, together with the remaining Western bases and the enormous Western-controlled oil reserves, might be overrun by a continuation of the drive of Abdel Nasser and the Soviets, each using the other. Blocking that drive and reversing it wherever possible became the immediate target of the United States.

Largely as a result of American initiatives, the Middle East became, from the beginning of 1957 to the middle of 1958, the arena of a brink-of-war diplomatic struggle between the United States, backed by some Arab governments, and Soviet-supported Arab nationalism of the variety identified with Abdel Nasser. In July

1958, after the Iraqi revolution, the balance sheet of the struggle was overwhelmingly unfavorable to the United States. American diplomacy had succeeded in retrieving Jordan for the Western camp, but had completely failed in the effort made to retrieve Syria; moreover, both Lebanon, formerly pro-Western, and Iraq, previously the mainstay of the Western position in the Arab East, were lost to the West. Had these setbacks been in equal proportion the gains of Abdel Nasser and Russia, the outcome would have been sheer disaster. Fortunately—though from no virtue of American policy—this did not turn out to be the case. For the elimination of the Western position in Iraq triggered a struggle in that country among Communists, Nasserists, and independents which ended in a victory for the last group, but not before it had set Moscow at odds with Cairo for the first time since they formed their tacit alliance in 1955. These events gradually led to a subtle diplomatic realignment resulting in a situation in which all the participants in the Middle East struggles checked one another into a delicate balance that has held to the present.

Throughout these events, Israel played a passive but important role. Her very presence tied down the armed forces of Abdel Nasser and restricted his freedom of action, thereby helping to prevent the struggles in the area from assuming the character of military conflicts which might have entangled the big powers. In other minor ways (to be seen later), she made indirect contributions to the emergence of the present balance which is tolerated by all concerned, and she continues to play an important role in its preservation.

1. THE POWERS' STRUGGLE, 1957–1958

The diplomatic offensive of the United States, designed to stem the tide of mounting Soviet influence and of Abdel Nasser's anti-Western nationalism, was launched with the promulgation of what came to be known as the Eisenhower Doctrine. This was a public law, approved by Congress in March 1957, by means of which the government sought: 1) to serve notice to the Russians that the United States would fight to prevent them from overrunning the Middle East; 2) to strengthen friendly governments menaced by Abdel Nasser and his followers; and 3) to provide a means other than treaties and alliances which governments that feared either the Soviet or Nasserist threat could use to associate themselves visibly with the United States. It is true that the Doctrine spoke of providing protection only against overt aggression, and only hinted at the Abdel Nasser threat by speaking of aggression on the part of "a nation controlled by international communism." But these, as events were to prove, were merely diplomatic phrasings designed to give the Doctrine the necessary international legal coating and to facilitate the aim of openly rallying friendly governments behind it; they did not restrict the freedom of action of the American government, which was, after all, free to interpret as it wished the meaning of its own Doctrine.

As soon as Congress approved the Doctrine, President Eisenhower sent Special Ambassador James P. Richards to the Middle East with the mission of rallying the area's governments behind it. Richards obtained warm endorsement for the Doctrine from Iraq, Lebanon, and Libya, and more reserved support from Saudi Arabia, Yemen and Israel. Significantly, he was not received in Egypt and Syria. His plan to go to Jordan was upset by the outbreak of a crisis in that country, which provided the first practical test of the American policy outlined in the Doctrine.

In March 1956, following the outbreak of violent demonstrations against Jordan's impending adherence to the Baghdad Pact, King Husayn had dismissed General Glubb, long-time British commander of Jordan's army and influential adviser to its rulers, and attempted to embark on a course more attuned to the wishes of the nationalist admirers of Abdel Nasser within his own country. In the following October, elections produced a government which committed itself to liquidating Jordan's treaty with Britain and signed an agreement placing the Egyptian, Syrian, and Jordanian armed forces under the command of an Egyptian Commander-in-Chief. In March 1957, after the Sinai-Suez War, the British and Jordanian governments agreed to abrogate the treaty between the two countries; and Saudi Arabia, Egypt, and Syria jointly undertook to provide Jordan with the annual subsidy of about $35 million which Britain had hitherto supplied. By then, the young king was having second thoughts about the course he was taking. He had sought to enhance his own position by following a pan-Arab nationalist line, but actually found himself pushed aside by his own government, which was bent on pursuing Abdel Nasser's lead to the point of turning the country into an Egyptian protectorate. On April 10, the king marshaled his courage and, using as an excuse his premier's declared intention of establishing diplomatic relations with Russia, denounced the machinations of international communism and dismissed his government. This act plunged the country into weeks of confusion, plots and counterplots, riots and repression. At several points in the crisis, the American President and the Secretary of State expressed the desire of the American government to "hold up the hands of King Hussein," invoked the Tripartite Declaration of 1950 and the Eisenhower Doctrine to warn all of Jordan's neighbors to keep their hands off, and declared the independence and integrity of Jordan to be "vital" to the national interest and world peace. To give the desired weight to these statements, the Sixth Fleet was ordered to the eastern Mediterranean. With this vigorous support, with help from Iraq, which kept troops poised on the frontier ready to move if Syria did, with backing from King Saud, who placed Saudi Arabian troops previously stationed in Jordan at the disposal of King Husayn, and with courage and some luck, the young Jordanian monarch mastered the crisis. A little while later, the United States took over and increased the subsidy which Egypt, Syria, and Saudi Arabia were supposed to provide to Jordan, and the country was safely brought back into the Western camp.

Whether American or other friendly intelligence services had been involved in planning Husayn's royal *coup d'état* is not known. But in the next test of American policy, in Syria, there is some evidence that something like the combination of moves that had detached Jordan from the Abdel Nasser camp was *deliberately* planned. Syria had been the one Arab state which had showed unflagging solidarity with Egypt's ruler and had followed him in seeking ties with Russia. During the Anglo-Franco-Israeli attack on Egypt, President Kuwatly had dashed off to Moscow to seek Soviet support; and, while there, he had arranged for Syria to receive large arms shipments, which were followed later on by agreements for trade and aid. Within the country, there was fierce maneuvering among half-a-dozen political groupings in which the pro-Nasser Ba'thists and the Communists had the upper hand. The plan for detaching Syria from the Moscow-Cairo axis seemed to call for a coup by some opposition factions supported by a few army officers inside Syria, to be backed by supporting military maneuvers on the Turkish, Iraqi, and Jordanian side of the frontier, and perhaps by another movement of the Sixth Fleet. But during the first half of August the plan was foiled by the discovery of the Syrian plotters, together with some evidence implicating American, British, and Iraqi intelligence groups. The American government's hasty attempts to improvise an alternative move boomeranged.

On August 13, 1957, the Syrian government requested the immediate departure of the American military attaché and two members of the American diplomatic mission, and followed this move by retiring ten senior army officers and replacing the conservative Chief-of-Staff by Brigadier Afif al Bizri, an alleged Communist. The United States reacted by declaring the Syrian ambassador in Washington *persona non grata* and sending Loy Henderson, Undersecretary of State, on a flying visit to the Middle East to consult with governments of the countries neighboring Syria, except Israel. On his return, Henderson reported the "deep concern" of these neighbors over the build-up of arms and the increase of the Communist threat in Syria, whereupon the President expressed his intention to carry out the policy expressed in the Eisenhower Doctrine to help the threatened nations. Orders were given to speed up arms deliveries to Jordan and other countries of the area, the Sixth Fleet held maneuvers off the Syrian coast, and the President called upon the Syrian people "to act to allay the anxiety caused by recent events." All of this amounted to an invitation to the Syrian people to revolt, and a promise of backing Syria's neighbors should they decide to take action to "protect themselves." But the Syrian people did not rise, and the only country among Syria's neighbors that made some move was Turkey—the one least plausibly threatened —which concentrated troops on her Syrian frontier. Lebanon and Jordan, which had received hurried shipments of American arms, presumably against the Syrian danger, acted to the contrary by expressing their devotion to Arab solidarity and making it clear they wanted no conflict from which only Israel could benefit. King Saud, who had lent a helping hand in Jordan, said he saw no threat. And the Iraqi premier, whose intelligence service was implicated in the discovered plot, visited Damascus where he announced that "full understanding" had been reached. The strong impression created in the Arab world that the United States, with the help of Turkey, was out to crush Syria made it impossible even for the Arab governments most loyal to Washington to take a public stand that could be understood as supporting this move.

As the American government sensed that it had overplayed its hand, it endeavored to beat as graceful a retreat as it could. But the Soviet Union and Egypt, once they realized that the danger of war was over, did their best to capitalize on the American government's miscalculation and to make its retreat as embarrassing as possible. The Soviet Union, which spoke at the beginning of the crisis in terms of "not being able to remain indifferent to what goes on in the Near East," now whipped up a real war scare, sent the Turkish government note after note of warning couched in the most vigorous terms, and spoke of contributing armed forces to crush the aggressors. Abdel Nasser, who had watched impotently while the Syrians went into a genuine panic over the initial American reactions, now made bold to send two Egyptian battalions to Syria, presumably to help stem the impending Turkish invasion. The crisis petered out in November, but not before Soviet Russia and Egypt had forced the United States to pass to the defensive, having "proved" that the Eisenhower Doctrine was just another instrument of imperialist domination. Substantively, the American moves not only failed to detach Syria from her alignment with Abdel Nasser, but they precipitated a chain of events in that country which resulted, in February 1958, in its complete merger with Egypt.

The formation of the United Arab Republic out of Egypt and Syria gave Abdel Nasser a dramatic, tangible success in his drive for Arab unity, and endowed him with a prestige in the Arab world that seemed well-nigh irresistible. Yemen immediately formed a confederation with the new state. King Saud, whom the Americans had tried to build up as a friendly mediator in the area's conflicts, was forced by an intensive Egyptian propaganda campaign against him to hand over active direction of domestic and foreign affairs to his brother Faisal, known to be more favorably disposed toward Abdel Nasser. Iraq and Jordan tried to deflect the Nasserite tide by forming a federation known as the Arab Union, which was promptly recognized by the Arab masses as the union of two frightened governments that it was. In May 1958, an intricate internal political struggle in Lebanon became converted, under the impact of Abdel Nasser's success in neighboring Syria, into a civil war which threatened to sweep away the country's pro-Western government, headed by President Chamoun. The United States rushed arms shipments to the beleaguered government, ordered the Sixth Fleet to the Lebanese waters, and increased the available Marine units in the Mediterranean, without producing any effect. As the American government pondered what to do next, a revolution broke out in Iraq, on July 14, 1958, which swept away the government that had brought that country into the Western alliance.

The United States, like all other nations, believed the Iraqi revolution to be another Nasserite coup and reacted immediately by landing the Marines in Lebanon, after having elicited an invitation to do so from President Chamoun. Simultaneously, Britain responded to a call from King Husayn and landed paratroops in Jordan in concert with the American action. The minimal object of the Anglo-American military moves was to protect the friendly governments of Lebanon and Jordan from being submerged by the revolutionary tide. At the same time, however, they were designed to place troops close to the Iraqi scene in case the opportunity presented itself to redress the situation there. This possibility so alarmed Abdel Nasser, himself surprised by the revolution but believing it to favor him, that he dashed off to Moscow and came back declaring he would fight to defend the revolutionary government. At the same time the Soviet government thundered against "imperialist piracy" in Lebanon and warned against any move on Iraq. For a few days the world seemed to be perched on the brink of war; but soon it became clear that no member of the "legitimate" government of Iraq remained alive or free to invite outside help, and that the new leaders held the whole country under firm control. From then on, it was all anticlimax. The Lebanese had reached a compromise agreement which restored their country's traditional neutrality, and Husayn had been saved; the problem now was to find a way that would allow Britain and the United States to withdraw their troops with as little embarrassment as possible. After long and bitter debates in the United Nations, the Arab states themselves produced the formula. This took the form of a resolution sponsored by all of them reminding themselves of their obligation to respect one another's system of government, and asking the Secretary General to help in making practical arrangements

which would uphold the principles of the U.N. Charter and facilitate the early withdrawal of foreign troops from Lebanon and
Jordan. The resolution was unanimously approved, and the American and British troops were out by November.

As the United States completed the withdrawal of her troops
from Lebanon, two years after Britain, France, and Israel had
begun to withdraw theirs from Egypt, the record of the intervening
period must have looked to her dismal indeed. She had attempted
to stem the tide of Nasserism, check Soviet influence, and rally the
governments of the area around her; in fact, Abdel Nasser was entrenched in Syria, the Baghdad Pact was dead and buried, together
with the friendly Iraqi government that had supported it; Lebanon,
formerly an ally, now became neutral; friendly King Saud, on
whom great hopes had been placed, was striving to become incon-
spicuous; and Jordan, rescued temporarily, was as insecure as the
life of her king. All the credit America had gained by opposing her
allies in 1956 had been dissipated, while Soviet influence had continued to increase and seemed now deeply entrenched on the shores
of the Tigris as well as the Nile and the Orontes. What must have
seemed worst of all to the American government, there was little if
anything that it could do to alter this disastrous outcome.

2. THE SHAPING OF A STALEMATE

Just when the United States' effort to shape the diplomatic-
strategic map of the Middle East had been acknowledged a complete failure, the area itself began to develop the elements of a
balance of power that was to check Abdel Nasser's drive, slow the
Russian advance, and give the United States an opportunity to re-
gain some of the influence she had lost. The key to the new balance
was Iraq. The new regime began its career by proclaiming its
allegiance to Arab solidarity and establishing close relations with
the Soviet Union and countries of the Soviet bloc. Its advent also
released a number of popular forces which had been oppressed
under the previous regime, chief among which were the Ba'thists,
the Istiqlal right-wing nationalists, and the Communists who,
though never a large group, were able to build up new mass
organizations very quickly. As soon as the danger of outside armed
intervention receded, the popular forces, each of which could count
on some support among the army officers who had made the coup,

began to contend for determining Iraq's course. The Ba'thists and the Istiqlalists pressed for immediate merger with the United Arab Republic and had the support of Colonel Arif, the second-in-command in the new regime. The Communists, fearing Abdel Nasser would suppress their party as he had done in Syria, were desirous of keeping Iraq free to steer her own course. They found a willing ear in General Kassem, the leader of the new regime, who for personal reasons as well as for reasons rooted in Iraq's economic interest and her ethnic and religious diversity, was opposed to a merger. The struggle between the two tendencies produced the usual plots and counterplots which resulted, four months after the revolution, in the arrest of Arif and Ba'thist and Istiqlalist leaders in and out of the army, an open break between Kassem and Abdel Nasser, and the strengthening of Communist influence. In March 1959, a pro-Abdel Nasser revolt by an army unit and tribesmen in the Mossul province, adjoining Syria, led by a certain Colonel Shawwaf, was suppressed by Communist partisans and loyalist forces at a great cost in lives. By that time, relations between Iraq and the United Arab Republic had degenerated into a cold war worse than the hostility between the two countries under the previous Iraqi regime; and the Iraqi Communists, having wiped out or silenced most of their enemies during the months of upheaval, seemed to have the country virtually in their power.

In the course of the widening conflict between the two countries, Abdel Nasser, for very good reasons, had singled out Kassem's collaboration with the Iraqi Communists as a special target for his attacks. The Communists had not only been instrumental in foiling the efforts of his partisans in Iraq and destroying many of them, but presented a threat to his own position in Syria. Abdel Nasser knew that there had been many in Syria who had favored merger with contiguous, oil-rich Iraq rather than with his own country, but had been handicapped by Iraq's monarchic regime and her alliance with the West. Now that Iraq was under a republican, nationalist, anti-Western regime, her attraction became very strong, and Kassem, along with the Iraqi and the Syrian Communists, tried to enhance it by playing on the discontent of the Syrians with the highhandedness of the Egyptians. In December 1958, soon after the arrest of Arif and other pro-United Arab Republic leaders in Iraq, Abdel Nasser extended his attacks beyond the Arab Communists to the interventionist policies of the Soviet Union. By the spring of 1959, after the Mossul debacle, he was charging the Communists with having hatched a plot at the 21st Congress of the Soviet Communist Party in Moscow to break up the United Arab Republic and create "a Red Fertile Crescent (the territory comprising Iraq, Syria, Jordan, and Palestine), with Baghdad as a command post of the counterrevolution against Arab nationalism."

Abdel Nasser's use of the Soviet and Communist threat in his power struggle with Kassem brought several sharp retorts from Moscow, including a humiliating rebuke by Khrushchev himself. Although the most severe verbal clashes were smoothed over each time by vague formulas and did not stop Soviet economic aid, it became quite obvious that in the new situation which was emerging in the area, the interests of Russia and of Abdel Nasser had begun to diverge. To get rid of Western power in the Middle East, the Russians had been willing to support Abdel Nasser's effort to extend his hegemony over Syria, Iraq, and Jordan, even if this meant the suppression of the local Communists. But once the revolutionary government of Iraq proved it could serve the same purpose while using the help of the Communists, the Soviets had every reason to favor it over Abdel Nasser. To be sure, the Russians were loath to drive the chief of the United Arab Republic into the arms of the West, and expected him to render further service in areas such as Saudi Arabia, Jordan, Libya, and Israel still under Western influence; for this reason, they refrained from pushing their quarrels with him too far and continued to provide him with economic and military aid. But they made it quite clear that they were not going to allow him to use them purely for his own self-aggrandizement and that they would oppose any effort he made to extend his power over areas that had already been pulled from under Western influence.

As Abdel Nasser understood better the terms of his relations with the Russians, he began to seek to improve his relations with the West in order not to be too dependent on Moscow. The United States was favorably disposed toward such moves for just the same reason, especially since Abdel Nasser's drive in the area as a whole had come to a standstill after his failures in Iraq. These failures, paradoxically, were also decisive in leading to the weakening of the position of Iraq's Communists. For, as Abdel Nasser's agitation against Kassem's "collusion" with the Communists subsided, the Iraqi chief felt more secure and no longer needed to rely heavily on Communist support. He therefore took every opportunity to whittle down the power of Communist organizations and succeeded eventually in undermining the party by splitting it and setting up a "national" Iraqi Communist party. At the same time, in an effort to retain a bridge to the West, Kassem used the fact that his army was equipped with British materiel as an excuse to seek British weapons, and the British government, after consulting the American, eagerly met this request in an effort to salvage some shred of influence in Baghdad.

By the summer of 1960, five years after the inauguration of the Baghdad Pact and the Soviet-Egyptian arms deal had transformed the Middle East into one of the main arenas of the Cold War, and two years after the Iraqi coup, the dust of these turbulent years had settled down to a general stalemate which was continued to the present (autumn 1962). Having failed to rally any bloc of Arab countries into the Western camp, the United States became more reconciled to seeing these countries neutral; she adopted a policy that sought to maintain friendly relations with them and help them economically so as to prevent them from becoming too dependent on Soviet Russia and to keep the way open for a more positive association. The Soviet Union, fearing that too bold a move to bring any one country unequivocally into the Soviet camp might drive the others into the camp of their enemies, was content with denying the West control over the area, and she too sought to keep its key countries from falling into the American camp by means of a policy of friendship and aid. As for Abdel Nasser, having been denied the prize of Iraq by Kassem and the Russians, he did not wish to antagonize the West by turning to some secondary target like Libya, a complex one like Jordan, or a very difficult one like Saudi Arabia. Moreover, since his drive had lost its momentum through the Iraqi setback, he found himself falling increasingly on the defensive in Syria itself. Indeed, in September 1961, a military coup in that country succeeded in breaking up the United Arab Republic, stopping his pan-Arab movement. Perhaps no clearer illustration of the general wariness of all concerned lest the delicately balanced stalemate become upset can be found than in the mildness of the repercussions caused by this last event. Washington, Moscow,

Jerusalem, and all the Arab capitals were intensely interested, but nobody mobilized any troops, moved any fleets, apprized the United Nations, exchanged angry warnings and sharp threats. Abdel Nasser sent 150 paratroopers to Latakia who were immediately captured and sent back home; Cairo and Damascus had some violent exchanges over the air-waves, and the broadcasts of other countries in the area were gleeful; but nothing more came of it in the end.

3. ISRAEL'S POSITION AFTER SINAI

Throughout the period between the early spring of 1957 and the late summer of 1962 Israel was only rarely impelled or called upon to make a move in connection with the events just described. That she could afford to remain relatively passive while the future of the area around her was being contested is an indication of her greater sense of security, and of the great improvement in her strategic and diplomatic posture that took place after Sinai and largely as a consequence of it.

At first glance, Israel's tangible gains from the 1956 War seem rather limited and hardly worth the military risks and the international condemnation she incurred. She was forced to disgorge all her territorial conquests, including the Gaza Strip, which the Egyptians claimed on no other basis than the frequently violated armistice agreement dating from seven years earlier. True, she was able to destroy or capture large quantities of Egyptian equipment, to rout and disorganize two Egyptian divisions, and to put the Egyptian military base in Sinai out of commission by ruining fortifications and facilities in that peninsula; but all this meant at the most a gain of a year or two and perhaps the infliction of some financial losses on Egypt. For immediately after the war, Egypt started rearming and reorganizing her forces with Russian help and rebuilding or replacing the destroyed installations in Sinai. Another apparent gain was the posting of a United Nations force on the Egyptian side of the frontier to prevent border incursions; but this was equally advantageous to Egypt, providing a screen behind which she could reorganize militarily with greater safety. In any case, the existence of that force has depended explicitly on the continued willingness of Egypt to let it remain on her territory. The only lasting tangible gain deriving directly from Sinai was the opening of the Gulf of Akaba for navigation, though even this achievement depended in the final account on Israel's continued capacity to deter Egypt from resuming her blockade rather than on Israel's having obtained any diplomatic or strategic guarantees capable of securing for her freedom of navigation. To these gains some observers add what they believe to be the salutary effect of disabusing Abdel Nasser and the Arabs about Egypt's real strength and about the prospects of liquidating Israel; but this can be counted as a blessing only on the very questionable assumption that the Arabs can be browbeaten into accepting Israel. It is at least as plausible to argue that by inflicting another humiliation on Egypt, the Sinai campaign further magnified the resentment of the Arab states toward Israel and made the chances of acceptance of her existence in their midst even more remote.

The real gains derived by Israel from Sinai were indirect and not immediately visible. They were not, for the most part, advantages so related to that operation that they could have been envisaged beforehand as goals to be attained by it. They may be credited to that campaign only in the sense that they occurred in the situation that emerged after it and were unlikely to have materialized if the campaign had not taken place. They can therefore be detected only by looking at the Sinai War in the context of the situation that preceded and the events that followed it.

First of all, the war blocked the movement to tighten the Arab semicircle around Israel that was under way before the hostilities began. It forced the postponement of Egypt's assumption of effective command of Jordan's troops, hampered the efforts of Abdel Nasser's supporters in that country to consolidate their position, and gave King Husayn the opportunity to launch his *coup d'état* in April 1957 without fearing military intervention from an Egypt still preoccupied with recuperating positions she had lost in the war. Jordan's successful escape from Egypt's control became all the more crucial for Israel after the Egyptian-Syrian merger a year later. It not only denied the very large armed forces of the United Arab Republic control of the strategically important Arab bulge in Palestine, but also deprived Abdel Nasser of a position from which he might have been able to foil Syria's secession from the United Arab Republic in 1961. The fact that the United States committed herself in very firm terms to the preservation of the independence and integrity of Jordan in the course of Husayn's struggle to escape Egyptian domination only enhanced the value and significance of the Jordanian countercurrent.

Secondly, the war provided the occasion for the formation and consolidation of a tacit Franco-Israeli alliance. This alliance has been of vital importance for Israel in that it secured for her an enduring source of first-rate military equipment to counterbalance the armaments received by the Arabs from Russia and added an advocate of her cause in the councils of the big powers. Initially an *ad hoc* affair, the Franco-Israeli cooperation has since become almost a tradition. When the French began selling arms to Israel in the spring of 1956, their purpose was strictly limited: they wanted to exert pressure on Abdel Nasser to cease helping the Algerian rebels militarily. In March of that year, Minister of Foreign Affairs Pineau had visited Cairo and tried to reach an understanding with Egypt's ruler on the question; but neither the implicit threat of helping Israel nor Pineau's expression of France's opposition to the Baghdad Pact, which was anathema to Abdel Nasser, had any practical effect on Nasser's position on Algeria. Still, the French were careful not to antagonize Abdel Nasser too much for fear of endangering their very substantial cultural and economic interests in Egypt and other parts of the Arab world, and confined their arms contracts with Israel to relatively small quantities. It was only after Egypt nationalized the Suez Canal in the summer of 1956, and after France and Britain began to consider in earnest military action against Abdel Nasser that the French government started to think of Israel as a partner in the envisaged operations, and to arm her accordingly. It would be surprising if, when that partnership was sealed and plans for the campaign were worked out, the French and the Israelis did not also agree on projects for consolidating the anticipated gains from the military campaign through far-reaching political and territorial revisions in the area surrounding Israel.

Many, including people in Israel and in France, thought that the failure of the Sinai-Suez War would be the prelude to the dissolution of the *mariage de convenance* between the two countries. In actual fact their relations only gained in strength and scope. For one thing, once direct French retaliation against Abdel Nasser was tried and failed definitively, support for Israel became all the more important since this became the only means left for France of exerting pressure on him in connection with Algeria. Secondly, Abdel Nasser's seizure of French property and his liquidation of the vast French cultural establishment in Egypt after the war brought France closer to Israel not only because of greater resentment against him, but also because there was nothing more to lose from a thoroughly hostile policy toward him. Thirdly, as is usual among highly articulate democratic societies, the fact of Franco-Israeli cooperation and "brotherhood in arms," however Machiavellian might have been its origins, called forth torrents of literature and oratory on both sides justifying it morally and dwelling on the transcendent ties underlying it, which contributed an added momentum to their tacit alliance while giving it a more positive character. Thus various projects of economic, technical, political, cultural, and scientific cooperation were started which went on expanding over the years. One such project alone has brought hundreds of French scientists and technicians to Israel where they have been working for years now with Israelis on the nuclear reactor near Beersheba. Finally, the espousal of Israel, especially supplying her with arms, was viewed by France as giving her the right to have a say in any big power discussion of the Middle East. The French were bitterly resentful of the fact that they had been completely left out of all the Anglo-American plans in connection with the Baghdad Pact. The two powers had assumed, quite rightly, that it would be difficult if not impossible for any Arab state to associate itself with France while she was suppressing the Algerians; but that they did not even consult her about the Pact was taken by her both as an insult and as a design of the Anglo-Saxons to exclude her altogether from an area in which she had had an important say for more than a century. With the loss of all her positions and influence in the Arab countries as a result of Suez and Algeria, the alliance with Israel became the most important means for asserting the *présence Française* in the Middle East.

A further gain which Israel derived indirectly from the Sinai War was a greatly improved understanding with the United States, and the initiation of a regular consultation procedure between the two governments which underscored continually the basic American moral commitment to Israel's security and integrity. In a certain sense, Israel's involvement in the Sinai adventure could be viewed as the outcome of a loss of confidence in the intentions of

the American government. As has been said before, the records that
have come to light so far show that the Eisenhower Administration
continued to uphold the United States' commitment to resist any
attempt to alter by force the territorial and political status quo between the Arab states and Israel. However, the manner in which
Secretary of State Dulles had pursued his Middle East policies until
the Suez-Sinai War, and his apparent willingness to accept the
disruption of the balance of armaments that resulted from the
Soviet-Egyptian deal had aroused strong suspicions among Israelis
that he was taking excessive risks with their security if he was not
actually working deliberately on a policy aimed at putting them in
a position in which they could be forced to make concessions. The
root of the trouble lay in a far-reaching difference in the assessment
of Arab attitudes and the possibility of modifying them. The Secretary of State no less than the Israelis recognized the importance of
solving the Palestine problem for the stability of the area. He was
inclined to believe, however, that American military and economic
cooperation with the Arab states was the best way of placing the
West in a position in which it could exercise a restraining influence
on them and perhaps induce them in due course to come to terms
with Israel. In the meantime, it would be in the Israelis' best interest if they would keep quiet, stop trying to press the United States
to identify herself openly with them and protesting against every
Western gesture toward the Arabs, and refrain from any action that
might exacerbate Arab feeling against them. The Israelis, on the
other hand, believed that the main motive of the Arabs in cooperat-
ing with any power was precisely to get arms and strengthen themselves for an eventual showdown with them; they did not share the
Secretary of State's confidence in the American government's being
able at some point to influence the Arabs decisively on the Palestine
question except through determined use of its power, and were convinced that American efforts to court the Arabs would be interpreted by them as an abandonment of Israel and would therefore
encourage them to persist in their intransigence. So sure were the
Israelis of their assessment of the situation that they were inclined
to suspect that, in taking a different view, Secretary Dulles was only
rationalizing his wish to woo the Arabs into the Western camp regardless of the perils to Israel's security involved in this process.
Therefore, when the Arab menace had seemed to assume dangerous

proportions, and when an opportunity for taking action to remove it had presented itself, they saw no alternative but to act.

The shock of the war and the acute international crisis it provoked impelled the American government to take Israel's assumptions in regard to her security more seriously. The Secretary of State came to a clearer realization that whether or not these assumptions were correct, it was important to try to give them greater consideration because the Israelis would ultimately act on them, and this might lead to another dangerous international crisis. This new approach found its clearest expression in the Israeli-American discussions on the withdrawal of Israeli troops from the Gaza Strip and the part of the Sinai peninsula controlling the entry to the Gulf of Akaba. The Israelis feared that these territories would be used again by the Egyptians to launch raids against Israel and to block passage to her ships, and they therefore refused to withdraw unless they were given some international guarantee against such eventualities. The American government did not believe that Israel's fears would materialize and was not, at the same time, prepared to give any formal guarantee which might unnecessarily antagonize the Arabs and appear as a reward for aggression. As the American government prepared to support a United Nations' resolution for sanctions against Israel, it seemed that the difference in estimating the situation was about to lead once more to a grave crisis. This time, however, a way out was found at the eleventh hour. An exchange of correspondence was arranged in which President Eisenhower told Premier Ben Gurion, in effect: We urge you to withdraw; we don't think your fears are justified, and we take the responsibility for giving you this advice. This formula restored the confidence of the Israelis in American intentions and established a pattern for subsequent relations between the two governments. From then on, there was closer consultation on all Middle East issues affecting Israel's security based on a renewed moral commitment on the part of the United States to Israel's integrity and independence, and an earnest endeavor not to allow a gap in the assessment of events and possibilities to widen to a point that might lead to an open clash of positions.

This improved understanding between the United States and Israel was greatly enhanced by the course of events in the years after the Sinai-Suez War. In 1957–1958, the United States gave up the effort to please Abdel Nasser and developed instead a policy aimed at containing his influence and rolling it back, which created an obvious harmony between America's immediate objective and Israeli interests. This harmony was reflected in the welcome accorded by Israel's government to the Eisenhower Doctrine—the first American diplomatic initiative in the Middle East that sought openly to enlist the cooperation of several Arab states as well as Israel—and allowed that government to take a more sophisticated view of the American moves in the Middle East. Not only did it not embarrass the American government with the usual representations every time it rushed arms or economic aid to some Arab country, but it actually did what it could to facilitate the American efforts to create a loose pro-Western Arab bloc to counter the Cairo-Moscow axis. Thus, when Iraq and Jordan formed the Arab Union with Western blessing in order to counter Abdel Nasser's United Arab Republic, the Israeli government warned against the introduction of Iraqi troops into the west bank of the Jordan but otherwise refrained from making further difficulties on this issue which it had always considered as vital. A few months later, when the Iraqi revolution brought about the almost complete encirclement of Jordan by hostile states, Israel allowed British paratroops to fly over her own territory to bring succor to King Husayn's embattled regime. She also allowed American tanker-planes to use Israeli air space in order to replenish Jordan's exhausted fuel reserves after the "brotherly" Arab government of Saudi Arabia had refused to allow help to come from its side.

In the situation that developed after the Iraqi revolution, the agreement of American and Israeli immediate objectives became even more harmonious, creating at least a promise of enhanced cooperation between the two governments. Ever since 1950, the United States had attempted to pursue a Middle Eastern policy that included two contradictory elements: she had tried to separate the Arab-Israeli problem from the East-West struggle in the area and to take a conservative position in regard to the former, and a revisionist position in regard to the latter. Whatever ultimate theoretical unity may be thought to exist between the two courses, in practice they proved irreconcilable and hampered each other. The American commitment to preserve the status quo on the Palestine issue tended, by identifying America with Israel's interest, to handicap the effort to rally the Arab countries into the Western camp. At the same time, the effort to lure these countries into a Western alliance with diplomatic, economic and, especially military, inducements tended, both directly and indirectly, to undermine the foundations of the status quo in the Arab-Israeli conflict, and to raise doubts in the minds of Israelis about the strength of the American commitment to them. The decisive collapse, after the loss of Iraq, of the American government's effort deliberately to organize the Arab East, and its conversion to a position that accepted the status quo in the area as a whole as well as in Palestine, finally removed that contradiction and eliminated a source of friction between the United States and Israel. America's initiatives from that time on to gain the friendship and promote the economic development of the Arab countries no longer appeared so threatening to Israel; on the contrary, to the extent that they tended to preserve the general balance in the area, they redounded to her benefit by helping to maintain the status quo between her and her neighbors. Similarly, the commitment to Israel ceased to appear as burdensome to the United States as when she was trying to build an alliance with the Arabs; indeed, to the extent that this commitment has meant supporting the balance of forces between Israel and her neighbors, it could not fail to contribute to the general balance by helping to deter one neighbor from overrunning a weaker one in the name of Arab unity and thus perhaps upset the general balance. The fact that, in both its application to the area as a whole and to the Arab-Israeli conflict, the policy of preserving the basic status quo is in practice beneficial to most of the Arab states as well as to Israel, and seems to be acceptable even to Russia, gives grounds for hoping that it will continue for some time, which is perhaps an added reason for Israel to feel gratified at the transformation that has taken place since Sinai.

4. ISRAEL AND AFRO-ASIA

The improvement in Israel's situation after Sinai gave her government the chance to turn its attention to a field of international activity which has received wide publicity and gained much praise for Israel. We refer, of course, to Israel's endeavors in the field of technical aid for the benefit of developing countries, especially the new nations of Africa and Asia. Israel's efforts in that sphere had their beginning several years before Sinai; but it was not until after that campaign that they assumed the dimensions of a deliberate, large-scale program. For one thing, these efforts could not have prospered without the reopening of the short route to east Africa and Asia through the Gulf of Akaba. For another thing, the overwhelming preoccupation with the immediate Arab threat had claimed all of Israel's attention, and it was not until that threat abated after Sinai that she could devote some of her means and energies to diplomatic activities that bore no *immediate* relevance to security. Finally, Israelis had to learn first that there was no short cut to long-range security through an alliance or other formal agreement with the United States or the Western powers before they could feel psychologically disposed to try in earnest to reach their goal through a long and uncertain detour.

Israel's first venture in foreign assistance began almost accidentally in Burma. In 1953, Foreign Minister Sharett, while representing Mapai at the First Asian Socialist Conference in Rangoon, managed to persuade the Burmese government to exchange diplomatic representation with Israel. Up to that time, Israel had failed to induce any Asian country except Turkey to establish normal diplomatic relations with her. The Muslim countries of Asia had avoided such a step out of solidarity with the fellow-Muslim Arab states; and the non-Muslim ones had lacked any positive inducement, moral or material, to establish connections with her. Non-Muslim Asian peoples had had for the most part no contact with Jews, no real appreciation of the problem of anti-Semitism and Jewish persecution, and were unaware of the strong Jewish ties to Palestine, which was stock knowledge among the Western peoples brought up on the Bible. Asian intellectuals who had heard something about Zionism were on the whole inclined to consider it as an instrument of Western imperialism aimed at imposing an alien people on the indigenous population, rather than a genuine nationalist movement. This indifference or antipathy of the Asians was reinforced by the fact that up to the mid-1950's Israel had had almost no commercial intercourse with any Asian country but Turkey. In view of all this, Israel considered the breakthrough achieved in Rangoon as of some importance and sought to consolidate it. Since the conventional motives for close, friendly relations among nations—such as cultural affinity or community of political or economic interest—were lacking in this instance, Israel endeavored to create artificially some tangible bonds between the two countries. Shortly after the establishment of diplomatic relations, Israel sent to Burma teams of medical personnel, engineers, conservation specialists, and various technicians of which that country was short. This reinforced the friendship between the two countries and led to the acceptance by Prime Minister U Nu of an invitation to visit Israel in the spring of 1955, which in turn led to an expansion of the cooperation program. Scores of Burmese ex-servicemen and their families were brought to Israel to spend extended periods in cooperative and collective villages in order to learn advanced agricultural techniques and to assimilate the Israeli experience in setting up settlement-outposts for application in Burma's jungles. After the opening of the Gulf of Akaba, cooperation between the two countries was further extended into new areas. Burmese enterprises, such as the Five Star Shipping Line, were established under Israeli management; Israeli enterprises entered into agreements to market Burmese products in Asia and Africa; and joint Burmese-Israeli companies were established in Burma, such as the public construction company formed in partnership with Solel Boneh.

The idea of using technical assistance and economic cooperation to justify and cement friendly diplomatic relations, first applied by Israel in Burma, and the patterns of cooperation developed in the course of its application there were extended after 1957 to many other countries. Thailand, the Philippines, Nepal, Laos, Cambodia, South Vietnam, and Japan established diplomatic relations with Israel and all but the last have participated in greater or lesser degree in various aid and cooperation projects. Iran did not formally exchange diplomatic representation with Israel, but the two countries developed very extensive and fruitful connections. In addition to Israel's providing technical assistance, the two countries have discovered that they had important political and economic interests in common. Israel now obtains most of her oil from Iran through Eilat, where a 16-inch pipeline carries it to the refineries in Haifa; and sends to Iran increasing amounts of export goods. A project to add a new Eilat-Haifa pipeline of a diameter double the first, now under consideration, should give a tremendous impetus to the trade relations between the two countries while providing Iranian oil with a short route to European markets that might prove of vital importance if the Suez Canal should be closed for political or technical reasons. In addition to these trade and aid benefits, Israel has come to be viewed by Iran as an important counterpoise to Abdel Nasser, who has incurred the Shah's hostility for his cooperation with Moscow and his war on the Baghdad Pact, of which Iran had been a member.

These remarkable successes of the Israeli diplomacy of friendship-through-aid in Asia have been overshadowed by the successes attained in Africa. Among the emerging nations of that continent, Israel did not have to contend with any of the prejudices she encountered in several Asian countries. Most of the black states of Africa had had no special bond with the Arabs (some have known them only as slave traders) and were ready to view Israel on her own present merits. The first black African state to achieve independence, Ghana, accepted the Israeli offers of aid and exchange of diplomatic representation; and the success of this experiment in cooperation set the example for the other countries. Henceforth the arrival of Israeli diplomatic missions and technicians became almost an integral part of the independence ceremonies marking the birth of each new African state. According to the Israeli Foreign Office, over 900 Israeli experts in a score of fields were engaged in technical assistance projects throughout Africa by the middle of 1962. The same source indicated that one thousand Africans were at that time undergoing training in Israel and that three thousand had already completed courses of varying duration and returned to their respective countries. Altogether, Israel was said to be lending assistance of one sort or another to sixty-five countries in Africa, Asia, and Central and South America. The program has been highly flexible throughout, and its extent, coverage, and quality have been continually adjusted to meet the needs of the beneficiary countries.

Why has Israel's aid program been so popular? What does Israel expect to gain and what has she actually gained from it so far? The first question is fairly easy to answer. Israel is a small country so that her aid is not suspected as an instrument of domination. Moreover, being a small developing nation, Israel's experience is often more relevant to the problems and needs of the recipient countries than is that of the big and advanced powers. Furthermore, Israeli technicians are usually low-paid, eager, accustomed to making do with the means available, and are generally obtainable on very short notice. No less important, Israelis are willing to move out of a venture without any fuss as fast as they move in. Thus, for example, two years after they had established a jointly owned shipping company with Ghana—the Black Star Line—they were ready to sell their interest to their partner and remain to help manage and run the company. Finally, among the race-conscious African peoples the Israelis are easier to accept psychologically. Though Israelis are Caucasian, they are not suspected or resented as members of the "master race" in view of the suffering and persecution they have undergone themselves at the hands of the white man.

Less easy to assess are Israel's motives for engaging in the aid program and the rewards she has drawn from it. With respect to motives, the psychological need to be accepted and liked in the international community is certainly an important factor. This need is felt particularly strongly in view of the Arab efforts to isolate Israel morally and depict her in the eyes of the African-Asian world as an offspring and protégé of Western imperialism thrust forcibly upon the Middle East nations. As an immediate aim, Israelis hope that establishing friendly and helpful relations with the Afro-Asian nations will at least neutralize them in the Israeli-Arab conflict. In the long run, many Israelis entertain the hope that their acceptance by the bulk of the non-Western countries may exert a salutary psychological influence on the Arabs and induce them in due course to accept Israel. Some even dare to expect that friendly African and Asian nations may exert here and now an active moral pressure on the Arab states to come to terms with Israel. The desire to explore the possibilities of fruitful economic activities for their own sake has been an additional factor; but the actual modest trade figures between Israel and African countries and the specialization of Israel's economy in highly processed and expensive products should serve as a warning against attributing too much weight to this "real" factor. Probably as important as the economic motive has been the extension of the pioneering drive beyond the frontiers of Israel and the sense of pride at being able to serve as "a light to the Gentiles." If there is any "realistic" motive in Israel's program of foreign aid it is probably to be found in the hope that it will draw tangible rewards from the United States by serving, coincidentally with her own interests, the same objects that that country seeks to promote through its aid program.

The extent to which these purposes have been served so far is difficult to establish because it is not often possible to relate effects to the cause of assistance, or even to assess the significance of the effects themselves. This is why it might be best, given the limitations of this book, simply to recall the salient facts that might be related to this question, leaving it to the reader to form his own impression of the degree of their dependence on the aid program and of their importance. Israel has established diplomatic relations on an ambassadorial level with twenty African countries in the last four or five years without any difficulty; not long before, it was considered an achievement by her to have established such relations with one non-Western country. Where in the first decade of statehood U Nu was the only chief of state to pay an official visit to Israel, ten heads or chiefs of state came on official visits in the course of one year in 1961–1962. At the "summit" United Nations General Assembly in 1960, President Nkrumah of Ghana called upon the Arab states to accept a "realistic and practical solution" of the Palestine problem based upon the acceptance of "the political realities that prevail there today." At the Belgrade Conference of Neutralist Powers in 1961, Premier U Nu of Burma made an impassioned speech against an anti-Israel resolution submitted by President Abdel Nasser and caused it to be withdrawn. Most important, perhaps, at the General Assembly session of 1961, a group of sixteen nations, mostly African, submitted a resolution calling for direct negotiations between the Arab states and Israel to solve all the problems outstanding between them—an object which had been fervently sought by Israel for years. On the other hand, Israel is still not included in the caucus of African-Asian nations at the U.N. and is not invited to the social functions sponsored by these delegations. An Afro-Asian conference in Addis Ababa, Ethiopia, in 1960, was successfully pressured by the United Arab Republic to pass a resolution expressing support for the Arabs of Palestine. A "summit" meeting of the rulers of the United Arab Republic, Morocco, Ghana, Mali, and Guinea, which took place in Casablanca in 1961, inserted in the final communiqué a denunciation of Israel as a tool of imperialism not only in the Middle East, but also in Africa and Asia. Two of the signatories—Ghana and Mali—were receiving at that time substantial technical assistance from Israel. Each of these setbacks, particularly the last one, naturally disappointed the Israelis and caused the skeptics among them to grumble about the usefulness of foreign assistance; but the Israeli government did not allow its disappointment to interfere seriously with the continuation of its program.

Summarizing, we may say that by the summer and early fall of 1962, Israel's diplomatic-strategic position was and had been for some years better than at any previous period since independence. The borders had been relatively quiet since the end of the Sinai campaign; the Arab ring around Israel had been loosened by the defection of Jordan, and then of Syria, from the Egyptian camp; her tacit alliance with France secured for her the heavy arms and equipment she needed to keep abreast of the increase in Egypt's power; the competition between East and West, the one supporting Abdel Nasser's drive and the other endeavoring to build an Arab bloc allied to itself, had abated since 1959, reducing the danger of the emergence of threatening combinations against her; finally, relations with the United States had constantly improved as the two countries' immediate objectives became more compatible. All these advantages have not yet resolved the issue of Israel's long-term security, which can only rest in the final account on a genuine peace with her Arab neighbors; but the longer the present non-violent stalemate continues, the better the chances are that the Arabs may reconcile themselves to her existence, especially if she and the powers concerned with the peace of the area use every opportunity to reach across the frontiers with gestures of understanding and generosity rather than of insult and provocation.

XVI

The United States and Israel: An Analytical Precis

In several parts of this work, we have had occasion to discuss different aspects of American-Israeli relations in a topical or chronological context. In this, the concluding chapter, we shall attempt to draw a comprehensive summary of these relations in an analytical context, focusing on the various factors that have significantly affected them. These may be conveniently discussed under five headings: 1) the intrinsic bonds between the United States and Israel; 2) the connections between American Jews and Israel; 3) the impact of American Jews on United States relations with Israel; 4) the impact of American interests in the Arab countries on these relations; 5) the implications of the Arab-Israeli conflict for the future of American-Israeli relations.

1. THE UNITED STATES AND ISRAEL: INTRINSIC BONDS

Although the direct bonds connecting the United States and Israel cannot be separated in practice from the other factors affecting the relations between the two countries, it is possible, with an effort of the imagination, to visualize these bonds more or less independently for analytical purposes, even if one cannot gauge their proper dimensions or their exact significance. The United States, for example, has a long tradition of sympathy for peoples striving to attain sovereign nationhood generally, and for persecuted peoples in particular which was likely to bring forth a friendly attitude toward the aspirations of Jewish nationalism. And while it is true that Jewish nationalism conflicted with Palestinian Arab nationalism, American opinion, quite apart from the influence of powerful Jewish propaganda, was apt to give priority to the Jewish claim to national restoration in Palestine, because of its connection with the Bible, over the Arab case about which it knows very little even today. Then, there is the element of mutual sympathy deriving from the affinity of regimes and the commitment of the two countries to democracy which, in the context of the popular American conception of the present international situation as a struggle of principles between "free" and "totalitarian" states, automatically places Israel in the camp of the "forces of light" led by the United States. Furthermore, there is an appreciation of the pioneering spirit that has built Israel which is reminiscent of the youthful days of America, a sense of respect for the drive and achievements of the young state in the economic, social, scientific, and military spheres, and an admiration for its recent efforts to help other small nations in Africa, Asia, and Latin America. One could cite perhaps other elements in this connection but they would all be of this same moral nature; they would not include any "real" mutual interests between the two countries, such as the oil bond between the United States and other Middle Eastern countries, the common interest of the United States and Turkey in defense against traditional Russian ambitions in that area, the links of contiguity, economic interest, and hemispheric defense with the countries of Latin America, and so on.

Israel's geographic position at the junction of three continents might have been of strategic value to the United States were it not that her isolation by Arab hostility considerably discounted the usefulness of that position. Israel's separating of the land connections between the Arab world in Africa and in Asia could be of political-strategic value, but only on the assumption, hardly ever entertained in the United States, that keeping that world divided was an important and lasting objective.

The fact that Israel offers the United States little if any tangible material attraction has had much to do with the attitude of some Americans in positions of power and influence who sought to reduce as much as possible any embarrassing commitments of their country toward Israel. This attitude has always stumbled over its own assumptions, especially the assumption that the factor of the American Jews and all its multifarious implications could and should be ignored. The separation between the Jewish factor and what we have called the "direct attitudes" of the United States toward Israel, artificially introduced here for purposes of analysis, is taken quite seriously by this school of thought, and the suggestion is made that the United States should conduct her relations with Israel independently of the Jewish factor. At the same time, proponents of this position have tended on the whole to minimize the practical implications that ought to follow from "mere" moral bonds and to stress the significance of countervailing "real" considerations. Because of the imperfect realism of this self-styled "realistic" approach, because of its failure to take into account the magnitude of the Jewish factor, and to give appropriate weight to the real influence of the moral element, this position never prevailed fully in the American government, though it often did have the effect of injecting an element of hesitation and doubt in American policies toward Israel and the Arab countries.

That the moral element can be "realistically" viewed as centrally relevant to the American national interest is well illustrated in the argument presented by W. W. Rostow, Counselor for the State Department and Chief of its Policy Planning Council, in a book he published before assuming his present post. (See his *The United States in the World Arena,* New York, 1960, Appendix A.) Rostow insists that the United States' supreme interest is not only to protect the national territory but also the basic humanistic democratic values of American society. The protection of the national territory requires that the United States should strive to prevent any potentially hostile power, or combination of powers, from dominating the Eurasian land mass (defined to include Asia, the Middle East, Africa, as well as Europe) or a sufficient portion of it to threaten the United States or any coalition she can build and sustain. Protection of the humanistic democratic values of American society requires, quite apart from the military situation, that Eurasia should not be coalesced under totalitarian dictatorships which would threaten the survival of democracy both in the United States and elsewhere. In the context of the present world situation, in which Russia and China control vast portions of Eurasia, the pursuit of the supreme national strategic objective is reduced in effect to preventing these two powers from swinging the balance of forces in their favor by acquiring control over a few key countries, such as West Germany and France or Italy in the West, and India or Japan in the East. Similarly, in a world in which antithetical ideologies prevail in many areas even outside the Sino-Soviet bloc, the protection of the humanistic democratic values of American society hinges on a balance which a few—in this case not clearly defined—areas may tilt. Viewed in this context, Israel's commitment to the same humanistic democratic values as the United States becomes of real importance for the American national interest, especially since her achievements in many fields of endeavor provide for the very many emerging nations a rare example of a successful democracy in a new state.

2. THE AMERICAN JEWS AND ISRAEL

The relations of American Jews with Israel and their influence in the United States have been crucial factors in building up an extraordinarily extensive and cohesive network of political, economic, moral, and cultural bonds between the two countries. We have already referred (see Chapters II and IV) to the process by which organized American Jewry had moved from supporting various "nonpolitical" aspects of the Zionist endeavor in Palestine, through supporting the Zionist struggle for keeping that country open for large-scale immigration, to supporting vigorously the recommendations of the United Nations commission to terminate the Mandate and create a Jewish (and an Arab) state. During the year of struggle in which Israel was born, American Jews gave proof of the extent of their enthusiasm for that state by sending to it aid in cash and kind valued at over $200,000,000. This incredibly large sum represents a per capita contribution by American Jews almost equivalent to the per capita receipt of the federal government in that year. In the following years, assistance given by American Jews to Israel continued on a relatively diminished scale, but it still added up to the very impressive total of about a billion dollars over the entire period since Israel's declaration of independence. In addition, American Jews bought during that period more than half-a-billion dollars' worth of bonds of various sorts issued by the Israeli government, and invested about half that amount directly in enterprises in Israel.

During those years, the attitude of American Jews toward Israel changed significantly but imperceptibly under the momentum of their practical relations with her and the impact of changed circumstances. For decades before the establishment of the state, American Jews had been divided between a Zionist minority, consciously striving to establish a Jewish commonwealth, and a majority that supported specific activities in Palestine and specific issues relating to it on various grounds, but explicitly shunned identification with the political-sociological conclusions and the philosophy of Zionism. The establishment of the state of Israel has tended to eliminate the difference between the two groups and to set their relation to it on a new basis. The Zionists, whose political philosophy logically implied that they should, now at last, take the path of "personal realization" and emigrate to the Jewish state, began by wavering and ended by stressing increasingly a new version of an old minority brand of Zionism associated with the name of Achad Haam (1856–1927) which had emphasized the primary role of the movement as the building of a *cultural* center in Palestine aimed at saving *Judaism* from extinction (rather than *Jews* from inevitable anti-Semitism) and giving the Jewish ethical genius an opportunity to express itself in new creations. With its stress on the cultural role of the Jewish state, this version minimized, *pari passu,* the importance of emigration for Jews who did not feel pressed to do so by their environment. This accorded perfectly well with the views of the non-Zionists who had always supported religious, cultural, and philanthropic endeavors in Palestine; and once they too came to support the creation of a Jewish state as the only means of insuring a refuge for persecuted Jews in the postwar world, the differences between them and the Zionists were almost obliterated. Of course, the old differences have continued to provide grounds for dispute among leaders of the two groups, especially since the separate communal institutions that were built on the basis of these differences have survived to the present day; but for the bulk of organized American Jewry these quarrels have become quite meaningless, and a sense of attachment to Israel and a willingness to help have come to be generally shared and appreciated all the more because they transcended denominational and other divisions. Working for Israel—collecting and giving money, following the country's news and development, caring about its problems and taking pride in its achievements, listening to lectures and sermons about it, attending meetings and rallies and social and cultural benefit functions, promoting and participating in specific pet schemes, and so on—has become increasingly a focal point of Jewish community life in America. Quite apart from the merits of the case itself, such work has provided a satisfying outlet for the natural desire of men and women to identify themselves with a cause transcending their life routine, has given members of an affluent society a psychologically needed "right" to enjoy their affluence by sharing it with others less fortunate, and it has perhaps helped to alleviate a faint sense of "guilt" on the part of American Jews because they had an easy time while their brethren in Europe and elsewhere suffered want and persecution. Against this evolution of attitudes toward Israel, the strictures of the small anti-Zionist American Council for Judaism have been completely ineffective.

The attachment of American Jews to Israel has worked in various ways to draw the two countries closer to each other. The massive economic aid they have provided to the Jewish state is only the most obvious of these ways; it has entailed care on the part of Israel's government not to undertake, except *in extremis,* any action that might cause the American Jews embarrassments vis-à-vis their fellow citizens and their government, and it has helped reduce the alternative of a pro-Soviet foreign policy orientation suggested by extreme left-wing parties to purely academic significance. By the forms of aid they have given and by their own visits, American Jews have also done much to bring a sense of American "presence" into every corner of Israel. There is, indeed, hardly an important educational, cultural, social, or philanthropic institution in Israel today which is not supported in some degree by American Jewish (as well as governmental) aid, including the four institutions of higher learning (the Hebrew University, the Haifa Institute of Technology, the Weizmann Institute of Science, and the Bar Ilan University), the main museums, the Israel Philharmonic Orchestra, the national theater, the Hadassah Medical Center, almost the entire vocational school system, the Histadrut, and scores of religious schools, orphanages, and culture and sports centers throughout the country. American Jewish tourists have flocked to the country at a mounting rate, recently exceeding 60,000 a year, and have not only spent money but brought to the masses of Israelis an awareness of the ties between their country and the United States. Indirectly, the relations of American Jews with Israel have been instrumental in bringing to the country scores of movie, theater and sports stars, artists, scientists, scholars, journalists, politicians, and other VIP's from the United States. In a reverse direction, they have brought to this country practically every member who ever sat in the Israeli cabinet, dozens of Knesset Members, almost every high officer, every self-respecting official above a certain rank, most artists and thousands of students and trainees of all sorts. Together with the impact of American movies, which have a near monopoly in that country of avid moviegoers, American books, magazines, and records, which are consumed at rates approaching those of some parts of the United States, the impact of the American Jews has been to make Israel easily one of the most "Americanized" and most America-conscious countries today. And the cultural-psychological web thus constructed over the years has become an added moral bond to those that already linked the United States and Israel.

3. THE AMERICAN JEWS AND UNITED STATES POLICIES TOWARD ISRAEL

The American Jews have affected American-Israeli relations not only through their influence on Israel, but also through their impact on American politics and the American government. So much nonsense has been written and said in this connection that it seems necessary to stress a few points on the subject. First of all, it is a fact, much as it has been denied, that American Jews have been influenced in their voting behavior by the attitude taken by political candidates on matters relating to Israel, and that candidates have frequently taken a stand on such matters with an eye to this fact. For although the Jews constitute only a small minority of the American electorate, they are concentrated in such large cities as New York, Chicago, Philadelphia, and Los Angeles, which often hold the key to the pivotal states they are in. Secondly, the Jews are not the first ethnic or religious group in America that has sought to influence American foreign policy in favor of kinsmen or coreligionists abroad. For example, in 1794, the Irishmen in America presented massive opposition to the Jay Treaty; in 1888 they played a major role in defeating a fisheries treaty with Canada, and eleven years later played a similar role in defeating the Anglo-American Arbitration Treaty of 1897. German-Americans attempted in 1888 to get the United States to settle a dispute between Germany, England, and the United States over the island of Samoa in a way favorable to Germany. At the turn of the century, Americans of Dutch ancestry tried to get the United States to intervene in the Boer War. Nonintervention in the Spanish Civil War was, to some extent, pressed on the United States by Catholic opinion. Americans of Polish descent have urged the denunciation of the Yalta agreements and, together with other Americans of Eastern European origins, have been particularly responsive to slogans about rolling back the Iron Curtain. Ethno-religious politics, like the politics of interest groups in general, have been an inescapable consequence of the pluralism and multiplicity of interests in American life and are therefore a fact to be reckoned with. Thirdly, the desire of minority groups to promote their particular views and interests, and the efforts of politicians to organize a variety of such views and interests into a winning majority are integral aspects of the American democratic process today. To exhort the voters to put the national interest above their particular group interest and the candidates to put integrity above the desire to catch votes is often insulting and always futile. For rarely do either perceive any clear-cut conflict between the national interest or personal integrity and the cause they espouse; on the contrary, in most cases they are convinced that their particular cause is in the best interest of the nation and, what is more, they are not always necessarily wrong. Finally, the point should be made in the particular case of the American Jews, that though they have undoubtedly exerted a great deal of influence in inducing favorable American attitudes and policies toward Israel, the degree and "danger" of this influence have been greatly exaggerated. For one thing, their pressure in one direction has often been checked by opposing pressures on the part of less vocal but nonetheless effective groups. For another thing, the American policy-makers have not been mere automatons responding to pressures and counterpressures; they have had a will of their own which has increased in firmness along with the increase in

American involvement in the Middle East as a whole. In fact, the case can be made that they have sometimes "overcompensated" for the Jewish pressure by resisting or adopting certain measures largely because they have been suggested or opposed by American Jews.

Having placed the "Jewish pressure" in some perspective, we can now look back and try to assess roughly the actual impact of American Jews on American attitudes and policies toward Israel in the last fourteen years. In general, we can say that, through their own interest in Israel and through the operation of the law of demand and supply in the political field as well as in the world of the media of communications, the American Jews have created a climate in which American sympathies toward Israel have been enhanced to the utmost and have been made to yield as many practical results as they could. But the capacity of American sympathies to yield practical results has apparently varied according to whether they applied to the economic and general sphere, or to the diplomatic-strategic. In the economic and general sphere, the impact of the American Jews has led to a uniformly and unequivocally friendly and helpful attitude toward Israel. With the United States giving economic aid to more than two score countries, not all formally allies, one would expect Israel too to be among the beneficiaries; but the level of aid given to her has been quite exceptional. During the first fourteen years of Israel's existence, the United States government has in fact awarded her close to $850,000,000 of aid in various forms, mostly outright grants of one kind or another. On a per capita basis of the recipient country, this is probably the highest rate of American aid given to any country. Moreover, the American government never seriously attempted to question the classification of the billion dollars of donations made by American Jews as tax-exempt "charity," though this money went, in effect, into the general development budget of Israel. Without this massive aid, given or sanctioned by the American government, Israel would have been unable to develop her economy on the scale she did, absorb as many immigrants, or perhaps even defend her existence. As part of the American aid programs, Israel has received all sorts of benefits on a scale proportional to her share in aid. Thus hundreds of American technicians and Israeli trainees have been exchanged; dozens of Israeli cultural, educational, and philanthropic institutions have enjoyed American assistance from counterpart funds (funds in Israeli currency accumulated by the American authorities in exchange for agricultural surpluses from the U.S.); and the Israeli public has been allowed to buy American educational and cultural material payable in Israeli currency at the official rate. In short, Israel has been given the status of a most favored nation, and not only in the technical sense in which the term is used in international trade. Any benefit the United States has granted to other countries has been awarded to Israel on a generous scale and promptly. No sooner had the United States launched the Atoms for Peace Program, for example, than Israel began building a small atomic reactor with American help within the framework of that program.

In the diplomatic-strategic sphere, however, the impact of the American Jews on American attitudes and policies has not been nearly so uniformly successful. The American Jews played a vital role in inducing the United States to support the partition plan. (It should be remembered that though this support was justifiable in terms of the Palestine problem as it presented itself at the time, it was not on these grounds that it was given.) Their influence was also important in bringing about the immediate recognition of Israel, in inducing President Truman to veto any suggestion to alter the partition plan against Israel's interest, and in prompting the American government to issue, together with Britain and France, the Tripartite Declaration which guaranteed Israel's gains and insured her against Arab attack. Under the Eisenhower Administration, Jewish influence contributed to preserving the American commitment to the existence and integrity of Israel at a time when a greater involvement of the United States in the Middle East and the intensification of the Cold War there threatened to undermine it. But at no time was Jewish influence sufficient to induce the American government to give Israel what she wanted most—a bilateral or multilateral formal alliance that would guarantee her security. Moreover, on many specific issues, the strongly expressed wishes of the American Jews did not prevail with the American government. Thus American Jews were unable to move their government to exert pressure on the Arab countries to cease their boycott of Israel or to desist from blocking the Suez Canal to Israeli shipping and trade. They failed to dissuade the American government from providing some Arab countries with economic and military aid despite their hostile practices against Israel, and to prevent American formal condemnations of Israel for her retaliatory raids across the armistice lines. During the crisis that began with the Soviet-Egyptian arms deal, an incredibly intense campaign of persuasion and lobbying failed to move Secretary of State Dulles to allow the sale of American arms to Israel to counter the Arab threat. Later, when Israel launched her attack on Egypt at the end of October 1956, the American government did not hesitate to initiate a condemnatory resolution in the Security Council even though its own fate was about to be decided in a national election; and in the following months, it made it clear that it would join other members of the United Nations in voting sanctions against Israel unless she withdrew from positions she had occupied in the course of the campaign. If, in the years since, United States policies and measures have not clashed as often with actions and desires of Israel, this has been due much more to a change of circumstances in the Middle East than to a reassertion of Jewish influence, or to the change of administration in the United States. Long before the 1960 elections, the Eisenhower Administration, anxious to preserve the balance of power that had emerged in that part of the world after 1958 and to forestall any "preventive attack" on the part of Israel, had set the pattern of closer consultation which characterizes the relations between the two countries today, and had given tokens of its understanding for Israel's legitimate defense concerns by supporting her right of free navigation in the Gulf of Akaba and by selling her substantial quantities of military equipment.

4. THE IMPACT OF AMERICAN INTERESTS ON THE ARAB COUNTRIES

The effect of the American sympathy toward Israel and the influence of the American Jews have been limited by considerations of direct and indirect American interest in the Arab countries and, to a lesser extent, by the moral counterclaims of the Arabs in regard to Palestine. The moral case for the Arabs never enjoyed a decent hearing in the United States by comparison with the Jewish case for many reasons. Nevertheless, among the few it reached there were some persons who had influence and status partly because of familiarity with the Arab world acquired through educational, scientific, and missionary work, and these were able to produce moral arguments which occasionally had the effect of strengthening those who favored a pro-Arab or less pro-Israel course on some practical grounds. The indirect American interest in the Arab countries relates to the existence of a sea or several seas of oil underneath some of them. According to estimates made in 1960, the Middle East had about two thirds of the proven oil reserves in the world, concentrated mainly in the countries bordering on the Persian Gulf. Output of crude oil from the Middle East constituted 17 per cent of the total world production in 1952, 23.7 per cent in 1959, and is still on the rise. Middle East oil production is carried chiefly by American, British, Dutch, and French companies, with the American companies drawing about half the total profits (that half was estimated roughly at between $600 million and $700 million in 1961).

The influence of oil on American policy toward Israel and the Arab countries, like the influence of American Jews, has been the subject of bitter controversy into which we need not enter here. We shall confine ourselves to making a few observations on the subject. First, the United States herself has not drawn much on the Middle East oil resources. Oil imports from that source have accounted for only 3 per cent of the American oil supply, and even these have been unwelcome to domestic producers. In March 1959, the American government actually imposed a compulsory restraint on crude oil imports from anywhere. Secondly, in contrast to these facts, there have been in the course of the last fifteen years periodic warnings, sometimes traceable to American companies operating in the Middle East, that American domestic oil resources were becoming depleted at a dangerous rate and that extra care should therefore be taken by the American government to ensure undisturbed access to the vast resources of the Middle East. Thirdly, the United States' allies in Europe draw most of their oil needs (86 per cent in 1958) from Middle East sources. Fourthly, the preceding fact has been mentioned always in the context of stressing the indirect importance of Middle East oil for the United States, but it has seldom been added that oil contributed (in the same year of 1958) "only" 25 per cent of the total energy supply of the European allies, or that there existed surplus capacity in the United States and in other non-Arab oil-producing areas. Moreover, there has been a tendency to equate access to Middle East oil with the perpetuation of the present ownership and royalty arrangements and the existing political regimes in the host countries. The near certainty that these countries would be bound to seek to dispose of their oil, because of their dependence on its revenues, no matter what changes in ownership and regimes might take place, has very rarely been discussed. Fifthly, notwithstanding the implication of manipulative handling of information, the oil companies have as much right as any interest or group to plead with their government for a policy that would protect their interests. It is to be noted in this context that, notwithstanding allegations to the contrary, the oil companies do not seem to have enjoyed an exceptionally easy access to the ear and mind of the government. Congressmen and agencies of the United States government have frequently attacked the oil companies publicly, have accused them of participation in an oil cartel, and have summoned their men for investigation. Finally, though the American oil companies operating in the Arab countries have lobbied against American support for the creation of a Jewish state, and though the United States' continued backing of Israel might cause them some embarrassment with the host Arab governments, their *objective* relation to Israel has altered a great deal since the mid-fifties. For one thing, the drastically increased dependence of the Arab governments on oil revenues and the "lesson" taught to host governments by the failure of nationalization in Iran have given the oil companies a greater sense of security against any rash action or retaliation by those governments. For another thing, since Abdel Nasser espoused the cause of pan-Arabism and since he embarked on a policy of nationalization and state socialism, the chief threat to the companies' position has derived from him rather than from the American entanglement with Israel. In fact, insofar as Israel became interested in preserving the status quo that emerged in the area after 1958, her interest has come to coincide with theirs. This does not mean, however, that the oil companies would regard with equanimity any new measure that would bind the United States even more tightly to Israel; such measures would put them and the host Arab governments under added pressure from other Arab quarters.

The direct interest of the American government in the Arab countries derives mainly from their strategic location and their weakness. These countries occupy an area that constitutes a cross-road between Europe, Asia, and Africa and controls the shortest routes from Europe to East Asia and the Far East. They lie at the eastern flank of the NATO countries to the south of Russia, from which they are separated on the east only by the weak and unstable Iranian buffer. Besides these attractions of the Arab countries to strategists of both East and West, their demonstrable weakness and the doubt this raises about their ability to resist pressures and blandishments have provided an added impulse to each of the power camps in the Cold War to interest itself in these countries if only to prevent their falling under the control of the other.

The bearing that this interest has had on American-Israeli relations in the diplomatic-strategic sphere has fluctuated a great deal. At its weakest, it was still strong enough to rule out a formal American-Israeli alliance, just as Jewish influence at its weakest was strong enough to retain the basic American moral commitment to Israel. Within this range, its actual impact has varied from time to time according to several factors: the extent and nature of actual American involvement in the area, changes in the estimates of Soviet intentions, the course of events in the area itself, and the modifications in the global strategic position of the United States. We have already analyzed in detail the shifts that have taken place in the course of American-Israeli relations under the impact of these considerations in the order in which the shifts occurred. Here we shall confine ourselves to a few general retrospective observations on the subject by way of summary.

American-Israeli relations seem to have gone through three phases connected with the American strategic interest in the Middle East as a whole and the Arab countries in particular. The first phase, extending from the end of 1947 to about the end of 1951, was marked by American support of Israel on practically all the vital issues affecting that country, including the partition resolution itself, recognition of the Jewish state, condemnation of Arab aggression, opposition to plans aimed at reducing the territory allocated to Israel by the partition resolution, support for Israel's claims to territory she gained beyond the partition boundaries, a security guarantee covering the territory occupied by Israel, and a promise to provide her with arms on an equal footing with the Arab states given in conjunction with the British and the French. During this phase, and especially in the early part of it, proponents of the American strategic interest in the Arab countries (together with defenders of the oil interests and advocates of the Arab moral cause) contended against this tendency of American policy, but in the final account failed to prevent it. Sympathy for Israel and the influence of the American Jews were, of course, important factors in this context; but an equally important consideration was the fact that the momentum for the pro-Israel policy had been set at a time when Britain had the primary responsibility for the defense of the Middle East as a whole (except for Turkey and Greece, whose protection was taken over by the United States in 1947). Indeed, the increased involvement of the United States in the area, as a consequence of the weakening of Britain's position in it and of the intensification of the pressure of world Communism (Berlin, Czechoslovakia, Yugoslavia, Korea), set the stage for the modification of American policy vis-à-vis Israel in the following years.

The second phase, lasting from the beginning of 1953 to the beginning of 1957, was marked by a mounting strain in American-Israeli relations as the United States assumed an active role alongside Britain in trying to secure the Middle East for the Western camp. Israeli pleas backed by American Jews against specific American measures deemed harmful (such as granting military aid to Arab states and seeking military alliances with them), or for specific American measures to reinforce Israel's threatened security (such as signing an alliance with her or selling her arms to counter massive Egyptian rearmament), foundered repeatedly against the determination of the American government to draw the Arab countries into a regional alliance under the aegis of the West and to avoid anything that might hamper the attainment of this goal. The fact that a Republican administration had been installed in Washington with new men, unencumbered by precedent and momentum in regard to Israel, was certainly an important factor in this development; but even more important was the change consummated during this period in the global strategic relationship between East and West. The Soviet Union was already in possession of the atomic and hydrogen bombs, and the peace of the world came to rest on the balance of terror. The new administration in Washington had given up the containment policy with considerable fanfare, and had come to stake the defense of the non-

Communist world on "massive retaliation." The effectiveness of massive retaliation depended on American ability to survive a first strike and to have enough power left to reach most important targets in the Soviet world; and this, in the primitive age before ICBM's, IRBM's, and fleets of Polaris-launching atomic submarines, depended on having a whole string of bomber bases around the Soviet perimeter; hence the importance of drawing the Middle East into the Western defensive network. The coming to power of a new regime in Egypt in 1952 which was eager in its early, uncertain years to gain American support both to insure itself against reaction assisted from outside and to facilitate its impending negotiations with Britain, seemed to offer reasonable hope that, with good management on the part of Washington, Egypt and the entire Arab East might be brought into the Western orbit. And while it is true that the American government reaffirmed on several occasions during this phase the United States' basic moral commitment toward Israel, its position on several specific issues affecting that country seemed to many responsible Israelis calculated to encourage the Arabs to think that the purport of that commitment was flexible and negotiable once they made up their mind to join the Western camp. The Israelis' suspicion of Washington's intentions, especially after the United States refused to sell them arms in the wake of the Soviet-Egyptian arms deal, was a crucial factor in Premier Ben Gurion's decision to launch a "preventive war" against Egypt in 1956, which brought United States-Israeli relations to their nadir.

The third phase of American-Israeli relations began in 1957 and has continued to the present (fall of 1962). To the extent that the United States' attitude toward Israel until that time had been characterized by a continuous inner conflict between considerations of American strategic interest in the Middle East, on the one hand, and sympathy toward Israel and the influence of American Jews, on the other, this conflict has since been greatly mitigated. At first, the causes for the alleviation of the conflict were essentially negative. Israel's Sinai adventure in coordination with the Franco-British action in Suez drove home to the American government a clear notion of the great international dangers, not to speak of the embarrassment at home, that could result if Israel were again made to feel driven to the wall. On the other hand, the United States also became convinced that Abdel Nasser had his own game to play in the Arab East which conflicted with American objectives in the area. Not only was he not to be drawn into any Western alliance, but he was bent on doing his utmost to prevent other Arab governments from entering or staying in such an alliance, and was, in this endeavor, working in tacit alliance with Russia. The Sinai development made support of Israel appear not just a matter of yielding to sentimentality and Jewish influence but also one of diplomatic prudence; while the realization that Abdel Nasser had his own vast ambitions dealt a crushing blow to the notion that the United States might be able to attract Egypt if she could only prove that she was not bound by Jewish influence at home always to take Israel's side.

By 1958–1959, developments in the Middle East and in the strategic balance in the world further reduced the grounds for conflict between American objectives in the Arab East and American support for Israel, and even began to allow a certain degree of positive meshing of the two. When the effort to rally at least some of the Arab countries into the Western camp finally collapsed in the wake of the Iraqi revolution of July 1958, the United States' objective was reduced to preventing the Soviet Union from extending *her* influence and power in that part of the world. This scaling down of goals, though prescribed by the failure of more ambitious designs, was nevertheless in keeping with developments in the weaponry and arsenals of the two giant powers which greatly reduced the need for an extensive string of bases and hence discounted the importance of direct control over the Middle East. To realize the revised goal, it became apparent that the best means was to attempt to preserve the stalemate, or balance, that emerged spontaneously in the area at the beginning of 1959. Israel had as much interest as the United States in such a policy and, moreover, she could bring to it an important positive contribution (see Chapter XV). And while the policy of preserving the status quo required also that the United States should develop and maintain bridges of friendship with the Arab governments and refrain from any initiatives that might needlessly embarrass some of them or provoke others into seeking closer relations with Russia, it at least involved a real element of mutuality of interest between the United States and Israel in the diplomatic-strategic sphere which had been patently absent since the establishment of the Jewish state.

5. THE ARAB-ISRAELI CONFLICT AND THE FUTURE OF AMERICAN-ISRAELI RELATIONS

American-Israeli relations at present stand on a firmer and friend-lier footing than at any time in their fourteen-year history. The bonds of sympathy and friendship which marked the beginning of American-Israeli relations have been transformed in the course of these years into a tradition of economic cooperation and intensive cultural intercourse which has been enhanced by the many-faceted mediating role played by American Jewry. At the same time, the renunciation by the United States of her efforts to build an Arab bloc allied to the West and the conversion of the two countries to a conservative position in regard to the area as a whole have weak-ened or eliminated several grounds for conflict between them. We might conclude on the basis of this record that the future of American-Israeli relations is as assured as that of America's re-lations with any other friendly country, if it were not for the per-sistence of the problem of Arab-Israeli hostility. The United States has shown as much interest as Israel in resolving this problem, if for no other reason than that the Russians have used it on nu-merous occasions to undermine the position of the West in the Middle East and gain a foothold there for themselves; and suc-cessive administrations have tried many and diverse methods to bring about peace between Israel and the Arabs, or at least to in-duce the two sides to cooperate on projects of common benefit, or to solve the refugee problem. But despite the agreement between the United States and Israel on the goal of peace, the failure of efforts to bring it nearer has left the problem of Arab-Israeli hos-tility to plague their relations periodically. It was because of that hostility that American and Israeli policies clashed in the past, and its persistence into the present makes the future of American-Israeli relations much more problematic than it might have been.

Because of the importance of the problem, it might be appro-priate to consider at this point the present prospects and possibilities of overcoming it. We cannot, of course, engage here in the com-prehensive and very complex analysis required to answer this ques-tion; but insofar as certain views relating to this subject have been implied or are strongly suggested in our study, we feel bound to try to make them explicit.

In explaining the failure of the Arab-Israeli negotiations for peace in 1949–1950, we have attributed it ultimately to the lack of any important incentive for the Arabs to make peace, and to the existence of intrinsic and internal reasons for them to oppose it. The years that have elapsed since have produced many momentous events in the Middle East—a dozen *coups d'état* or revolutions in the five Arab states that invaded Israel in 1948; changes of regime in three of them, with all the rulers at the time of the invasion killed or overthrown; all treaties between these states and Western Powers abrogated, the Baghdad Pact come and gone; American and Soviet influence waxing and waning; hundreds of millions in annual revenues from oil and Suez Canal tolls enriching the economies of some of the Arab countries—but they have not added a single important positive incentive for the Arabs to make peace but, on the contrary, have only strengthened the grounds for their wanting to oppose it.

During those years the Palestine problem became intricately involved with the twists and turns of several Arab societies caught for decades in a severe crisis of identity marking their efforts to adjust to modern existence. As Arab leaders related the malaise of their societies to their political-military weakness and sought to remedy it through the pursuit of power, the challenge of Israel's existence became all the more galling, and the urge to subdue the Jewish state rather than come to terms with it became all the more pressing. And as the deeply rooted desire of the Arabs for unity, strengthened by their striving for political-military power, became manifest in rival schemes for mergers, the obstacle persented by the existence of Israel to some of these schemes provided another reason for the wish to remove the Jewish state. It follows from all this that as long as Arab societies continue to seek a remedy for their problems in external manifestations of power rather than in internal intellectual and practical endeavors, and as long as there are leaders among them who hope to achieve Arab unity along axes that cut across Israel, any effort to coax or press the Arab governments to make peace is bound to prove futile. For the United States to engage in such an effort would be even worse than futile since it might very well nullify the capacity she has to alleviate the problem of Arab-Israeli hostility in more modest ways. It is fortunate in this connection that President Kennedy did not choose the falsely simple way of attacking the problem directly to redeem the pledge he had made as a presidential candidate, before a Zionist assembly in 1960, when he promised to make renewed efforts to secure Arab-Israeli peace.

Although the prospects of resolving the problem of Arab-Israeli hostility seem at the moment to be worse than they were twelve or thirteen years ago, the chances of checking dangerous manifestations of that hostility seem to be brighter now than ever before. For almost five years the borders between the Arab states and Israel have been quieter than in any comparable period in the past. Infiltration and shooting incidents, which had served before to trigger a vicious circle of violence, have been successfully localized with few exceptions. No attempt has been made by the Arabs to interfere with Israeli shipping in the Gulf of Akaba, and Israel has not renewed her pressure to secure free passage in the Suez Canal. The Arab boycott of international firms doing business with Israel, which has acted as an added irritant to Arab-Israeli relations, has been slowly but surely losing its effectiveness. The Egyptian government, after a partial disillusionment with Soviet Russia and the setbacks it suffered in Iraq and Syria, seems to be turning its attention increasingly to internal development. There are also faint indications that Egypt is beginning to feel the strain on its resources from trying to keep ahead in the arms race with Israel. All these trends are not only welcome in themselves but also offer the best hope for a peaceful settlement in the long run. They give the chance for feelings on both sides to subside; they help the Arabs to become accustomed to the idea of the existence of Israel in their midst; they provide a favorable climate for resolving specific problems, and they give the political and intellectual leaders of the Arabs the opportunity to reconsider calmly their diagnosis of the ills of their own societies—all of which constitute necessary preliminaries to the acceptance of even the most ingenious peace plan. However, these trends are also very unstable and uncertain, and it is by working for their consolidation and their advancement that American diplomacy can make the most practicable and fruitful contribution toward meeting the problem of Arab-Israeli hostility.

How the United States might go about this work is something which depends a great deal on the course of events and cannot therefore be set down in advance. A few examples of what could be done now may, however, be mentioned by way of illustration. It is an accepted fact that the refugee problem constitutes the thorniest and most tragic aspect of the Arab-Israeli conflict. In the past the United States has promoted or joined several efforts to solve this problem separately, both for humane reasons and in the hope of advancing piecemeal toward an Arab-Israeli settlement, but these efforts have been fruitless. It seems clear by now—at least it should be clear—that these efforts failed precisely because the refugee question was so linked with the issue of over-all peace in the minds of all concerned that unless they agreed on peace first they could not possibly agree on any compromise terms on the refugee question. But if the issue were approached indirectly, if the United States, together with other interested countries, were to promote on a truly large scale the economic development of Jordan, where most of the refugees dwell, would not the forces of the market themselves be likely to induce many refugees, particularly the younger men, to give up living on the dole of the relief agencies and try to reconstruct their lives? The greater the economic development and the higher the standard of living outside the refugee camps, the more refugees would be induced to take advantage of the new opportunities. Those who decide to do so should be helped in their effort to resettle, but no attempt should be made to press the reluctant; above all, nobody should be asked to renounce formally any political rights or claims against Israel. The program would be explicitly one of economic development of Jordan, not of refugee resettlement as such; yet in another fourteen years the bulk of the refugee problem might be on its way to solution as a result of it, instead of becoming aggravated as it has become in the past fourteen years.

A successful program of large-scale economic development for Jordan might also make an immense contribution to the peace and stability of the area as a whole. One of the most likely and gravest threats to the area at the present is the weakness and inviability of the Jordanian state. The separate existence of Jordan depends entirely on the life of her brave young king and the subsidy and political support provided by the United States. The removal of the king by assassination might well leave nobody with the means, will, or courage to preserve Jordan's independence or even to appeal for help; and the result is very likely to be a scramble for territory by

Jordan's neighbors which could lead to war. By developing the country and making it economically viable, the will to live as a political entity could be strengthened among Jordan's people and be made less dependent on the life of her king.

Another measure that could consolidate and advance the current favorable trends in the Middle East is economic aid to Egypt. The United States has been helping that country again since 1959 and has increased the size of the aid given to her recently. This should be continued and expanded. Helping Egypt in the realization of her economic and social development programs is apt to encourage the tendency her government began to manifest after the Iraqi and Syrian setbacks to concentrate on internal improvements, and is in any case certain to increase its responsiveness to American counsels of restraint. The American government should, however, be cautious this time not to repeat the error committed in 1953–1955 of allowing the Egyptian rulers to nurture the dangerous misinterpretation that American sympathy and aid for their internal programs implies necessarily a cooling-off toward Israel, nor should the United States feel bound by a false consistency to refrain from taking strong exception to those aspects of Egyptian foreign policy of which it disapproves.

With regard to Israel there seems to be no need now for any new initiative, but it is necessary to continue close consultation to avoid the repetition of the tragic crisis of confidence of 1955–1956. The Israeli government should be reassured by word and deed that aiding the Arab countries does not imply courting them to Israel's detriment. An effort should be made to cultivate its confidence that, though the United States cannot, for obvious reasons, give it the security guarantee it seeks in the form of an alliance, she will stand by her moral commitments in a time of crisis; and the United States must be ready, for instance, if a situation like the one that followed the first Soviet-Egyptian arms deal should recur, to back her word with deed by selling arms to Israel. Provided this is successfully done, the record of recent years indicates that Israel would be amenable to suggestions of restraint in dealing with border incidents, passage through the Suez Canal, and similar issues.

All the favorable trends of recent years, and all the measures one might advocate and the United States might adopt, should not be understood as offering any assurance that serious problems in the relations between the United States and Israel can be avoided altogether even in the near future. The Middle Eastern scene, comprising an intra-Arab conflict, an inter-Arab conflict, and an East-West conflict, all meshing with the Arab-Israeli conflict, and with the multitude of factors affecting them all, is extremely vulnerable. Among the issues likely to arise and put the relations between the two countries to a test are the collapse of some Arab regime, a clash between two Arab states, a renewal of the Soviet drive in the area, an outbreak of fighting with Syria over the diversion of Jordan waters by Israel, the discovery that either Egypt or Israel is engaged in projects to produce mass destruction weapons. But if the unfolding of American-Israeli relations in the past and the motives behind them as analyzed in this work convey any expectation to this writer, it is that they will pass any such test and will continue to prosper.

Appendix I: Facts About Israel

Table 1. Population, by Population Groups, 1949–1960
(Estimates, Thousands)

Year (end)	Total population	Jews	Moslems	Christians	Druze
1949	1,173.9	1,013.9	111.5	34.0	14.5
1950	1,370.1	1,203.0	116.1	36.0	15.0
1951	1,577.8	1,404.4	118.9	39.0	15.5
1952	1,629.5	1,450.2	122.8	40.4	16.1
1953	1,669.4	1,483.6	127.6	41.4	16.8
1954	1,717.8	1,526.0	131.8	42.0	18.0
1955	1,789.1	1,590.5	136.3	43.3	19.0
1956	1,872.4	1,667.5	141.4	43.7	19.8
1957	1,976.0	1,762.7	146.8	45.8	20.5
1958	2,031.7	1,810.1	152.8	47.3	21.4
1959	2,088.7	1,858.8	159.2	48.3	22.3
1960	2,150.4	1,911.2	166.3	49.6	23.3

Source: *Statistical Abstract of Israel, 1961*, p. 27.

Table 2. Jewish Population by Continent of Birth, 1948–1960
(Absolute Numbers and Percentage)

Mo. Day Yr.	Total		Israeli-born		Asia		Africa		Europe and America	
	Number	%	Number	%	Number	%	Number	%	Number	%
11 8 1948	716,678	100.0	253,661	35.4	57,768	8.1	12,236	1.7	393,013	54.8
12 31 1949	1,013,871	100.0	279,173	27.5	132,493	13.1	56,159	5.5	546,046	53.9
12 31 1950	1,202,993	100.0	311,100	25.8	188,578	15.7	80,542	6.7	622,773	51.8
12 31 1951	1,404,392	100.0	353,220	25.2	289,565	20.6	98,576	7.0	663,031	47.2
12 31 1952	1,450,217	100.0	393,873	27.1	292,603	20.2	105,965	7.4	656,776	45.3
12 31 1953	1,483,641	100.0	433,298	29.2	292,017	19.7	109,725	7.4	648,601	43.7
12 31 1954	1,526,000	100.0	470,811	30.9	292,860	19.2	121,033	7.9	641,305	42.0
12 31 1955	1,590,519	100.0	509,979	32.1	292,349	18.4	152,859	9.6	635,332	39.9
12 31 1956	1,667,455	100.0	548,273	32.9	293,474	17.6	196,207	11.8	629,501	37.7
12 31 1957	1,762,741	100.0	588,191	33.4	296,923	16.8	218,920	12.4	658,707	37.4
12 31 1958	1,810,148	100.0	625,969	34.6	302,372	16.7	220,980	12.2	660,827	36.5
12 31 1959	1,858,841	100.0	666,466	35.9	303,736	16.3	224,058	12.1	664,581	35.7
12 31 1960	1,911,189	100.0	708,140	37.1	303,480	15.9	228,141	11.9	671,428	35.1

Source: Statistical Abstract of Israel, 1961, p. 43.

Table 3. Jewish Immigrants by Continent of Birth, 1919–1960
(Absolute Numbers and Percentage)

Period	Absolute Numbers					Percentage				
	All Continents	Asia	Africa	Europe	America and Oceania	All Continents	Asia	Africa	Europe	America and Oceania
1919–5/14/1948	452,158	40,776	4,033	377,487	7,579	100.0	9.5	0.9	87.8	1.8
5/15/1948–12/31/1960	968,748	507,074		442,248		100.0	53.4		46.6	
5/15/1948–12/31/1948	101,819	4,739	8,192	76,554	478	100.0	5.3	9.1	85.1	0.5
1949	239,076	71,624	39,156	121,753	1,344	100.0	30.6	16.7	52.1	0.6
1950	169,405	57,771	25,525	83,632	1,006	100.0	34.4	15.2	49.8	0.6
1951	173,901	103,326	20,123	49,533	671	100.0	59.5	11.6	28.5	0.4
1952	23,375	6,701	10,024	6,131	516	100.0	28.7	42.9	26.2	2.2
1953	10,347	2,871	4,889	2,025	549	100.0	27.8	47.3	19.6	5.3
1954	17,471	3,305	12,188	1,325	641	100.0	18.9	69.8	7.6	3.7
1955	36,303	1,323	32,143	1,942	620	100.0	3.6	89.3	5.4	1.7
1956	54,925	2,739	44,878	6,674	631	100.0	5.0	81.7	12.2	1.1
1957	69,733	5,249	24,112	38,889	874	100.0	7.6	34.9	56.2	1.3
1958	25,919	7,597	3,893	13,626	802	100.0	29.3	15.0	52.6	3.1
1959	22,987	7,635		15,348		100.0	33.2		66.8	
1960	23,487	6,801		16,684		100.0	29.0		71.0	

Source: Statistical Abstract of Israel, 1961, p. 86.

Table 4.   Summary Estimates of Gl
($ million)

Item	1952		1953		1954		1955	
	Credit	Debit	Credit	Debit	Credit	Debit	Credit	Debit
Goods and services	393.1	86.5	365.2	102.3	376.5	135.2	426.6	143.9
Transfer payments	0.5	191.7	1.6	174.4	4.1	264.8	5.1	215.5
Capital transactions	—	116.4	—	75.3	—	1.0	17.7	94.1
Total transactions	393.6	394.6	366.8	352.0	380.6	401.0	449.4	453.5
Net errors and omissions	1.0	—	—	14.8	20.4	—	4.1	—
TOTAL	394.6	394.6	366.8	366.8	401.0	401.0	453.5	453.5

Source: Statistical Abstract of Israel, 1961, p. 308.

obal Balance of Payments, 1952–1960

1956		1957		1958		1959		1960	
Credit	Debit	Credit	Debit	Credit	Debit	Credit	Debit	Credit	Debit
534.5	177.9	557.2	222.0	573.1	238.7	581.1	266.8	670.9	331.8
3.8	244.3	5.7	251.1	4.9	255.9	4.7	255.7	7.0	306.5
73.3	173.7	103.3	181.9	168.0	237.5	181.4	236.2	217.7	262.6
611.6	595.9	666.2	655.0	746.0	732.1	767.2	758.7	895.6	900.9
—	15.7	—	11.2	—	13.9	—	8.5	5.3	—
611.6	611.6	666.2	666.2	746.0	746.0	767.2	767.2	900.9	900.9

Table 5. Balance of Payments, 1961[a]
($ million)

	Credit	Debit	Net Credit or debit
A. Commodities and Services			
(1) Commodities	237.8	569.9	−332.1
(2) Tourism and foreign travel	30.1	16.4	+ 13.7
(3) Transport	84.5	52.9	+ 31.6
(4) Insurance	25.3	25.7	− 0.4
(5) Capital servicing	13.1	69.0	− 55.9
(6) Government (n.e.s.[b])	7.5	60.5	− 53.0
(7) Miscellaneous	18.1	24.4	− 6.3
TOTAL (1) to (7)	416.4	818.8	−402.4
B. Unrequited Transfers			
Private			
(8) Gifts and transfers by immigrants and residents	44.1	1.3	+ 42.8
(9) Personal restitution from West Germany	111.5	1.0	+110.5
Government and Public Institutions			
(10) German reparations	90.9	2.6	+ 88.3
(11) U.S. government aid	19.7	—	+ 19.7
(12) U.N. technical assistance	0.4	0.2	+ 0.2
(13) Transfers by the Jewish Agency and other institutions	87.6	—	+ 87.6
TOTAL (8) to (13)	354.2	5.1	+349.1
TOTAL A + B	770.6	823.9	− 53.3

Table 5 (Continued)

	Credit	Debit	Net Credit or credit
C. Net Capital Movements			
(14) Long- and medium-term loans			
(14.1) Independence and development loans	63.3	31.2	+ 32.1
(14.2) U.S. government loans within frame of grant-in-aid	29.2	2.5	+ 26.7
(14.3) Other Long- and medium-term loans	100.1	64.5	+ 35.8
(14.4) Foreign investments	54.0	8.5	+ 45.5
TOTAL (14)	246.6	106.6	+140.1
(15) Short-term Capital Movements			
(15.1) Short-term loans	8.0	—	+ 8.0
(15.2) Clearing accounts	—	0.4	− 0.4
(15.3) Foreign deposits in local banks	18.5	—	+ 18.5
(15.4) U.S. government deposits	12.3	—	+ 12.3
(15.5) Other short-term capital	—	4.9	− 4.9
(15.6) Foreign currency reserves	—	85.0	− 85.0
(15.7) Monetary gold	—	9.9	− 9.9
TOTAL (15)	38.8	100.2	− 61.4
TOTAL (14) + (15)	285.4	206.7	+ 78.7
TOTAL A to C	1,056.0	1,030.6	+ 25.4
Net Errors and Omissions	—	25.4	− 25.4

Source: Bank of Israel, *Annual Report, 1961,* pp. 30–31.

[a] The data in this and other other tables in Appendix I became available when this book was in the final stages, after earlier data had been incorporated into the discussion.

[b] Not elsewhere specified.

Table 6. Main Commodity Exports, 1960–1961
($ million)

	1960	1961
Agricultural Products		
Citrus fruit	46.6	40.5
Eggs	10.7	12.2
Groundnuts	2.1	2.3
Other products	3.8	8.0
TOTAL	63.2	63.0
Industrial Products		
Citrus products	7.8	7.9
Edible oils	3.6	4.1
Other foodstuffs	3.6	3.8
Potash	3.4	4.1
Other minerals	3.4	5.0
Automobiles	2.7	1.4
Tires	8.2	8.7
Machinery, metal goods and electrical appliances	11.6	14.7
Cement	2.5	2.0
Plywood	4.2	4.4
Chemicals and pharmaceuticals	4.1	4.8
Textiles: yarns, material and clothing	17.8	24.4
Other products	12.4	13.8
TOTAL	89.0	103.4
Diamonds	56.4	64.9
Miscellaneous	1.7	6.5
GRAND TOTAL	210.3	237.8

Source: Bank of Israel, *Annual Report, 1961*, p. 34.

Table 7. Commodity Exports, by Main Categories, 1958–1961
(in percentages)

	1958	1959	1960	1961
Agricultural products	40	32	30	26
Industrial products	34	40	43	44
Diamonds	25	27	26	27
Miscellaneous	1	1	1	3
TOTAL	100	100	100	100

Source: Bank of Israel, *Annual Report, 1961,* p. 33.

Table 8. Commodity Exports, by Main Markets of Destination,
1960–1961
($ million)

	1960		1961	
	$ million	%	$ million	%
European Common Market	64.6	30.7	68.4	28.7
Great Britain	36.1	17.2	35.7	15.0
Eastern Europe	4.0	1.9	6.4	2.7
Other European countries	45.0	21.4	47.5	20.0
United States	29.4	14.0	39.0	16.4
Africa	10.5	5.0	13.0	5.5
Other countries and unclassified exports	20.7	9.8	27.8	11.7
TOTAL	210.3	100.0	237.8	100.0

Source: Computed from Bank of Israel, *Annual Report, 1961,* p. 37.

Table 9. Export of Services, 1960–1961
($ million)

	1960	1961
Tourism	26.9	30.1
Transportation	68.5	84.5
Insurance	22.0	25.3
Capital servicing	7.7	13.1
Government (n.e.s.)	6.4	7.5
Miscellaneous	15.1	18.1
TOTAL	146.6	178.6

Source: Bank of Israel, *Annual Report, 1961,* p. 38.

Table 10.   Commodity Imports, by Economic Destination, 1960–1961
($ million)

	1960	1961
Commodities for Direct Consumption		
Food	18.6	17.0
Current consumption	15.4	18.2
Durable goods	14.4	14.9
Total	48.4	50.1
Raw Materials		
For food industry	50.2	57.8
For other industries	189.3	206.6
For agriculture	28.8	26.7
Building materials	15.7	15.0
Total	284.0	306.1
Investment Goods		
For industry and construction	52.7	66.7
For agriculture	8.4	11.5
For transportation	18.3	24.2
Ships and aircraft	36.5	62.2
Other equipment	7.3	14.6
Total	123.2	179.2
Fuel	34.9	34.2
Miscellaneous	0.3	0.3
Grand Total	490.8	569.9

Source: Bank of Israel, *Annual Report, 1961*, p. 40.

Table 11.   Commodity Imports by Main Supply Centers, 1960–1961
($ million)

	1960		1961	
	$ million	%	$ million	%
European Common Market	146.0	29.8	173.7	30.5
Great Britain	59.3	12.1	76.6	13.5
Eastern Europe	4.0	0.9	6.2	1.0
Other European countries	58.6	11.9	61.4	10.8
United States	146.4	29.8	167.9	29.6
Africa	17.8	3.6	20.8	3.6
Other countries	58.7	11.9	63.3	11.0
TOTAL	490.8	100.0	569.9	100.0

Source: Bank of Israel, *Annual Report, 1961,* p. 41.

Table 12.   Import of Services, 1960–1961
($ million)

	1960	1961
Foreign travel	11.4	16.4
Transportation	43.6	52.9
Insurance	22.4	25.7
Capital servicing	51.2	69.0
Government (n.e.s.)	53.0	60.5
Miscellaneous	18.3	24.4
TOTAL	199.9	248.9

Source: Bank of Israel, *Annual Report, 1961,* p. 41.

Table 13. Capital Import, 1949–1959
($ million)

Total Capital Import (= surplus import of goods and services)	3,295
A. Unrequited Transfers (net)	
1. Gifts and capital transfers by immigrants	309
2. Personal Restitution from West Germany (began in 1954)	232
3. Reparations from West Germany (began in 1953)	491
4. U.S. aid (began in fiscal year 1951–1952)	454
5. Transfers by U.J.A. and other institutions (85% American)	881
Total A	2,367
B. Capital Movements (net)	
6. Development and independence loans (began in 1952)	359
7. Loans from Export-Import Bank	98
8. Other medium- and long-term loans	71
9. Other investments from abroad	229
10. Use of foreign currency balances	− 17
Total B	740
Grand Total: A + B	3,107
Errors and omissions	188

Source: M. Michaeli, *Riv'on Lekhalkala,* June 1961.

Table 14. U.S. Government Economic Aid to Israel
May 1948 to 1961 (Fiscal Years) (Obligations in $ million)

Year	Technical Aid	Special^a Assistance	Total MSP Assistance	DLF	Public Law No. 480			Exim bank	IMG	Grand Total
					Title I	Title II	Title III			
1950	—	—	—	—	—	—	1.2	135.00^c	—	136.2
1951	—	—	—	—	—	—	21.5	—	—	21.5
1952	0.9	63.5	64.4	—	—	—	—	—	—	64.4
1953	2.5	70.0	72.5	—	—	—	0.04	—	0.9	73.44
1954	1.4	52.5	53.9	—	—	—	20.7	—	2.1	76.7
1955	1.4	39.7^b	41.1	—	12.7^f	—	0.4	—	2.0	56.2
1956	1.4	25.5^d	26.9	—	27.7	—	1.6	—	2.6	58.8
1957	1.7	25.0^e	26.7	—	10.5	—	2.3	—	1.5	41.0
1958	1.4	7.5	8.9	15	39.2	—	2.3	27.55^g	0.6	93.55
1959	1.6	7.5	9.1	10	38.3	—	1.7	—	0.5	59.6
1960	1.4	7.5	8.9	15	37.6	—	0.5	—	0.3	62.3
1961	1.0	7.5	8.5	16	25.9	—	0.8	35.9	0.3	87.4
CUMULATIVE TOTAL OBLIGATIONS	14.7	306.2	320.9	56	191.9	—	53.04	198.45	10.80	831.09

Source: Compiled by the Economic Section, American Embassy, Tel Aviv.

a Development Assistance 1952–1957. Includes Relief Assistance in 1952 and 1953.

b Fifty per cent ($20 million) was extended to Israel on a loan basis.

c These credits were authorized in calendar year 1949. A total of $86.4 million of principal has been repaid, leaving the principal outstanding as of June 30, 1961, at $48.6 million.

d Includes $5 million of third-country currencies. Of $25.5 million total, $12.5 million was available on a loan basis.

e Of $25 million total, $10 million was made available on a loan basis.

f Values are carried at costs to the Commodity Credit Corporation and not at market prices.

g Includes $24.2 million for irrigation; $0.35 million for research atomic reactor (has been repaid); and $3.0 million for privately owned paper mill.

[306]

Table 15. Sources of Capital Import, 1949–1959
($ million)

	$ million	%
1. World Jewry	1,469	47.3
2. U.S. government	552	17.8
3. German government	723	23.3
4. Others	363	11.6
TOTAL	3,107	100.0

1. Includes: United Jewish Appeal and other institutions, Independence and Development Loans, and "other sources."

2. Includes: American government aid plus loans from Export-Import Bank minus repayments.

3. Includes: Restitution and reparation payments by the West German government.

4. Includes: Transfers by immigrants and use of foreign currency balances.

Source: M. Michaeli, *Riv'on Lekhalkala,* June 1961.

Table 16. Import Surplus (Capital Import) in Relation to Gross National Product in Economies of High Capital Import

The Economy	Period	Proportion (%)
Southern Rhodesia	1946–1952	31.3
Israel	1950–1959	24.5
Korea (South)	1949–1954	14.5
Ireland	1946–1954	11.1
Greece	1949–1954	10.9
China (Formosa)	1951–1952	4.6
Austria	1948–1954	4.5
Italy	1950–1954	1.7
The Philippines	1946–1954	1.6
France	1949–1954	1.2

Source: M. Michaeli, *Riv'on Lekhalkala,* June 1961.

Table 17. Public Financing of Investment, by Sectors, 1958–1961
(at current prices)

Sector	1960			1961			1958	1959
	Total investment	Public financing^a	Share of public financing	Total investment	Public financing^a	Share of public financing	Share of Public financing in investment	
	I.L. million^a		%	I.L. million^a		%	%	
Agriculture and irrigation	176	148	84	189	155	82	74	72
Industry	184	72	39	244	81	33	42	32
Mining	14	7	50	16	3	19	75	71
Electric power	37	2	5	44	3	7	69	54
Transportation	155	119	77	229	123	54	59	68
Commerce and services	164	93	57	205	97	47	48	56
Residential housing	306	116	38	391	133	34	44	44
TOTALS	1,036	557	54	1,318	595	45	54	52

Source: Bank of Israel, *Annual Report, 1961*, p. 65.
^{a} 1 I.L. (Israeli pound) = $0.33

Table 18. Saving and Investment, 1950–1959
(I.L. million at 1956 prices)

	1950	1951	1952	1953	1954	1955	1956	1957	1958	1959	1950–1959
A. Net domestic investment (saving)	−157	−127	−175	−147	−107	−59	−178	4	−32	34	−944
B. Net investment from foreign sources (Import Surplus)	592	610	495	486	495	538	643	538	623	568	5,628
C. Depreciation	122	128	113	107	123	133	150	168	186	206	1,436
D. Gross total investment (A + B + C)	557	611	533	446	511	612	615	750	777	808	6,220
E. Gross National Product	1,330	1,629	1,710	1,706	2,089	2,318	2,509	2,855	3,099	3,469	22,914
F. Gross investment in relation to Gross National Product (D/E) (%)	41.9	37.5	31.2	26.1	24.5	26.4	24.5	26.3	25.1	23.3	27.1

Source: Compiled by M. Michaeli, *Riv'on Lekhalkala*, June 1961.

Table 19. Per Capita National Product and Occupational Distribution for Selected Countries

Per capita net national product ($)	Countries	Agriculture, forestry, fishing, mining (1)	Industry, Electricity, gas (2)	Cols. (1) + (2) (3)	Construction (4)	Services (5)	Cols. (4) + (5) (6)
1,870	United States	13.3	29.2	42.5	6.5	51.0	57.5
1,310	Canada	20.7	27.4	48.1	6.6	45.3	51.9
1,000–1,010	Switzerland, New Zealand	20.9	30.5	51.4	7.2	41.4	48.6
950	Australia, Sweden	19.5	30.7	50.2	1.8	42.0	49.8
800	Belgium, United Kingdom, Iceland, Denmark	16.6	39.5	56.1	5.9	38.0	43.9
740–780	France, Norway	24.4	28.9	53.3	7.0	39.7	46.7
670	Finland	34.6	26.5	61.1	7.7	31.2	38.9
500–510	Germany, Holland	18.9	33.7	52.6	7.3	40.1	47.4
410–460	Porto Rico, Ireland, Austria, Chile, Cuba, Italy	40.5	15.6	56.1	5.4	38.5	43.9
300–370	Malaya, South Africa	43.1	19.1	62.2	4.1	33.7	37.8
110–150	Mexico, Portugal, Philippines, Peru, Egypt, Ceylon	55.7	12.9	68.6	2.1	29.3	31.4
80	Thailand	75.6	3.9	79.5	0.2	20.3	20.5
647	Israel, 1954	18.4	23.9	42.3	9.7	48.0	57.7
757	Israel, 1957	15.7[a]	24.8[a]	40.6	9.2	50.2	59.4

Sources: For Israel, *Statistical Abstract of Israel*, various years. For other economies: (1) occupational distribution data taken from Colin Clark, *The Conditions of Economic Progress* (New York, 1957), pp. 510–520; (2) per capita National Product data taken from *Per Capita National Product of Fifty-five Countries, 1952–1954* (New York: United Nations, 1957). Compilation made by M. Michaeli, *Riv'on Lekhalkala*, June 1961. ᵃ For 1957, mining is included under industry.

Table 20. Distribution of Personal Income of Income Units;
Israel and Some Other Countries
(in percentages)

Income Group (decile)	Israel 1957–58 urban population	Sweden 1958		West Germany 1950[a]	Netherlands 1950	Great Britain 1952	United States 1952
		Urban Population	Entire Population				
Bottom tenth	1.6	1.4	1.6	1.0	1.3	2	1
2nd tenth	3.3	2.8	2.9	3.0	2.9	3	3
3rd tenth	5.0	4.3	4.1	4.0	4.0	5	5
4th tenth	7.0	6.1	5.9	4.5	5.6	7	6
5th tenth	8.9	8.1	7.7	7.5	7.2	8	8
6th tenth	9.3	9.6	9.8	9.0	8.5	9	9
7th tenth	10.7	11.3	11.5	11.0	9.8	10	10
8th tenth	12.5	13.0	13.6	12.0	11.7	12	12
9th tenth	17.5	15.8	15.9	14.0	14.0	14	15
Top tenth	24.2	27.6	27.0	34.0	35.0	30	31
TOTAL	100.0	100.0	100.0	100.0	100.0	100	100

Source: The Falk Project for Economic Research in Israel, *Fifth Report, 1959 and 1960*, p. 40.
[a] Percentages for West Germany, Netherlands, Great Britain, and the United States are for the entire population of each country.

311

Table 21. Family Personal Income, by Country of Origin;
Urban Wage and Salary Earners' Families:
1951–1960

Country of Origin	Average income (I.L. per month)				Indexes (Total = 100)			
	March 1951	Year 1954	Years 1956–57	Oct. 1959–Mar. 1960	March 1951	Year 1954	Years 1956–57	Oct. 1959–Mar. 1960
TOTAL	78.0	216.0	274.2	373.3	100	100	100	100
Asia-Africa: Total	69.3	164.7	214.9	282.6	88.8	76.2	78.4	75.7
Europe-America: Total	78.9	233.0	294.5	418.4	101.2	107.9	107.4	112.1
Israel-Born: Total	80.3	223.9	288.5	416.2	102.9	103.7	105.2	115.5
Income ratio: $\frac{\text{Asia-Africa}}{\text{Europe-America}}$					88%	71%	73%	68%
Cost of Living Index (IX 1951 = 100)	93	220	254	280				

Source: Extracted from Falk Project for Economic Research in Israel, *Fifth Report, 1959 and 1960*, p. 57.

Table 22. State Budget, 1960/1961
Composition of Revenue and Expenditure According to Source and Purpose

Source of revenue	Amount I.L. million	%	Purpose of expenditure	Amount I.L. million	%
TOTAL	1,689.3	100	TOTAL	1,689.3	100
Income and property taxes	358.4	21.2	Social services	263.8	15.6
Taxes on expenditure	571.7	33.9	Economic and administrative services	121.7	7.2
Fees for licenses and services	35.9	2.1	Security services and reserves	461.5	27.3
Collections on account of interest and miscellaneous revenue	132.3	7.8	Subsidies and contributions for export	149.0	8.8
Internal loans and miscellaneous receipts	337.2	20.0	Payment of debt and special expenditure	246.3	14.6
Counterpart funds (revenue from abroad)	253.8	15.0	Development of branches of the economy	447.0	26.5

Source: Israel Government Year Book 5721 (1960/1961), p. 175.

Table 23.   The Tax Burden, 1958–1961

	1958	1959	1960	1961
	(I.L. million)			
(1) Direct and indirect taxes	810	989	1,155	1,439
(2) Subsidies	112	153	187	239
Net tax	698	836	968	1,200
Taxes as percentage of:				
National income	29.5%	31.9%	33.6%	35.3%
Private income	27.0	29.0	30.0	31.8
Net taxes as percentage of:				
Net National Product	21.5	22.3	23.4	24.5
Gross National Product	19.8	20.6	21.5	22.5

Source: Bank of Israel, *Annual Report, 1961,* p. 85.

Table 24. Composition of Receipts and Payments of
Public Sector Authorities, 1961
(Percentage)

	Government	National institu- tions	Local authorities	Total
Receipts				
Taxes	68.5	—	45.6	61.3
Collections and miscel- laneous	10.6	7.8	22.6	12.1
Unrequited receipts from abroad	8.0	50.7	—	11.2
Long- and medium-term loans	16.7	12.9	11.3	16.2
Short-term credit (net)	− 3.8	21.2	2.7	− 0.8
Intrasector transactions (net)	—	7.4	17.8	—
TOTAL	100.0	100.0	100.0	100.0
Sources				
Domestic	(80.2)	(37.3)	(98.3)	(77.9)
Foreign	(19.8)	(62.7)	(1.7)	(22.1)
Payments				
Current purchases	43.7	34.6	50.0	44.9
Transfer payments and subsidies	23.3	12.9	11.6	21.6
TOTAL	67.0	47.5	61.6	66.5
Purchases on capital account	5.4	10.6	33.6	9.5
Loans and participation in share capital	18.0	32.7	—	17.7
Redemption of long-term loans	6.1	9.2	4.8	6.3
Intrasector transactions (net)	3.5	—	—	—
TOTAL	100.0	100.0	100.0	100.0

Source: Bank of Israel, *Annual Report, 1961*, p. 86.

[316]

Table 25. Results of Elections to the Knesset, 1949–1961, and to Local Authorities, 1959

Party	First Knesset 1/25/1949 % of vote	First Knesset No. of seats	Second Knesset 7/30/1951 % of vote	Second Knesset No. of seats	Third Knesset 7/26/1955 % of vote	Third Knesset No. of seats	Fourth Knesset 12/3/1959 % of vote	Fourth Knesset No. of seats	Fifth Knesset 8/15/1961 % of vote	Fifth Knesset No. of seats	Elections to local auth. 11/3/1959 % of vote
All eligible voters	506,567		924,885		1,057,795		1,218,483		1,274,280		1,037,811
Valid votes	434,684		687,492		853,219		969,337		1,006,964		821,257
Percentage of valid votes cast	85.8		74.2		80.6		79.5		79.0		79.0

Percentage distribution of valid votes among parties and number of Knesset seats won

Party	% of vote	No. of seats	% of vote	No. of seats	% of vote	No. of seats	% of vote	No. of seats	% of vote	No. of seats	% of vote
Mapai	35.7	46	37.3	45	32.2	40	38.2	47	34.7	42	34.7
National Religious Front:											
Mizrachi and Mizrachi Workers ⎱	12.2	16	8.3	10	9.1	11	9.9	12	9.8	12	9.9
Agudah and Agudah Workers ⎰			3.6	5	4.7	6	4.7	6	5.6	6	5.2
Herut	11.5	14	6.6	8	12.6	15	13.5	17	13.8	17	11.4
Mapam	14.7	19	12.5	15	7.3	9	7.2	9	7.5	9	5.9
Achdut Haavoda					8.2	10	6.0	7	6.6	8	5.6
General Zionists	5.2	7	16.2	20	10.2	13	6.2	8 }	13.6	17	11.1
Progressives	4.1	5	3.2	4	4.4	5	4.6	6 }			4.5
Communists	3.5	4	4.0	5	4.5	6	2.8	3	4.2	5	2.4
Minorities lists	3.0	2	4.7	5	4.9	5	4.7	5	3.9	4	3.7
Other lists	8.4 }	7	3.0 }	3	1.6	—	2.2	—	0.3	—	5.6
Other religious lists	1.7 }		0.6 }		0.3	—	—	—	—	—	—
TOTAL	100.0	120	100.0	120	100.0	120	100.0	120	100.0	120	100.0

Source: Compiled from *Statistical Abstract of Israel,* 1961, p. 486 and p. 490.

Table 26. Towns with More than 20,000 Inhabitants
at the End of 1960

Tel Aviv-Yafo	390,000
Haifa	179,500
Jerusalem	164,000
Ramat Gan	87,000
Petach Tikva	52,500
Holon	43,000
Beersheba	42,500
Bnei Berak	41,000
Natanya	39,000
Givatayim	30,000
Rehovot	30,000
Bat Yam	28,500
Rishon Letzion	27,000
Herzliah	26,100
Nazareth	25,500
Hadera	25,100
Akko	24,500
Ramla	23,500
Tiberias	21,000
Lod	20,200

Source: *Statistical Abstract of Israel*, 1961, p. 36.

Table 27. Production and Consumption of Electricity
(million kw-h)
(1952–1960)

	1952	1953	1954	1955	1956	1957	1958	1959	1960
Production	809	914	1,076	1,308	1,410	1,416	1,766	1,968	2,313
Consumption	669	759	896	1,097	1,204	1,189	1,496	1,665	1,970
Irrigation	140	172	201	254	255	263	371	365	431
Industry	177	207	270	351	402	463	532	630	770
Other Uses	352	380	425	492	547	463	593	670	769

Source: Statistical Abstract of Israel, 1961, p. 229.

Appendix II: Suggested Reading

The purpose of this bibliography is not to provide an exhaustive account of the literature on the subjects treated in this book but rather to help the reader who may wish to pursue any of these subjects further with some suggestions. In most instances, where there is abundant material, our suggestions will consist primarily in pointing out some key works and we shall count on the reader who wishes to go still further with the subject to use the bibliographies appended to these works and the general bibliographical references we shall make below. In other instances, where the material is scant, the items we shall mention may come close to exhausting the English sources on the subject, excluding periodical literature.

1. Bibliographical References

A most comprehensive listing of books, pamphlets, and articles on all subjects touching upon or relating to Palestine and Israel has been produced since 1945 by the Zionist Archives and Library, New York, under the title *Palestine and Zionism: a Bimonthly Bibliography of Books, Pamphlets and Periodicals*. The Archives and Library, incidentally, keep many of the items listed in the foregoing publication, some of which cannot be easily obtained elsewhere. An inevitable limitation of this kind of compilation is that it cannot and does not provide a clue to the content of the material listed, apart from its full title. This is why the reader will find the *Middle East Journal* (1947–) and *Middle Eastern Affairs* (1949–) extremely useful. Both of these journals carry annotated bibliographies of books and articles on the Middle East and produce a chronology and reprints of important documents in addition to relevant articles. Richard Ettinghausen has compiled a substantial annotated bibliography on the Middle East which, unfortunately, stops at December, 1953: *A Selected and Annotated Bibliography of Books and Periodicals in Western Languages Dealing with the Near and Middle East* (Washington, 1954). For books relating to the international relations of the Middle East, very broadly conceived,

Foreign Affairs, the quarterly of the American Council of Foreign Relations, which has just celebrated its Fortieth Anniversary, provides a very useful listing with brief comments and/or description. A well-selected annotated bibliography has been produced by the American Universities Field Staff, Inc. (New York, 1960), under the title, *A Select Bibliography; Asia, Africa, Eastern Europe, Latin America,* including sections on Israel and the Middle Eastern countries.

2. *Reference Works*

Unlike most developing countries, Israel offers the inquirer a wealth of statistics and facts. Israelis have measured almost everything that can be measured and classified it in many imaginative ways. The *Israel Government Yearbook* and the *Statistical Abstract of Israel,* issued annually since the establishment of the state, put much of this material at the disposal of the public. The reader will have to be careful in using this material, particularly the economic and financial data, because it comes from different sources within Israel sometimes using different criteria, and because of the complication of the economic data by the changing value of Israel's currency. These two sources, however, are invaluable. The *American Jewish Yearbook,* published by the American Jewish Committee since the beginning of this century, includes a great deal of material about Jews in the United States and in the world, and about Zionism and Palestine. After 1950, it also includes a useful bibliography of books published in the United States touching upon Jews, which comprises, of course, books on or relating to Israel. The Europa Publications Limited (London) issues a very good survey and directory of the Middle East, including Israel, comprising geographical, historical, and economic surveys and concise information about political, industrial, financial, cultural, and educational organizations, as well as a "Who's Who" of the Middle East. The eighth edition of the survey appeared in 1961 under the title *The Middle East, 1961.*

3. *Jewish History*

The material on this subject is immense and varied. The ambitious or scholarly reader wanting to pursue this subject can do no better than start with Salo W. Baron's magisterial work, *A Social and Religious History of the Jews* (8 vols., New York, 1952–1960). The reader will also be able to draw from this study ample bibliographies for any specific topic and period within that subject. For those who would like something more general and more lively there is the crisp one-volume history by Abram L. Sachar, *A History of the Jews* (New York, 1953), which carries the story past the establishment of Israel, and Cecil Roth's excellent *A Short History of the Jewish People* (rev. and enl. ed., New York, 1948), which brings the social history of the Jews to the end of World War II. Max Margolis and Marx Alexander have also written a good *History of the Jewish People* (New York, 1958). An interesting philosophical-historical work by an Anglican clergyman who has devoted his life to the study of Judaism is James W. Parkes' *The Foundations of Judaism and Christianity* (Chicago, 1960). Parkes has also written among many other works a remarkable book on the history of Palestine, *A History of Palestine from A.D. 135 to Modern Times* (New York, 1949), and a profound essay relating the new state of Israel to the traditions of Jewish culture and to Jewish-Gentile relations: *End of Exile* (London, 1954). For a good text on the ancient Jewish states in Palestine, Albert Bailey's and Charles Kent's *History of the Hebrew Commonwealth* (rev. ed., New York, 1949), is the standard work. For the place of Palestine in the Jewish tradition there is a good book edited by Abraham S. Halkin, *Zion in Jewish Literature* (New York, 1961). Rabbi Elmer Berger, the Executive Director of the anti-Zionist American Council for Judaism, has provided a dissenting view of Jewish history in his *A Partisan History of Judaism* (New York, 1951).

4. Zionism

The literature on Zionism is as abundant as the material on Jewish history. Fortunately, some excellent synthetic works are available to the student or reader which enable him to acquire a very good idea of this movement without too much toil, while providing at the same time valuable bibliographical guidance for those who wish to pursue some particular aspect in greater detail. Among these works, the most notable is Ben Halpern's *The Idea of the Jewish State* (Cambridge, Mass., 1961). Halpern analyzes the rise of Zionism and its strategy and tactics in the context of the political, social, and cultural conditions of the Jews in the nineteenth century and in that of the movement's relation to non-Zionists, anti-Zionists, non-Jews, and the great powers. An excellent companion to Halpern's book is *The Zionist Idea,* edited by Arthur Hertzberg (New York, 1959), which provides a first-class compilation of the views of Zionist leaders from the nineteenth century to the present and conveys a strong sense of the depth and variety of intellectual trends and motives that went into the making of the Zionist movement. Editors B. J. Vlavianos and F. Gross have compiled in their *Struggle for Tomorrow: Modern Political Ideologies of the Jewish People* (New York, 1954) a series of articles and documents expressing a variety of modern Jewish ideologies which places Zionism in juxtaposition with alternative and rival philosophies and movements such as Assimilationism, Bundism, Territorialism, and so on. On the side of political history, Israel Cohen's *A Short History of Zionism* (London, 1951) provides a standard concise text, and Israel Goldberg's (Rufus Learsi, pseud.) *Fulfilment; the Epic Story of Zionism* (Cleveland, 1951) gives a more vivid account, including a description of the contribution made by American Zionists to the success of the movement. Alan R. Taylor, in his *Prelude to Israel; an Analysis of Zionist Diplomacy 1897–1947* (New York, 1959), supplements the previous two works with a critical examination of Political Zionism.

The preceding books should give a very good idea of the Zionist movement and its historical development; but to obtain a *feeling* for the world of Zionism one must turn to the autobiographies, memoirs, and biographies of some of its leading figures. The following are only the most important works one may wish to consult: Israel Cohen, *Theodor Herzl: Founder of Political Zionism* (New York, 1959), the life and career of the Zionist leader based on personal acquaintanceship and access to private papers; Alexander Bein, *Theodor Herzl: A Biography* (New York, 1941), a standard work; M. Lowenthal, ed., *The Diaries of Theodor Herzl* (New York, 1956), covering the period from June 1895 to May 16, 1904, from Herzl's musings on the Jewish problem to his death as leader of the World Zionist Organization; Isaiah Berlin, *Chaim Weizmann* (New York, 1959), a brilliant essay by the noted historian and friend of the foremost leader of the World Zionist Movement for nearly three decades; Chaim Weizmann, *Trial and Error* (New York, 1949), the invaluable and perhaps indispensable autobiography of the Russian Jewish boy from Motl who grew up to win for his people the right to a national home in Palestine and to preside over its realization (to paraphrase Chaim Weizmann himself); Sir Leon Simon, *Ahad ha-Am* (Philadelphia, 1960), the biography of Asher Ginsberg, the Russian-born Zionist philosopher and exponent of a philosophy of Zionism which, though never held by any but a small minority, had nevertheless a pervasive influence on the movement; Simcha Kling, *Nachum Sokolow* (New York, 1961), a biography of the publicist from Warsaw, president of the Zionist movement after Herzl's death and an influential figure in its councils, Joseph Schechtman, *Rebel and Statesman* (New York, 1956), and *Fighter and Prophet* (New York, 1961), a two-volume biography of Vladimir Jabotinsky, one of the most colorful, talented, and fanatic leaders of Zionism, the founder of the New Zionist Organization—a militant splinter organization that eventually begot the *Irgun Zvai Leumi* and the *Lochamei Herut-Yisrael* known to the outside world as "terrorist organizations"; Marie Syrkin, *Nachman Syrkin* (New York, 1960), a biographical study of the ideological father of non-Marxist Zionist Socialism by his daughter; S. Goldman, ed., *The Words of Justice Brandeis* (New York, 1953), the views of the greatest figure of American Zionism on such subjects as the American Jewish community, the Bible, and Zionism; Stephen S. Wise, *Challenging Years* (New York, 1949), the recollections, written during the last years of his life, of the distinguished rabbi and powerful leader and tribune of American Zionism for many years; Norman Bentwich, *For Zion's Sake* (Philadelphia, 1954), a biography of Judah L. Magnes, another eminent American Jewish leader and Zionist who became the first Chancellor and the first President of the Hebrew University in Jerusalem. This book is particularly interesting because Magnes espoused and advocated a minority view which was willing to renounce Jewish sovereignty in Palestine for the sake of Arab-Jewish understanding.

Other important works on leading figures of Zionism are Rose Zeitlin, *Henrietta Szold* (New York, 1954), the record of the life of a saintly American woman who became the moving spirit of *Youth Aliyah,* an organization that saved thousands of children and helped them reconstruct their life in Palestine; Barnett Litvinoff, *Ben Gurion of Israel* (London, 1954), a useful if somewhat awestruck biography of the leader of Israel, and her Prime Minister during twelve of her fourteen years of existence; Robert St. John, *Ben Gurion* (New York, 1959), a lively and sensitive portrait by an experienced journalist, which is better than Litvinoff's, but still tentative; David Ben Gurion, *Rebirth and Destiny of Israel* (New York, 1954), selections from the speeches and writings of Israel's leader reflecting his philosophy and "vision"; Richard H. S. Crossman, *A Nation Reborn* (New York, 1960), a brief but very perceptive analysis of the roles of Weizmann, Ben Gurion, and Bevin in the creation of Israel by a British Labor MP and an editor of the *New Statesman* with long firsthand experience with the Palestine question; Menachem Begin, *The Revolt; Story of the Irgun* (New York) 1951, a lively and dramatic account of the dissident underground military organization by its Commander-in-Chief which reflects the thinking of the author who now heads Israel's second largest political party; Yaacov Meridor, *Long is the Road to Freedom* (New York, 1961), the experience of one of Begin's lieutenants in the underground and in exile; Marie Syrkin, *Way of Valor* (New York, 1955), a biography of Golda Myerson (now Meir), the young woman from Milwaukee who became Israel's ambassador to Moscow, Minister of Labor, and has been for many years Israel's Foreign Minister; Robert St. John, *Tongue of the Prophets, the Life Story of Eliezer Ben-Yehuda* (New York, 1952), the life of the man who did more than anyone else to revive the Hebrew language and adapt it for daily use as the national idiom of Israel. This biography reveals the fanatic singleness of purpose which has characterized so many of the leaders of the national renaissance of the Jews in various spheres.

5. *The Balfour Declaration and the Mandate*

Here, as in the case of Zionism, a vast literature has been fortunately assimilated and synthesized in a few first-class works which also contain very extensive bibliographies. For the Balfour Declaration we have Leonard Stein's book, *The Balfour Declaration* (New York, 1961). This is probably the definitive work on the subject and contains, moreover, very useful data about the Zionist movement in the years before and after the Declaration, as well as perceptive biographical sketches of the leading Zionist, Jewish, and British personalities involved in the birth of that historical document. For an analysis of the Palestine problem in the Mandatory period as it moved toward its climax in tragedy and war in 1948, Jacob C. Hurewitz's *The Struggle for Palestine* (New York, 1950) is a superb work, thorough, impartial and—chilly. A fuller textual documentation and a warmer but less impartial analysis is provided in the two-volume study sponsored by the ESCO Foundation for Palestine, *Palestine, a Study of Jewish, Arab and British Policies* (New Haven, 1947). John Marlowe (pseud.), in *The Seat of Pilate* (London, 1959), has given an account of the Palestine Mandate underscoring the dilemmas faced by the British in their effort to muddle through an impossible situation. Most of the biographies listed above and many of the works on Israel listed below include valuable additional material on various aspects of the Mandatory period viewed from many perspectives.

6. *General Works on Israel*

A large number of general books, mostly of the impressionistic type, have been written about Israel by journalists, rabbis, creative writers, and miscellaneous visitors. A few of these are surprisingly good but most of them are somewhat parochial or superficial and are of interest more as a reflection of the apparently insatiable market for books on Israel than for what they have to say. There is no purpose in listing and assessing works of this sort here. The few works that follow are samples of the exceptional best. Arthur Koestler, in *Promise and Fulfilment* (New York, 1949), studies intelligently and provocatively the political forces and the military events leading to the establishment of Israel and analyzes the cultural and religious forces struggling to shape her orientation. Hal Lehrman's *Israel: The Beginning and To-*

morrow (New York, 1952) is a competent journalistic account of the early years of the state which makes interesting reading now, as one compares his "tomorrow" with *today*. Frank D. Waldo's *Bridgehead; The Drama of Israel* (New York, 1957) is a sensitive and well-drawn portrait of Israel in terms of the people who compose it and their faith. Horace M. Kallen's *Utopians at Bay* (New York, 1958) is a perceptive study of the problem of creating an Israeli people or nation out of the global miscellany of Jews and non-Jews who live in Israel. Laurence F. R. Williams, a member of the editorial staff of *The Times* (London) who had visited Palestine when it was under Turkish rule and under the British Mandate and then visited Israel twice since her establishment, gives in *The State of Israel* (New York, 1957), an impressionistic account from his uncommon perspective. Abraham M. Heller's *Israel's Odyssey: A Survey of Israel's Renaissance* (New York, 1959) is a very good account of the achievements and problems of the Jewish state. In *Israel: a Blessing and a Curse* (New York, 1960) H. V. Cooke, former American Consul in Jerusalem, has written a book full of insights and sound judgments which, however, are too often stated in a frustrating capsule form.

7. *The War of Independence and Military Matters*

A definitive account of the Israeli War of Independence (as Israelis call the War of 1948) remains to be written, though some good books on the subject have been published. On military and defense matters since 1949 there is very little reliable material. The Sinai Campaign of 1956 has brought to light some important information but even this has been largely overtaken by rapid developments since. There is practically nothing on the subject of "militarism" except for a piece by Ben Halpern in the collective work edited by John J. Johnson, *The Role of the Military in Underdeveloped Countries* (Princeton, 1962). Israel's response to the challenge to her national security and the implications of that response have to be pieced together from bits of scattered material and require a "sense" of the subject which can be acquired only through long observation. Among the few good books on the War of Independence is Netanel Lorch's *The Edge of the Sword,* translated from the Hebrew (New York, 1961). The author has the advantage of firsthand experience of the Israeli army and some of the events he writes about. Major E. O'Ballance has given another competent detailed military account in his *The Arab-Israeli War, 1948* (London, 1956). Jon and David Kimche's *A Clash of Destinies* (New York, 1960) provides a well-written account of the War of 1948 which combines military and political developments and reveals some very interesting facts about frictions within the Israeli defense establishment of the time. Less vivid but often more judicious is Harry Sacher's *Israel: The Establishment of a State* (New York, 1952). Of the many personal accounts by participants in that war, Dov Joseph's *Faithful City* (New York, 1960) is one of the most interesting. The author, presently Minister of Justice, was military governor of Jerusalem during its siege by the Arab armies. Daniel Spicehandler's *Let my Right Hand Wither* (New York, 1950) is a good sample of the accounts written by American volunteers on Israel's side. For the subsequent period, an article by Major General Moshe Dayan, former Israeli Chief of Staff, in *Foreign Affairs* (January 1955), "Israel's Border Security Problems," gives a brisk analysis of the subject which manages to convey between the lines the Israelis' mood of unflinching determination to go their own way in matters of national security. Commander E. H. Hutchinson, of the United Nations' Truce Supervision Organization, has given a very critical account of his experience with the Israelis in this matter in the years 1951–1955 in his *Violent Truce* (New York, 1956). A less condemnatory though still critical view is provided by the chief of the Truce Supervision Organization and subsequently the Commander-in-Chief of the United Nations' Emergency Force stationed in Gaza and Sinai, Major General E. L. M. Burns, in his *Between Arab and Israeli* (London, 1962). This book is altogether an excellent chronicle of and commentary upon the history of Arab-Israeli hostility as reflected in the intermittent border violence, and is cast in the framework of political developments in the area. Information about Israel's armed forces, their size, spirit, and quality is provided in several books on the Sinai Campaign, notably in Major E. O'Ballance's *The Sinai Campaign of 1956* (New York, 1960), and in the book by General S. L. A. Marshall, the noted American military historian, *Sinai Victory* (New York, 1957). Amos Lev, *With Plowshare and Sword* (New York, 1961), gives a glimpse of the Israeli army from within and of the state of mind of a soldier killed in the Sinai war.

8. *The Country and the People*

The most important source on the country, its geography, climate, and resources is the magnificent and luxuriously produced *Atlas Yisrael* (Jerusalem, 1961), written in Hebrew, of which an English version is now in preparation. A businesslike treatment of the same subject is provided in W. B. Fisher, *The Middle East: A Physical, Social and Regional Geography* (New York, 1950), and a concise summary is available in the survey by the Europa Publications mentioned in section 1 of this bibliography. A good current description of the country is provided by Zev Vilnai's *Guide to Israel*, of which a revised edition is now in preparation. For statistical data relating to the land, natural resources, and their use, the *Statistical Abstract of Israel* and the *Israel Government Yearbook* contain the latest information. These same sources provide also the latest demographic data and give a quantitative profile of Israel's people. On the problems involved in the absorption of immigrants, Shmuel N. Eisenstadt, Professor of Sociology at the Hebrew University, has written an excellent study, *The Absorption of Immigrants: a Comparative Study Based Mainly on the Jewish Community in Palestine and the State of Israel* (Glencoe, Ill., 1955). Raphael Patai, in *Israel Between East and West* (Philadelphia, 1953), has dealt imaginatively, sometimes too much so, with the clash of cultures between the various ethnic groups in Israel, particularly between the Orientals and the Europeans. Abraham Shumsky treats the same problem, with specific reference to education, in *The Clash of Culture in Israel: A Problem for Education* (Columbia Studies in Education, New York, 1955). On the position of the Arabs in Israel, Walter Schwartz's book, *The Arabs in Israel* (London, 1959), is a fair and well-written account. Don Peretz, in *Israel and the Palestine Arabs* (Washington, 1958), explores the proposals and counterproposals for settling the Arab refugee problem that have been made since the establishment of Israel, in addition to the position of the Arab minority.

9. *Government and Politics*

There is already a fairly large literature on this subject, references to which are to be found in the few works we mention here. Though much of this literature is good, most of it is rather dry and dull. Marver Bernstein's *The Politics of Israel* (Princeton, 1957) is an excellent study of Israel's political development with emphasis on institutions and the role of government in social and economic planning. Oscar Kraines's *Government and Politics of Israel* (New York, 1961) is a painstaking and very useful factual text with very little analysis. Emmanuel Rackman made a good study of the various constitutional projects and the controversy on the constitution during the early years of Israel in his *Israel's Emerging Constitution* (New York, 1955). The legal system is propounded in Henry S. Baker's *The Legal System of Israel* (Tel Aviv, 1955). Edwin Samuel's *Problems of Government in the State of Israel* (Jerusalem, 1956) dwells mainly on the administrative aspects. One of the few efforts to take an interpretive approach to Israeli politics is exemplified by A. Tartakover's "Sociology of Political Life in Israel," in *Jewish Social Studies* (April, 1960). The question of religion and state has been touched upon in many works but has seldom been satisfactorily dealt with. J. Badi's *Religion in Israel Today* (New York, 1959) is a rare monograph on the subject. Those who wish to pursue this subject further will have to assemble the data scattered over many books and periodicals, using the bibliographical aids we have mentioned.

10. *Economy and Society*

There is no single good comprehensive descriptive work on the economy of Israel though there are many excellent reports, articles, and studies covering various aspects of it. Alex Rubner's *The Economy of Israel* (New York, 1960) comes close to filling the gap but is marred by polemical excess. The *Reports* of the Falk Foundation for Economic Research in Israel, of which there have been five so far, provide excellent studies of various topics of Israel's economy and are indispensable. Equally valuable are the annual reports of the Bank of Israel, issued each year under the title *Bank of Israel, Annual Report,* which give comprehensive reviews and analyses of economic performance and submit recommendations to the government. The relevant chapters in Bernstein's book (*The Politics of Israel*), mentioned above, give a good description of economic institutions and tendencies which can serve as a starting-point for pursuing the developments analyzed or summarized in the previous sources. The Economist (London) Intelligence Unit issues from time to time an "Economic Review of Israel," the last two of which came out in June 1957 and July 1960 respectively. On agriculture, Haim Halperin has written a very good study, *Changing Patterns in Israel Agriculture* (London, 1957). Abraham Granott analyzes the pattern of land tenure in Israel in his *Agrarian Reform and the Record of Israel* (London, 1956). There is no recent satisfactory comprehensive study of the Histadrut in English. A. Revusky's *The Histadrut* (New York, 1938) is useful but is hopelessly outdated. Gerhard Münzer's *Labor Enterprise in Palestine; a Handbook of Histadrut Economic Institutions* (New York, 1947) provides a good survey of the development of the Jewish economy in Mandatory days and conveys a good notion of the importance of the Histadrut in that development, but the quantitative data are, of course, irrelevant to the present. Samuel Kurlan's *Cooperative Palestine: The Story of Histadrut* (New York, 1947) is mainly descriptive. Ferdinand Zweig's *The Israeli Worker* (New York, 1959) is an excellent sociological analysis of the Israeli workers, their conditions, and their ideology and devotes a section to the problems confronting the Histadrut now. Rubner, in his previously mentioned book, devotes several pages to the conflicts within the Histadrut, and between the Histadrut and the government, but he tends to exaggerate both the power and the dangers of the Histadrut. The article by M. L. Plunkett, "Histadrut: The General Federation of Jewish Labor in Israel," in *Industrial and Labor Relations Review* (1958), gives a good summary of the development and present condition of the Histadrut but contains little beyond what is mentioned in the present work. The collective settlements (kibbutzim) have been mentioned only occasionally in this book for reasons of economy of space. Perhaps it was a mistake not to dwell longer on this fascinating "Utopia that did not fail," in Buber's words. Fortunately for those who wish to pursue this subject there are several good works. Melford E. Spiro has written a two-volume anthropological study of the kibbutz based on firsthand experience: the first *Kibbutz; Venture in Utopia* (Cambridge, Mass., 1956), deals with the philosophy and way of life of a collective settlement; and the second, *Children of the Kibbutz* (Cambridge, Mass., 1958), concentrates on the generation born and brought up in the kibbutz. Esther Tauber, in *Moulding Society to Man* (New York, 1955), has written a history of the collective settlements and their organization, and Joseph Baratz, one of the founders of the first kibbutz half a century ago, has given his recollections in *A Village by the Jordan* (New York, 1955).

11. *International Relations*

There is a vast literature on various aspects of international relations having a direct and indirect bearing on Israel, and we cannot try to encompass it here. We shall mention only some key works and let the reader who wishes to pursue the subject further draw upon the bibliographies mentioned in these works and upon the general bibliographical sources mentioned at the beginning of this list. A basic reference text is George Lenczowski's *The Middle East in World Affairs* (3rd ed., Ithaca, New York, 1962). Another important text is the book edited by Sir Reader Bullard for the Royal Institute of International Affairs, *The Middle East: A Political and Economic Survey* (3rd ed., London and New York, 1958). On the Soviet Union, the Middle East, and Israel, a key book is Walter Laqueur's *The Soviet Union and the Middle East* (New York, 1959). *Israel in Crisis* (New York, 1950), by Abraham Magil, gives a Communist view of Israel's War of Independence during the honeymoon period in Israel-Soviet relations, while *The Kremlin, the Jews and the Middle East* (New York, 1957), by Judd L. Teller, dwells on the basic Soviet hostility to Zionism. Supplementing all these works is Guido Goldman's monograph, *Zionism Under Soviet Rule* (New York, 1960). Walter Eytan, the former Director General of Israel's

Foreign Ministry, presents the official Israeli view of Soviet diplomacy in the context of Israel's over-all foreign relations in his *The First Ten Years: A Diplomatic History of Israel* (New York, 1958). On the United States' relations with Palestine for nearly a century prior to the establishment of Israel, Frank Manuel has written a lively and scholarly account, *The Realities of American Palestine Relations* (Washington, 1949). In *Middle East Dilemmas; the Background of United States Policy* (New York, 1953), J. C. Hurewitz analyzes incisively and objectively the origins and growth of American interests and responsibilities in the Middle East. A first-rate history of the international relations of the Middle East and analysis of the evolution of American policy toward the entire area since the War of 1948 is provided by John C. Campbell in his *Defense of the Middle East* (rev. ed., New York, 1960). Campbell, as well as Hurewitz and Manuel, mentions and makes use of the main sources which anyone undertaking research on the subject under consideration would have to use. But even the merely interested reader is advised to look at least into some biographies, memoirs, and records of Congressional hearings if he wants to get a sense of Middle East problems as they are seen and acted upon by the policy-makers in moments of decision. Confining ourselves to a few examples only, we should mention: *The Forrestal Diaries,* Walter Millis, ed. (New York, 1951); Harry S. Truman, *Years of Trial and Hope* (New York, 1956); J. R. Beal, *John Foster Dulles: A Biography* (New York, 1957); R. Goold-Adams, *The Time of Power: A Reappraisal of John Foster Dulles* (New York, 1962); Sherman Adams, *Firsthand Report* (New York, 1961); Sir Anthony Eden, *Full Circle* (Boston, 1960); James G. McDonald, *My Mission in Israel, 1948–1951* (New York, 1952). All but the last, which deals exclusively with Israel, contain important sections on the Middle East and Israel. For an example of Congressional hearings we should select those conducted by the House and the Senate in connection with the issuing of the Eisenhower Doctrine because they raise the whole issue of American policy toward the Middle East in the preceding and following years. These may be found under the titles: *Economic and Military Cooperation with Nations in the General Area of the Middle East,* Hearings on H. J. Res. 117, U. S. House Committee on Foreign Affairs, 85th Cong., 1st sess., January 7–22, 1957 (Washington, D.C., G.P.O., 1957); and *The President's Proposal on the Middle East,* Hearings on S. J. Res. 19 and H. J. Res. 117, U. S. Senate Committees on Foreign Relations and Armed Services, 85th Cong., 1st sess., January 14–February 4, 1957 (Washington, D.C., G.P.O., 1957). Other interesting material concerning Israel, the Middle East, and the powers include the study put out by the Royal Institute of International Affairs, *British Interests in the Mediterranean and Middle East* (New York, 1958), and the collection of documents published by the State Department under the title *U. S. Department of State, U. S. Policy in the Middle East, September 1956–June 1957; Documents* (Washington, D.C., 1957). On the period of the Kennedy Administration there is the State Department *Bulletin,* and the interesting correspondence between President Kennedy and President Abdel Nasser, published in *Middle Eastern Affairs,* November, 1962. For the attitude of American Jews toward Israel and their political behavior, most of the works and many of the biographies and memoirs mentioned in section 4 above are relevant. Samuel Halperin's *The Political World of American Zionism* (Washington, D.C., 1960) is an excellent study of the process and methods by which Zionism mobilized Jewish and American opinion behind its claims, and contains, moreover, a comprehensive and largely original bibliography. Laurence H. Fuchs' *The Political Behavior of American Jews* (Glencoe, Ill., 1956) examines the influences that have affected Jewish voting, including the issue of Israel. The role of America in the creation of Israel is examined by Isaac Zaar, *Rescue and Liberation: America's Part in the Birth of Israel* (New York, 1954). A very critical and often exaggerated account of Jewish influence on American foreign policy and a warning about its consequences is given in two books by a member of the American Council for Judaism, Alfred M. Lilienthal, in *What Price Israel* (Chicago, 1953) and *There Goes the Middle East* (New York, 1957). On the importance of Middle East oil and its influence on foreign policy there is Halford L. Hoskins' *Middle East Oil and United States Foreign Policy* (Washington, D.C., 1950); Benjamin Shwadran, *The Middle East Oil and the Great Powers* (New York, 1955); J. E. Hartshorn, *Oil Companies and Governments* (London, 1962); Stephen Longrigg, *Oil in the Middle East* (2nd ed., New York, 1961); George Lenczowski, *Oil and State in the Middle East* (Ithaca, 1960); and Wayne Leeman, *The Price of Middle East Oil* (Ithaca, 1962). All the biographies and memoirs mentioned in this section contain material on the influence of American Jews and/or of oil on American policy considerations.

12. On the Lighter Side

To conclude this rather demanding list of suggested reading we may mention two or three works which view Israel with a sense of humor. Shneor Zalman Cheshin, in *Tears and Laughter in an Israel Courtroom* (Philadelphia, 1959), discusses some of the cases over which he presided as magistrate and district judge in Tel Aviv. Charles Kariel Gardosh (Dosh, pseud.), the leading Israeli cartoonist, presents a good collection of his work in *To Israel with Love* (New York, 1960). Finally, Ephraim Kishon, a sometimes-hilarious Israeli satirist, presents a collection of his columns in *Look Back Mrs. Lot* (New York, 1961).

Index

DATE DUE

MAR 13 '64			
MAR 2 6 '64			
APR 2 4 '64			
MAY 2 2 '64 OCT 3			
OCT 1 7 1968			
MAR 4 1974 DEC 4 1974			
GAYLORD			PRINTED IN U.S.A.